te
ge
UK

uk

Protecting Human Rights in the EU

Tanel Kerikmäe

Editor

Protecting Human Rights in the EU

Controversies and Challenges of the Charter
of Fundamental Rights

 Springer

Editor
Tanel Kerikmäe
Tallinn Law School
Tallinn University of Technology
Tallinn
Estonia

ISBN 978-3-642-38901-6   ISBN 978-3-642-38902-3 (eBook)
DOI 10.1007/978-3-642-38902-3
Springer Heidelberg New York Dordrecht London

Library of Congress Control Number: 2013947801

Springer is part of Springer Science+Business Media (www.springer.com)

Contents

Contributors

Marco Botta Institute for European Integration Research, University of Vienna, Austria

Archil Chochia Tallinn Law School, Tallinn University of Technology, Tallinn, Estonia

Pawan Kumar Dutt Tallinn Law School, Tallinn University of Technology, Tallinn, Estonia

Edita Gruodytė Law Faculty, Vytautas Magnus University, Lithuania

Ondrej Hamulák Faculty of Law, Palacký University in Olomouc, Czech Republic

Kristi Joamets Tallinn Law School, Tallinn University of Technology, Tallinn, Estonia

Kari Käsper Tallinn Law School, Tallinn University of Technology, Tallinn, Estonia

Tanel Kerikmäe Tallinn Law School, Tallinn University of Technology, Tallinn, Estonia

Stefan Kirchner Law Faculty, Vytautas Magnus University, Lithuania

Katrin Merike Nyman-Metcalf Tallinn Law School, Tallinn University of Technology, Tallinn, Estonia

Katarina Pijetlovic Tallinn Law School, Tallinn University of Technology, Tallinn, Estonia

Lehte Roots Tallinn Law School, Tallinn University of Technology, Tallinn, Estonia

Alexandr Svetlicinii Tallinn Law School, Tallinn University of Technology, Tallinn, Estonia

Introduction: EU Charter as a Dynamic Instrument

Tanel Kerikmäe

The wording of the European Union Charter of Fundamental Rights starts with an ambitious vision: "The peoples of Europe, in creating an ever closer union among them, are resolved to share a peaceful future based on common values". The Charter, containing 54 articles, is not only often glorified but also severely criticised by its overwhelming character. It cannot be denied that, despite some doctrinal controversies and scholarly debates on the binding effect of the Charter, it has already a significant impact to the general policy of the European Union, including citizen's Europe, common market, relations with third countries, enlargement, etc. The economic environment and legal environment are changing rapidly, and fundamental rights should be interpreted and protected in the light of these "changes in society, social progress, scientific and technological developments" as stated by the Charter. Therefore, the discussions related to the text of this innovative instrument are necessary and useful in the process of modelling the future of the protection of fundamental rights by the Union. The Charter cannot be static and rigid by its nature. It should rather be seen as a dynamic instrument that can never challenge the very core of the rights and values protected but must still be "living" legal text, i.e., allowing developments that are in correspondence with the aims of the Charter (stated by its preamble). This is a responsible task for implementators and interpretators of the text that is a part of European Union primary law. The authors of the book do not overemphasise the arguments that relate the Charter to the vision of federal Europe and constitutional patriotism or as a tool for readjusting nation-state based Europe to the citizen's Europe. However, the Charter is inherently a phenomenon to strengthen still fragile democratic legitimation of policymaking in Europe.

European Union as an institutional framework has often been a good example for the rest of the world. Furthermore, Europe has already proven its dedication to

T. Kerikmäe (✉)
Tallinn Law School, Tallinn University of Technology, Akadeemia tee 3, 12618 Tallinn, Estonia
e-mail: tanel.kerikmae@ttu.ee

T. Kerikmäe (ed.), *Protecting Human Rights in the EU*,
DOI 10.1007/978-3-642-38902-3_1, © Springer-Verlag Berlin Heidelberg 2014

1

the protection of human rights and fundamental freedoms by several legal instruments, including constitutions of European states and intergovernmental conventions such as ECHR. The developments within the European Union related to the Lisbon treaty and the Charter are also very much followed by global thinkers. I was intensively questioned by the Cambodian professors and students in Phnom Pehn at the seminar on ASEAN declaration of human rights, a text that was adopted recently. I can assure that European practice and visions continue to be a pattern and a source for inspiration for many politicians and scholars in other regions. It was also visible in Mysore, at the 2013 conference of International Association of Law Schools that dedicated its annual meeting to human rights issues.

The book does not claim to be an exhaustive set of analysis of all challenges and problems deriving from the Charter. It would be quite an impossible task. However, main issues have been discussed. The first chapter, written by myself, is dedicated to the background, legal nature, and innovative character of the Charter. One of the peculiar topics relates to horizontal legal effect—a problem that is probably one of the most discussed among lawyers when the Charter becomes an issue. Besides the legal nature, one of the popular subject matters is certainly the question of balancing of universal and particular rights in the Charter. Besides being innovative, I also label the Charter as "intricate". This is not even because there are many newly recognised rights introduced (some of them specific to EU internal market) but rather because of the normative character of the legal text. The Charter contains rights and principles that have different normative value and implementation mechanisms. Depending on the willingness of the beneficiaries, Member States and the EU itself ensure whether the "new perspective for horizontal effect" can be implemented in a way that would meliorate the dialogue within multilevel constitutional law.

As Prof. Metcalf points out in her chapter, the Charter contains "unusual rights" (such as the right to conduct business, the right of access to placement services, etc.) that cannot be found in other human rights instruments. The author suggests that the European Union is expected to act as a pioneer in providing new understanding of basic rights. She emphasises the relevance of contextuality of social developments and culture. Under developments issue, rights affected by technology have also been discussed in detail. Prof. Metcalf concludes with interesting remark on European exceptionalism: instead of limiting human rights, "the European version consists of adding a new layer onto existing rights and interpreting the 'old' rights through a new prism". Prof. Metcalf, with her co-authors Pawan Kumar Dutt and Archil Chochia, is also contributing to another substantial chapter titled "The freedom to conduct business and the right to property", where the EU technology transfer block exemption regulation and the relationship between intellectual property and competition law are discussed. The chapter is trying to find a ground for a debate on relationship between technology transfers, economic efficiencies, and fundamental rights possibly regulated by the EU Charter.

Professors Gruodyté and Kirchner deal with effective access to the judicial system and right to legal aid—core issue of any legal system and rule of law in general. By them: "nowadays States should guarantee access to justice as a human right which requires the state to take a positive action, a *status positivus* obligation". The principle of fair trial is a litmus for ensuring the human rights and freedoms in real life and demonstrates the capacity to ensure the right to legal aid protecting any other human rights. The authors make comprehensive comparative overview and interlink the practice of EU member states with case law on the issue of legal aid under Article 47 of the Charter.

Several of the chapters are devoted to the fields, directly influenced by the Charter: issues related to the impediment of marriage are covered by Kristi Joamets. This issue is a perfect example of a rapidly changing society. As the author herself puts it: "this is the character of our society today – quick changes in society have put policy-makers and implementers of law in a rather difficult situation" related to same-sex marriages. The chapter is focusing on an element inherent to European integration—free movement and its linkage to marriage. The author indicates that there are visible principles that develop the area, but it is still unclear whether the rights can be implemented at national level, especially in the context of "social and cultural differences of member states" in the field of regulation. The further guidelines would be derived from the CJEU case law that should also take account of the changing nature of "marriage".

Marco Botta and Alexandr Svetlicinii are discussing the enforcement of EU competition law, the freedom to conduct business, and the right to property. By them, there is a growing relevance of fundamental rights protection in competition law enforcement. Again, the principle of fair trial is having a central role, especially in the light of "progressive criminalization of competition law enforcement". Mainly, the case of Menarini, adjudicated by ECtHR, is taken as a model for further developments in EU competition law and the interpretation of the EU Charter.

Some of the parts of the current collection of articles are bound to the specific target groups or beneficiaries of the regulation such as asylum seekers and refugees. Dr Lehte Roots screens the possible interpretative development of the EU Charter through the jurisprudence of both CJEU and ECtHR and finds that "after the accession of EU to the European Convention of Human Rights and the development of the case law there might emerge a need for the review of the situation". The complicated interrelationship between the EU Charter, ECHR, and the constitutions of the Member States is very much obvious here as in some other fields of regulation of fundamental rights.

This is also evident in case of free movement of students in the EU, a topic presented by Kari Käsper. As the author indicates, education is "the area which Member States have wanted to exclude from harmonisation". That is why the "soft measures" have been preferred. The issue is still very much related to the EU Charter as the right to education and the anti-discrimination policy are concerned. The author points out that the area (and the free movement of students) is "under intense debate in the EU" and one possible development would be the shift of Luxembourg court ideology from economic to fundamental rights-based arguments. The Charter would be a good basis to clarify and detail the rules in the field.

Katarina Pijetlovic is addressing the new competences of the EU concerning the rights of athletes as specific target group of the EU Charter. Sports law as developing area of regulation is increasingly inevitably bound with aspects of fundamental rights. However, the concept of "specificy of sports" places the rights of athletes into context that differentiates them from other beneficiaries rights. The author creates a hypothetical example to prove that the EU Charter can be used as an innovative tool to counterbalance against the aforementioned concept and makes reference to several regulation areas of the Charter that can be used to protect athletes' rights such as right to representation, fair trial, and privacy. The last author, Ondrej Hamuläk, gives a synoptic insight to the constitutional nature of fundamental rights at supranational level.

The current book is an outcome of excellent research cooperation. Most of the contributors are my colleagues from Tallinn Law School, Tallinn University of Technology. I am also happy that several of our academic friends joined us to design an academic research book that would be a helpful tool for professionals, academics, and students in various fields, especially legal science, human rights and constitutional law, political science, international relations, and European integration.

I would like to express my great gratitude to all of the contributors and hope that the current collection of articles will find many readers and commentators.

EU Charter: Its Nature, Innovative Character, and Horizontal Effect

Tanel Kerikmäe

1 Theoretical and Practical Pre-requisites to the EU Charter of Fundamental Rights

European Union law includes well-developed rules on the four fundamental economic freedoms (free movement of goods, workers, services, and capital), and for a
while, these were the "rights" that the EU was aggressively safeguarding. However,
as the EU legal order has matured to a fuller, more complete system, human rights
could no longer be ignored. The intrinsic clash between economic interests and the
protection of human rights became more apparent and required action on the part of
both the European Court of Justice and other EU institutions.[1]

It has long been an issue that, alongside the European Union, the Council of
Europe's regional system of human rights protection has developed relatively
effective jurisprudence under the European Convention of Human Rights and
Fundamental Freedoms. All EU Member States are also parties to the Convention,
which may place them in a difficult position, for example, if an alleged human
rights violation arises from a legal act or an action undertaken by a Member State
pursuant to the EU law.[2]

The birth of the European Charter and its nature can be explained by two and
interrelated important ambitions—first, somewhat ambivalent EU constitutional
developments and, second, the emerging human rights case law of the European
Court of Justice that has aimed to solve the potential conflict between dogmatic
common market approach and dynamism of the EU as related to the citizens of

---

[1] Kerikmäe and Käsper (2008).

[2] Ibid.

T. Kerikmäe (✉)
Tallinn Law School, Tallinn University of Technology, Akadeemia tee 3, 12618 Tallinn,
Estonia
e-mail: tanel.kerikmae@ttu.ee

T. Kerikmäe (ed.), *Protecting Human Rights in the EU*,   5
DOI 10.1007/978-3-642-38902-3_2, © Springer-Verlag Berlin Heidelberg 2014

Europe. The Charter is a great piece of compromise between desires and reasonably possible mechanisms that can be introduced in the area. While some wanted it to make the existing human rights more visible in the EU level, others preferred to extend the scope and include new rights and spheres that were not covered before but are of great importance and innovative character. This document resembles the long-standing differences between different philosophies and ideologies and the way to find a compromise in this complex situation and get to the outcome in the form of the Charter.[3] Human rights (beside criminal jurisdiction) have always been a symbol of independence and sovereignty of the statehood. This is the principal reason for a long-lasting discussion over the EU catalogue of fundamental rights, in particular regarding its form and content. Another challenge continues to be a matter that basic rights can be related to any issue regulated by law, which makes the division of the powers in multilevel system rather sophisticated at first glance. Even in post-Lisbon EU, the borderline between exclusive, joint, and Member State competence is far from being clear due to different political and interest groups that still have distinguishable aspirations of the Union's future.

It is still relevant to emphasise that both of the aforementioned ambitions are carefully taking into account the constitutional values of the Member States. Therefore, case law of the CJEU can also be seen as an achievement to the integration that prepares the next stage in the EU development.

2   CJEU Case Law and the Charter

At least through the CJEU case law, the EU has not shown that principles of EU law may have an impact also on the issues outside of the areas, however, within the competence of the EU. Thus, there is a "sneaking", secondary impact of the law that may be wider than the primary, explicit one. In the Mangold case,[4] the CJEU found a common principle of prohibition of discrimination based on age, which is not easy to establish from reading the Constitutions of the Member States.[5] Nevertheless, such a principle potentially restricted the behaviour of Member States in areas outside the EU competence.[6]

Another important aspect is that the CJEU has also referred to the European Convention of Human Rights[7] in its several judgments. In the 1990s, the Court had

---

[3] Bellamy and Schonlau (2012).

[4] See ECJ Case Mangold v. Helm (2005) C-144/04.

[5] Eriksson (2009), p. 736.

[6] See Kerikmäe and Nyman-Metcalf (2012b).

[7] A reference to the European Convention of Human Rights and Fundamental Freedoms was inserted into EU law by Article 6(2) of Treaty of European Union (Maastricht Treaty) adopted in 1992, according to which the "Union shall respect fundamental rights, as guaranteed by the European Convention for the Protection of Human Rights and Fundamental Freedoms signed in

to consider the impact that human rights had on the EU rules. In one of the relevant landmark decisions, the Schmidberger case,[8] the CJEU had to rule on a sharp conflict between human rights and one of the basic economic freedoms, the free movement of goods. In that case, an Austrian environmental organisation blocked part of a busy motorway as a form of political protest for environmental protection. The Court was asked to consider whether the failure of Austrian authorities to prevent this blockage constituted a specific justification for restrictions on the free movement of goods. In its judgment, the CJEU stated that "measures which are incompatible with observance of the human rights thus recognised are not acceptable in the Community". The Court went on saying that protection of human rights, namely the freedom of expression and the freedom to assembly, can outweigh even a fundamental community right, such as the right to free movement of goods.[9]

In his paper, Schermers concludes the following: "Already now violation of human rights will be a ground for annulment of a Community act. The CJEU applies fundamental human rights as general principles of law. Acceptance of the Charter will offer a clearer and more binding foundation to the existing case-law..."[10] The Charter would weld the jurisprudence of the CJEU and relate it to the EU constitutional developments that were prepared more than a decade ago.

3 Charter-Relevant International Law and Practice

The EU proposed drafting of the Charter at the Cologne European Council in June 1999 based on the Commission's report from earlier that year.[11] The draft text was approved by the Biarritz European Council in October 2000 and subsequently by the European Parliament, Council, and Commission. It was drafted with a view to including it in the Treaty of European Union. Later, it was included as one of the main components of the Constitutional Treaty, which after that has become the Reform Treaty and then the Lisbon Treaty. As the idea of having a European Constitution was regarded as too elitist, the Charter was separated from the text of the Treaty and exists in the form of an independent legal act. Such an outcome also was affected by the results of the referenda in the Netherlands and France in 2005. In general, the Charter was well received, and right after its adoption some

---

Rome on 4 November 1950 and as they result from the constitutional traditions common to the Member States, as general principles of Community law".

[8] See ECJ Case Eugen Schmidberger, Internationale Transporte und Planzüge v Republik Österreich (2003) C-112/00.

[9] Kerikmäe and Käsper (2008).

[10] Schermers (2001), p. 8.

[11] Report of the Expert Group on Fundamental Rights, the European Commission. Affirming Fundamental Rights in the European Union: Time to Act. Brussels, February, 1999.

courts of the Member States have mentioned it as a subsidiary source of law.[12] In most cases, the European Court of Human Rights, for its part, is referring to the EU Charter descriptively in the part of a judgment called "relevant international law and practice".

4 Innovative and Intricate Character

The content of the Charter is manifold.[13] Some might consider that too many newly recognised rights have been introduced. The text includes "traditional" civil and political rights such as protection of human dignity (Article 1), right to life (Article 2), prohibition of torture and inhuman or degrading treatment or punishment (Article 4), and prohibition of slavery and forced labour (Article 5). It also contains traditional freedoms such as right to liberty and security (Article 6), respect for private and family life (Article 7), and freedom of thought, conscience and religion (Article 10). The Charter lists the social and cultural rights: right to education (Article 14), freedom to choose an occupation and right to engage in work (Article 15). It also pays special attention to cultural rights in the form of freedom of the arts and sciences (Article 13).

Some of the rights are specific to the EU internal market, among them is freedom to conduct business (Article 16), workers' right to information and consultation within the undertaking (Article 27), and right to collective bargaining and action (Article 28). An entire section is devoted to non-discrimination: equality before the law (Article 20). The rights of children and the elderly (Articles 24–25) are mentioned separately. Article 33 on family and professional life declares that "the family shall enjoy legal, economic and social protection". Special attention is paid to social security and social assistance (Article 34), health care (Article 35), access to services of general economic interest (Article 36), environmental protection (Article 37), and consumer protection (Article 38).

Chapter V is a catalogue of citizens' rights: the right to vote and to stand as a candidate at elections to the European Parliament (Article 39), the right to vote and to stand as a candidate at municipal elections (Article 40), the right to good administration (Article 41), freedom of movement and of residence (Article 45), and diplomatic and consular protection (Article 46). Chapter VI concentrates on procedural rights such as fair trial, presumption of innocence, principles of proportionality, and legality.

The content of the Charter is a mixture of fundamental rights, principles and values, and ideas, some of which have clear frames and history of application,

[12] For example, the Estonian Supreme Court has stated in its decision on 17 February 2003 in Case No. 3-4-1-1-03 that the Charter is not legally binding but reflects certain principles of law that are common to all EU Member States; RTIII (7 March 2003) 5, p. 48.

[13] See Kerikmäe and Käsper (2008).

whereas others are novel concepts that have not yet found their clear place in the *espace juridique Européen* (European legal space).

5 In Between Human Rights and EU Standards

In general, the universality of human rights might be in danger. As I recently stated with my colleague Prof. Metcalf: "Maybe it is so that fewer rights but stronger ones which furthermore are really universal actually could mean more rights? The rights and the understanding and interpretation of rights may have to be purist. This may be the way universal human rights as a concept can survive at all. In the modern world there are different trends that to some extent conflict, like the trend of globalisation but also the re-emphasising in different parts of the world of traditional values, whether from a religious background or something else".[14] However, the EU Charter, even in its complexity, has to be seen as a European regional set of "fundamental rights" that are legally allocated to be supervised by external authority—reliable human rights protection system established by the Council of Europe, the European Convention of Human Rights and Freedoms.

The main problem related to the Charter is most likely related to its normative structure. The Charter contains *rights* and *principles* that are to be treated differently and were drafted as a mechanism to achieve consensus on the broad range of rights included in the Charter.[15] Blackstock asks, "What is a right and what is a principle then?" and finds that, in many cases, this is not a "clear cut". By her, the explanations do in some places identify the distinction, e.g., the "rights" of the elderly (Art. 25 CFR) and environmental protection (Art. 27 CFR). However, here Blackstock's conclusion proves it again—it is not a "clear cut": socio-economic rights can have as much importance as interference with civil liberties, e.g., the right to vote discourse. Furthermore, rights and principles may be expressed in the same article, e.g., right to family and professional life (Art. 33 CFR).[16] Article 52.5 of the Charter states that principles are justiciable only insofar as they are implemented by measures taken by Member States. The Explanations of the Charter clarify that principles do not "give rise to direct claims for positive action by the Union's institutions or Member States' authorities".

Some of the authors are straightforward in making reference to "the potential federal effect of the Charter". For example, by Groussot, Pech, and Petursson, "it is sometimes alleged that the new legally binding status of the Charter may eventually convince the CJEU to enforce common standards applicable right across the EU regardless of whether national measures fall within or outside the scope of

---

[14] Kerikmäe and Nyman-Metcalf (2012a).

[15] Blackstock (2012), April 17. http://eutopialaw.com/2012/04/17/the-eu-charter-of-fundamental-rights-scope-and-competance/.

[16] Blackstock (2012).

application of EU law".[17] A Charter is, from the perspective of international law, e.g., European Convention of Fundamental Rights and Freedoms, a set of constitutional rights and principles, a European national constitutional law. By de Sousa, "national measures applying to private relationships must be interpreted in accordance with the fundamental freedoms, or, if such '*interprétation conforme*' is not possible, those national measures must be disapplied".[18] The Charter would be seen as a step forward to establish a direct horizontal effect, as the collisions between human rights and the EU standards of fundamental rights and principles can be furnished by constitutional legal culture of Member States.

6 New Perspective for Horizontal Effect?

Lately, the phenomenon of the horizontal effect[19] has been intensively discussed in legal theory. The controversy in applying the horizontal effect doctrine is that the aim of fundamental rights was to protect individuals from violation of their rights by public authorities while exercising their powers. However, if an individual can invoke rights against another individual, fundamental rights become as a duty and requirement for the other person.[20] Tzevelekos finds that "with respect to human rights abuses by third parties the first-generation norm creates an affirmative 'quasi-horizontal' effect which imposes an obligation upon the state to adopt - for the benefit of subjects under its jurisdiction - the necessary positive measures for prevention and prohibition of human rights abuses by third parties".[21] He also adds that "the need for positive protection arises in situations where the enjoyment by citizens of their civil rights is threatened by something other than state acts".[22]

The text of the Charter itself, particularly Article 51, refers only to the EU institutions and to the Member States, excluding private groups or individuals as addressees. Moreover, the majority of Member States do not allow direct horizontal effect under their national law, therefore putting an obligation only to public authorities to respect the fundamental rights and become the addressees of the Charter.[23] Does it mean that the horizontal character of the Charter is not possible? Some authors remain quite suspicious, making references to CJEU Case C-282/10

[17] See Groussot et al. (2011), http://www.ericsteinpapers.eu/papers/2011-1.

[18] See De Sousa, http://www.academia.edu/2167103/Horizontal_Expressions_of_Vertical_Desires_-_Horizontal_Effect_and_the_Scope_of_the_EU_Fundamental_Freedoms.

[19] This part of the chapter is inspired by the last FIDE Congress in Tallinn. See Kerikmäe et al. (2012).

[20] Besselink (2012), p. 17.

[21] Tzevelekos (2010).

[22] Ibid.

[23] Besselink (2012), p. 18.

Maribel Dominguez,[24] Opinion of AG Trstenjak delivered on 8 September 2011, and British and Polish opt-out protocol to the Charter.[25] As an exception, some Member States do allow direct horizontal effect, however, only for a small list of certain fundamental rights, e.g., civil and political rights in Portugal.[26]

However, it seems that when implementing human rights, *expressis verbis* reference to inter- or supranational law in the field (such as ECHR and EU Charter) are not formally required. Rather, teleological interpretation deriving from the international and supranational jurisprudence can be expected. Being excluded from the Lisbon Treaty, the Charter can still be regarded to be a part of EU constitutional law, its set of fundamental rights and freedoms. According to Alexy, there are two constructions of constitutional rights: the rule construction and the principles construction, both of them representing two opposing ideas on which the solution of the constitutional rights doctrine turns.[27] Thus, the horizontal effect of the Charter can be explained by the idea of Alexy, namely, the horizontal effect is a matter of constitutional review, behind which the tension between constitutional rights and democracy is found.[28] The Charter would, therefore, be a unique opportunity to establish a dialogue between national and supranational levels, fill the gap of legal *lacunae* that was restricted by blind dogmatism, protectionism, or technical collisions within multilevel legal system. The dialogue between two constitutional levels is inevitable for securing rule of law if we hope to build up the EU as a *Rechtstaat* that has legitimacy in decision-making. European legal identity cannot be seen as a final but as an ongoing process.[29]

The horizontal effect of the Charter is a concept that is rather possible to develop further due to the constitutional traditions in the Member States. For example, the Federal Constitutional Court of Germany, when considering whether the basic law of Germany had horizontal effects, reasoned that rights have both subjective (existing to protect individuals) and objective aspects (effectuating values of the society).[30] The latter aspect would justify the normative complexity of the Charter that clearly consists of rights and principles, reflecting the values and aspirations of European community. This is a decisive question of whether the Charter becomes an effective and applicable instrument. The opponents of the vision of constitutional dialogue are referring to the conflicts in the past. According to Kokott, the European integration is supranational; Community law is directly applicable and claims primacy in application over national law. She also claims that one of the fundamental principles, prohibition against age discrimination, deriving from case

---

[24] See Groussot et al. (2011), p. 2.

[25] See pending Joined Cases C-411/10 and C-193/10 *N.S.* and Opinion of AG Trstenjak delivered on 22 September 2011.

[26] See Besselink (2012), p. 18.

[27] Alexy (2010).

[28] Ibid.

[29] See also Kerikmäe (2010).

[30] See Schor (2010) and Ferreres Comella (2009), p. 238.

law and the Charter, has a direct horizontal effect and, in the legal orders of the Member States, constitutes an ultra vires act, violating national sovereignty.[31] However, some of the fundamental freedoms (which are the core elements of EU policy) have been given direct effect in the EU level and, consequently, in the Member States. According to the existing ECJ case law, free movement of workers, freedom to provide services, and freedom of establishment have direct horizontal effect and these rights are also incorporated and protected in the Charter.[32]

7 Differences in Interpretation

Also, some authors refer to the inconsistencies between the CJEU's case law and that of the European Court of Human Rights. Van den Berghe states that "the Charter contains two provisions governing the relationship between the Charter and the Convention with a view to avoiding inconsistencies between both instruments. According to a number of Court of Human Rights judges, this recognition that the Convention's level of protection constitutes a minimum standard is 'a rule whose moral weight would already appear to be binding on any future legislative or judicial developments in European Union law'".[33] Again, human rights protection is not a novel area for the Member States of the EU as they have experiences with the ECHR system. The adjustment of their EU-related legal obligations with the Convention would be at least partly mediated by the EU Charter that can be seen as a highest constitutional text in protecting fundamental rights in the European Union. Furthermore, the aims of the principles deriving from the Charter can be implemented through the directives that also give certain margin of appreciation to the Member States. De Witte puts it as follows: "the European Union has conducted, during the last decade, an active policy of adopting anti-discrimination directives that aim at ensuring greater convergence between member-state laws in this domain. One aspect of this evolution is that the relevant EU legislation forces some states to reconsider their traditional view that fundamental rights should be binding and enforceable only against state authorities and not against private bodies and individuals. This Europe-driven 'horizontalisation' of anti-discrimination law is a major challenge for many national legal systems and contributes to the emergence of new but not uncontroversial conceptions of inclusive citizenship".[34] Besides concrete rights, also principles that are guidelines or frames for the EU institutions and the Member States in their legislative process both in supranational (directives) and national (implementation acts and measures) levels are set by the Charter.

---

[31] Kokott (2010).

[32] Besselink (2012), p. 19.

[33] Van den Berghe (2010).

[34] De Witte (2009).

In its Case C 555/07, *Seda Kücükdeveci v Swedex GmbH & Co. KG*, the Luxembourg court has developed a new doctrine. The CJEU safeguarded its case law with the Charter, stating that the Directive 2000/78 "does not itself lay down the principle of equal treatment in the field of employment and occupation, which derives from various international instruments and from the constitutional traditions common to the Member States" but "has the sole purpose of laying down, in that field, a general framework for combating discrimination on various grounds including age". At the same time, the Court also refers to the EU Charter of Fundamental Rights, which "prohibits any discrimination on the grounds of age".

8 Using a Private Law Approach?

There are also particular approaches to clarify the horizontal effect of fundamental rights. Private law experts see the solution in applying canons of private law. Irene Kull says that "the catalogue of fundamental rights that follows not only the principle of the freedom of contract, but also the principle of protecting the weaker party, binds the implementer of law and they are exercised via the indirect horizontal effect of fundamental rights with the help of private law principles (good faith, good morals, reasonableness, etc.). These principles guide judges in the interpretation of contract law provisions and in the elaboration of rules".[35] However, horizontal effect is different from the impact of rights on private law.[36] In addition, the horizontal effect has sometimes been analysed by the competence areas. As explained by Eurofound, "the impact of the doctrine of horizontal direct effect, when applied to provisions of the Treaties, has been limited in the fields of employment and industrial relations".[37] The inclusion of fundamental rights concerning employment and industrial relations in primary EU law, as was the case with equal pay for women and men (Article 157 TFEU), could lead the CJEU to attribute binding "direct effect", vertical and horizontal, to provisions of the Charter. Authors of the commentaries of the EU Charter are rather careful in describing the horizontal nature of the legal act, finding only that "Article 4 of the Charter may therefore potentially also be recognised a horizontal effect, imposing on the Union an obligation to act in order to prevent acts prohibited under this provision from being committed. Whether the institutions of the EU may be held responsible for torture and related forms of prohibited treatment conducted by private parties, organisations or individuals within the member states (where such preventive

---

[35] See Kull (2007), http://www.juridicainternational.eu/unfair-contracts-of-suretyship-a-question-about-the-horizontal-effect-of-fundamental-rights-or-about-the-application-of-contract-law-principles.

[36] Krzeminska-Vamvaka (2009), http://centers.law.nyu.edu/jeanmonnet/papers/09/091101.pdf.

[37] See Eurofound; the European Foundation for the Improvement of Living and Working Conditions is a European Union body. http://www.eurofound.europa.eu/areas/industrialrelations/dictionary/definitions/horizontaldirecteffect.htm.

measures have not been institutionalised or implemented otherwise), is an open question. However, it cannot be excluded a priori".[38]

De Sousa makes it clear that the terminology has often misunderstood that "the expression horizontal effect does not exclusively refer to relationships between private parties as horizontal effect can also be said to refer to the effect of Union law between Member States, while vertical effect also affects the relationship between the Union and individuals".[39] Thus, the horizontal effect should not, in the case of the EU Charter, be seen in a limited or narrow way but rather vice versa—giving the term much broader sense. In general, the progressive direction of accepting human rights application horizontally by EU Member States is a prerequisite in effective implementation of the EU Charter of Fundamental Rights. Certainly, every member state has still its own peculiarities in implementing EU law and fundamental rights.

9 Experience in Estonia

Leaving aside the examples of the "old member states", Estonia could become an example of German-oriented, conservative jurisdiction in explaining the progress of horizontal effect. The general acceptance of horizontal effect of fundamental rights in Estonia is visible, and one can find several analytical reports related to the issue. Already in 1998, the expertise presented by a governmental expert commission on constitutional issues[40] referred to the so-called construction problems related to horizontal legal relations, which could be solved by mechanisms of direct and indirect effect. Estonian experts were inspired by well-known German legal theorists Hans Carl Nipperdey and Günter Dürig.

However, the experts indicate another problem—collision—which leads to the contemporary discussion related to the norm hierarchy. The Commentaries to the Constitution of the Estonian Republic[41] do not add much to the discussion concerning horizontal effect, being just more open-minded and flexible when presenting the same theoretical doctrines. The parts that are related to the EU membership are praising the supranationality of the EU legal norms and values. Also, the well-known textbook on Estonian constitutionalism, written by the former head of the Supreme Court, former justice of ECtHR and current MP, describes the

---

[38] See The EU Network of Independent Experts on Fundamental Rights, Commentary of the Charter of Fundamental Rights of the European Union, p. 45. http://llet-131-198.uab.es/catedra/images/experts/COMMENTARY%20OF%20THE%20CHARTER.pdf.

[39] De Sousa, p. 3.

[40] By request of Estonian Parliament (*Riigikogu*), the Government composed a special commission of constitutional expertise (members: Uno Lõhmus, Kalle Merusk, Heiki Pisuke, Jüri Raidla, Märt Rask, Heinrich Schneider, Eerik-Juhan Truuväli, Henn-Jüri Uibopuu, Paul Varul). There were several experts included in the discussions, also the undersigned of the current report, Tanel Kerikmäe. http://www.just.ee/10725 (section 3).

[41] Eesti Vabariigi Põhiseadus. Kommenteeritud väljaanne. Juura. Tallinn 2008, para 19.

Drittwirkung only as a case when one of the private parties is having public functions deriving from State authority and violates the rights of another private party.[42]

As the legal order in Estonia has been integrated into the EU legal system, the aspect of horizontal effect has been getting more practical importance, just as it has in the entire European *espace juridique*.[43] This issue is closely related to the question of possible collisions between norms in the multilevel legal system. Liina Kangur, analyst of the Supreme Court, refers to great challenges for Estonian courts that consist of "implementation of both EU law and domestic law in the light of aims established by EU law".[44] Uno Lõhmus explains the ideology of CJEU that is generally accepted by Estonian judiciary, i.e., the court of an EU Member State in the process of applying a domestic legal norm must take into account the text and the goals of the EU law as much as possible.[45] It concerns mostly the EU secondary law where Member State has not only a certain margin of appreciation but also a certain part of the primary legislation, such as the regulations that require the establishment of special institutions and that require sanctions by the Member State.[46]

It can be assumed that the horizontal effect reflects the approach to the Constitution in general. Robert Alexy provides that "the question of which construction: the rule construction or the principles construction is to be preferred is, therefore, by no means a problem of theoretical interest alone".[47] It seems that Estonia is following the path of principles construction as the Supreme Court declared the undisputable harmonisation with the EU law, while lower courts are following the Supreme Court declarations. However, they are not taking the initiative to use EU law directly or even quasi-directly. The principle is also reflected by Estonian theorists: "...fundamental rights do not settle a specific legal dispute, but open themselves via the legal provisions regulating the relevant area of law. The direct horizontal impact of fundamental rights and constitutional principles implies the possibility to rely on them in private law claims".[48] Assuming that the horizontal effect is effective only if there is a visible positive obligation,[49] meaning enforceable rights, it is somewhat difficult to analyse whether the Estonian judiciary in general is inspired from ECHR and EU law or is just following the guidance of the

---

[42] Maruste (2004), p. 305.

[43] Brems (2005), p. 301.

[44] See Kanger (2007), http://www.riigikohus.ee/vfs/776/Analyys%20EL%20oiguse%20kohaldamine %20HK%20praktikas%20%28L_Kanger%29.pdf.

[45] See Lõhmus (2007).

[46] Ibid.

[47] Alexy (2010).

[48] See Kull (2007), http://www.juridicainternational.eu/unfair-contracts-of-suretyship-a-question-about-the-horizontal-effect-of-fundamental-rights-or-about-the-application-of-contract-law-principles.

[49] See Wiesbrock Development Case Note, ECJ Case Seda Kücükdeveci V Swedex GmbH & Co. KG., Judgment of the Court (2010) C-555/07.

Supreme Court. It seems that the Estonian Supreme Court likes the approach of the German Federal Court, where the horizontal effect of the Constitution itself is discussed[50] and not encouraging the lower courts to take action on the basis of higher norms than the Constitution. It has been deemed to be a good interpretation filter for the Supreme Court. The Estonian judicial approach then corresponds to the idea of exceptionality of horizontal effect, thus used directly "only if there are no appropriate statutory means of protection. Because constitutional rights and freedoms are at the core of the legal system, there should be a presumption that private law adequately protects them".[51]

Horizontal effect presupposes that the norm is directly applicable. There is no question about EU primary law. However, the discussion on direct effect of directives, considering their legal nature, has been intensive in European legal theory. As the conditions for direct applicability of directives has been agreed (Member State has failed the implementation, a directive is unconditional and gives certain rights to individuals), there exist diametrically different opinions on whether a directive can be horizontally effective.[52] Šipilov finds three categories of cases that can presuppose the horizontal effect of directives:

(a) Although a directive is addressed to an EU member state, right(s) of an individual deriving from State obligations may injure the right(s) of other individuals (case of public procurement);
(b) Disputes between private parties may entail indirect effect of the directives as they can be used as a basis for interpretation of domestic legal norm;
(c) Interpretation of domestic law in accordance with a directive (again, indirect effect).

This kind of test would well be applicable in the case of the EU Charter.

10 Conclusion

There is no doubt that the Charter will influence the whole *acquis communautaire*.[53] The extent of this impact is still somewhat unpredictable. Much depends on the political direction Europe is taking and the boldness of European judges in both Member States and, more importantly, the CJEU. Potentially, it can be used as a powerful tool to strengthen EU influence in the social

---

[50] Schor (2010), p. 238.

[51] Krzeminska-Vamvaka (2009), http://centers.law.nyu.edu/jeanmonnet/papers/09/091101.pdf.

[52] See Šipilov (2010) "Põhiõiguste kolmikmõju ja Euroopa Liidu õiguse horisontaalne kohaldatavus. Master thesis awarded by Estonian Ministry of Justice as the best research paper of 2010. http://www.just.ee/52952.

[53] Conclusion is inspired by Kerikmäe and Käsper (2008).

sphere (strikes, collective bargaining, working conditions, etc.), which has to be taken into account by anyone who wishes to do business in or with Europe.

An open question is how the Charter will work in areas where the EU and Member States share competences. There is no doubt that the Charter applies to the activities of the EU institutions, but the extent to which it also applies to Member States, when implementing EU law, is unclear. The distinction will be a difficult one, taking into account the fact that most areas are regulated by both the EU and national legislation and it is sometimes complicated to distinguish one from another. The question of the EU turning into a rights-based union then has to do with the status of principles and values, namely, "are some of them turned into basic rights – protecting human rights and democratic procedures unconditionally?"[54] Therefore, whether the Charter will open a new era in the development of the EU from limited economic cooperation to a full political, economic, and social union remains unclear. Future practice and, undoubtedly, emerging case law of the CJEU will provide more answers. In any case, the significance of the Charter should not be underestimated.

References

Books and Articles

Alexy R (2010) Rights, balancing and proportionality. The construction of constitutional rights. Law & ethics human rights. The Berkeley Electronic Press, Berkeley

Bellamy R, Schonlau J (2012) The normality of constitutional politics: an analysis of the drafting of the EU charter of fundamental rights. In: Corradetti C (ed) Philosophical dimensions of human rights. Some contemporary views. Springer, Dordrecht, pp 231–252

Besselink LFM (2012) The protection of fundamental rights post-Lisbon the interaction between the EU charter of fundamental rights, the European Convention on Human Rights (ECHR) and National Constitutions. Report of 25th FIDE congress

Blackstock J (2012) The EU charter of fundamental rights. Scope and competence, Eutopia Law. http://eutopialaw.com/2012/04/18/the-eu-charter-of-fundamental-rights-scope-and-competance-2/

Brems E (2005) Conflicting human rights: an exploration in the context of the right to a fair trial in the European Convention for the protection of human rights and fundamental freedoms. Hum Rights Q 27:294–326

De Sousa PC. Horizontal expressions of vertical desires – horizontal effect and the scope of the EU Fundamental Freedoms. http://www.academia.edu/2167103/Horizontal_Expressions_of_Vertical_Desires_-_Horizontal_Effect_and_the_Scope_of_the_EU_Fundamental_Freedoms

De Witte B (2009) The crumbling public/private divide: horizontality in European anti-discrimination law. Citizenship Stud 13(5):515–525

Eriksson A (2009) European Court of Justice: broadening the scope of European non-discrimination law. Int J Constitut Law 7(4):731–753

Ferreres Comella V (2009) Constitutional courts and democratic values: a European perspective. Yale University Press, New Haven

Fossum JE (2004) In: Closa C, Fossum JE (eds) Deliberative constitutional politics in the EU. Centre for European Studies, Oslo

---

[54] See Fossum (2004), http://www.arena.uio.no/cidel/Reports/Albarracin_Ch2.pdf.

Groussot X, Pech L, Petursson GT (2011) The scope of application of EU fundamental rights on member states' action: in search of certainty in EU adjudication. Eric Stein Working Paper No. 1/2011

Kanger L (2007) Euroopa Liidu õiguse kohaldamine Eesti halduskohtute praktikas: põllumajandustoetuste ja üleliigse laovaru tasu kaasuste näitel. Estonian Supreme Court, Legal Information Department

Kerikmäe T (2010) Estonia as an EU state: lack of proactive constitutional dialogue. In: Topidi K, Morawa AHE (eds) Constitutional evolution in Central and Eastern Europe expansion and integration in the EU. Ashgate Publishing Ltd, Farnham, pp 11–42

Kerikmäe T, Käsper K (2008) European charter of fundamental rights. Lexis Nexis Expert Commentaries. http://w3.nexis.com/sources/scripts/info.pl?326754

Kerikmäe T, Nyman-Metcalf K (2012a) Less is more or more is more? Revisiting universality of human rights. Int Comp Law Rev 12(1):35–51

Kerikmäe T, Nyman-Metcalf K (2012b) The European Union and Sovereignty: the sum is more than its parts? Temas de Integração, Junho, pp 5–16

Kerikmäe T, Nyman-Metcalf K, Roots L, Meiorg M, Popov A (2012) Estonian report: protection of fundamental rights post-Lisbon: the interaction between the EU charter of fundamental rights, the European Convention on Human Rights (ECHR) and National Constitutions. In: Laffranque J (ed) Reports of the XXV FIDE congress Tallinn 2012. Tartu Ülikooli Kirjastus, Tartu, pp 389–422

Kokott J (2010) The basic law at 60 – from 1949 to 2009: the basic law and supranational integration. German Law J 11:99–114

Krzeminska-Vamvaka J (2009) Horizontal effect of fundamental rights and freedoms – much ado about nothing? German, Polish and EU theories compared after Viking Line. Jean Monnet Working Paper No 11/2009

Kull I (2007) Unfair contracts of suretyship — a question about the horizontal effect of fundamental rights or about the application of contract law principles. Juridica International: Law Review of the University of Tartu, Estonia I 2007

Lõhmus U (2007) Kuidas liikmesriigi kohtusüsteem tagab Euroopa Liidu õiguse tõhusa toime. Juridica (3)

Maruste R (2004) Konstitutsionalism ning põhiõiguste ja -vabaduste kaitse. Juura, Tallinn

Schermers HG (2001) Drafting a charter of fundamental rights of the European Union. In: Kellermann AE, de Zwaan JW, Czuczai J (eds) EU enlargement: the constitutional impact at EU and national level. T.M.C. Asser Press, The Hague

Schor M (2010) New thinking about National High Courts. Tulsa Law Rev 45(4) (University of Tulsa)

Šipilov V (2010) Põhiõiguste kolmikmõju ja Euroopa Liidu õiguse horisontaalne kohaldatavus. Master Thesis

Tzevelekos V (2010) In search of alternative solutions: can the State of origin be held internationally responsible for investors human rights abuses that are not attributable to it? Brooklyn J Int Law 35:155–231

Van den Berghe F (2010) The EU and issues of human rights protection: same solutions to more acute problems? Eur Law J 16(2):112–157

Wiesbrock A (2010) Case Note – Case C-555/07, Kücükdeveci v. Swedex, Judgment of the Court (Grand Chamber) of 19 January 2010. German Law J 11:539–550

Official Material

Eesti Vabariigi Põhiseadus. Kommenteeritud väljaanne. *Juura* (Tallinn 2008)

Report of the Expert Group on Fundamental Rights, the European Commission, "Affirming Fundamental Rights in the European Union: Time to Act," Brussels (February 1999)

The EU Network of Independent Experts on Fundamental Rights, Commentary of the Charter of Fundamental Rights of the European Union

Case Law

European Court of Justice
Case C-112/00 *Eugen Schmidberger, Internationale Transporte und Planzüge v Republik Österreich* (12 June 2003)
Case C-144/04
Joined Cases C-411/10 and C-193/10 *N.S.* and Opinion of AG Trstenjak (22 September 2011)
Supreme Court of Estonia
Estonian Supreme Court Case No. 3-4-1-1-03 (17 February 2003)

The Future of Universality of Rights

Katrin Nyman-Metcalf

1 Introduction

From its start as a body set up for cooperation on coal and steel, the European Union (EU) has grown to be a major player in world affairs and an important influence in the daily life of its citizens. With influence comes responsibility. In some areas, the EU has such important competence that it replaces the Member States; in other areas, there is shared competence. In any case, even if the question of possible sovereignty of the EU is a controversial issue,[1] the role of the Union is such that it has to assume responsibility for the protection of fundamental rights within its areas of competence and activity. The EU has gone further than this, however: as is shown in the various chapters of this book, the EU, especially through the Charter of Fundamental Rights, introduces specific rights that the Member States must apply and provides a framework of rights as inspiration for the global discussion on human and fundamental rights. Almost the first words of the preamble of the Charter of Fundamental Rights mention the spiritual and moral heritage of the European Union.[2]

The Charter of Fundamental Rights includes several rights that are not found in earlier human rights instruments or in instruments of a wider geographical applicability. This is discussed in more detail elsewhere in this book, but such more unusual rights that may be mentioned include the right to conduct business, the right of access to placement services, and non-discrimination based on age or genetic features, as well as the rights of the elderly. The background to introducing new rights may be manifold. But it raises the question of whether it is part of a new development of rights that will lead to changes of also other instruments in order for more human

---

[1] Bieber (2009), Kerikmäe and Nyman-Metcalf (2012a), and Locke (2009).

[2] Charter of Fundamental Rights, Preamble (second paragraph).

K. Nyman-Metcalf
Tallinn Law School, Tallinn University of Technology, Akadeemia tee 3, 12618 Tallinn, Estonia
e-mail: katrin.nyman-metcalf@ttu.ee

T. Kerikmäe (ed.), *Protecting Human Rights in the EU*,
DOI 10.1007/978-3-642-38902-3_3, © Springer-Verlag Berlin Heidelberg 2014   21

rights instruments to include such "modern" rights or is instead a sign of a different trend that will lead to a lessening of the universality of rights and towards a concentration on more concrete and specific rights applicable to fewer and more homogenous countries, perhaps in just one region. There is also a third possibility, namely that there is neither the one nor the other change, but the Charter is a specific instrument in the rather specific setting of the EU and has no effect on general human rights law.

The use of the words "fundamental rights" rather than "human rights" can be read as a sign that the Charter is intended to be quite different from universal human rights instruments or even the European Convention on Human Rights and Fundamental Freedoms (ECHR). However, when seeing how not just in the public debate and by many authors but even by jurists the different terms related to rights are used interchangeably or at least without strict distinctions, not too much should be read into the titles of international rights instruments.[3]

The question of universality of human rights is the subject of debate in many contexts. This may be in relation to specific rights and the difference in their interpretation or more generally linked to cultural relativism. Both phenomena are exacerbated by globalisation and its different facets, such as (pertaining to the two contexts mentioned) that modern technologies mean that, for example, freedom of expression and privacy issues concerning the same media content can be relevant simultaneously in very different parts of the world. International assistance to state building further highlights cultural relativism issues. The important role of the EU in the world means that its policy on fundamental rights will have importance outside of the borders of the Union, if only as an example watched with interest in different parts of the world. The EU Treaties indicate the importance EU policies can have also outside of the EU in the Article on external action and foreign and security policy; Article 21 of the Treaty of the European Union (TEU) proclaims that the Union, in its action on the international scene, shall be guided by the same principles that inspired its own creation, one such principle being the universality and indivisibility of human rights and fundamental freedoms. The second paragraph of the same Article mentions support of human rights as a goal for external action.

Universality of human rights at first glance appears attractive: we all have human rights by nature, as we are all part of the human race, and we should all have the same rights just because we are indeed humans. Moving one step away from this philosophical approach to the actual embodiment of rights in legal instruments, universality is more problematic.[4] Robert Post is sceptical to universal standards generally because, in his view, such standards are generally articulated at such a high level of abstraction and have so many exceptions and qualifications that they lose the ability to guide and control state action.[5]

---

[3] In national law, the use of terminology, including the distinction between (the equivalents of) fundamental rights and human rights, is usually much stricter.

[4] Kerikmäe and Nyman-Metcalf (2012b).

[5] Molnar (2012), p. 30.

It can be argued if and in that case what rights can be universal. Even if the corpus of rights is in some instances universal, that same universality may be challenged in formulation and interpretation. Rights more often than not are neither historically nor cross-culturally universal but rather retain elements of specific historical, political, and economic circumstances.[6] Interpretation in a manner that suits the specific cultural context is the way by which to avoid an undesirable level of harmonisation because of international conventions. However, interpretation can only go so far: the more specific the rights are, the less scope is there to "interpret away" any differences.

In the EU itself, the Charter explicitly refers to common values while respecting the diversity of the cultures and traditions of the peoples of Europe and national identities.[7] The EU's respect for the cultural, religious, and linguistic diversities of the Member States is one of the rights of the Charter.[8] The question of how much of a common philosophy the EU actually possesses on which to build its understanding of rights that it wishes to implement among all the Member States and furthermore spread to the world adds yet another layer to the question of what the influence of the Charter can be for fundamental rights in general.[9]

2   Contextuality, Universality, or Something in Between?

Important academics, such as Robert Post, advocate a contextualist view on human rights: what is suitable in one country may not be so in another, and this should be accepted even if there are international conventions.[10] Traditions, general understandings, and practical situations are not the same so rights cannot be. Illustrating the state of flux that the universalism is in, Post in a recent interview[11] claimed surprise to have heard speakers at a media conference claiming that hate speech should be regulated by different countries in their own way. He claimed that, contrary to his own contextualist views, in most instances advocates of rights would rather claim and support universality of any rights that form part of international conventions on human rights—an internationalist doctrine of human rights that extend universally around the globe, a global vision of rights that would not allow that speech is constitutionally protected in one country but not another.

Ovey and White highlight human rights treaties—as opposed to some other international treaties—as treaties that must allow states a margin of appreciation if they are to be at all effective. Without such contextuality as state-specific social

---

[6] Heinze (2009), pp. 270–272.

[7] Charter of Fundamental Rights, Preamble (paragraph 3).

[8] Charter of Fundamental Rights, Article 22.

[9] On this see Williams (2009), p. 550.

[10] Molnar (2012), pp. 23–24.

[11] *Ibid.*

developments and culture entail, the rights may not be effectively enforceable and thus not fulfil their objective. This is not the same as questioning the autonomy of human rights, but it provides a necessary frame in which to interpret the rights that is indeed contextual.[12]

Even if the context may have to be considered, Krygier is just one of many influential authors who also warn against exaggerating the cultural context, as this lends itself to being used as an excuse for not tackling real problems and for eroding rights.[13]

Contextuality and the differences between different countries when it comes to interpretation of human rights that it should logically lead to is one thing. It may be complicated, but it is not new and is something on which there is an understanding since some time already, illustrated by cases in international human rights bodies. What, however, is a growing issue is cultural differences *within* one society, with different groups of people having very different cultures that affect their understanding of rights. To what extent this should influence interpretation of rights, affording respect for minority culture and traditions, even if these differ from those of the majority population, is a complex and politically challenging question. This issue is seen in many European states with large immigrant populations or national minorities. Politically, the view that people have the right to maintain their culture and traditions even when they have settled in another country has been growing for the past three or four decades, but more recently (about the last decade) the opposite view that everyone who lives in a country must adapt to the majority culture appears to gain ground, not least in many EU states (where this is a controversial political topic in many countries). In addition, even if the general view of respect for all cultures and for maintenance of traditions still has a lot of followers, the situation often looks different when a specific right is concerned. The wearing of Islamic dress is one such issue that has highlighted the tension between different rights and different interpretations of rights.

Finnis mentions the Shabina Begum case from the UK House of Lords, which accepted a school's ban on wearing the Islamic *jilbab* in school; as there were other schools with a policy that Shabina could attend, she was not deprived education. In Finnis' view, the House of Lords did not pay much attention to freedom of religion issues. He criticises the verdict as illustrating the unsatisfactory conceptual and argumentative state of contemporary human rights law.[14] The case was decided rather on a practical level, dodging the sensitive issue.

Achieving functioning universality through culture-specific interpretation is complicated by the fact that the view on what such interpretation should be—the context for it—and the understandings of the persons making the interpretation are determined by a specific community. In this way, there is a "correct" interpretation, although others may—depending on how much cultural relativism the commentator

---

[12] Ovey and White (2006), p. 55.

[13] Krygier makes this comment in relation to Afghanistan. Krygier (2011), pp. 30–31.

[14] Finnis (2009), pp. 430–431.

accepts—use a different way to reach this "correct" answer. The Charter of Fundamental Rights illustrates the setting in the EU for what the context of rights is. It complements the ECHR and the extensive case law accompanying that (and applicable to all EU Member States). How much room is allowed for culture-specific interpretations against this backdrop will be further shown through additional case law in the future. A more specific way to formulate rights, however, would appear likely to give less room for different interpretations. The Charter has decided several issues that may be culture-specific and narrowed the scope of interpretation on these issues in the EU. It is a liberal democratic view with social responsibility and importance of equality between sexes and ethnic groups, with respect for various minorities, that is the European setting for rights.

In a global context, to use such a setting as a starting point for what rights are or should be is much more complex. Malik calls the view naïve that liberal democracy is the panacea in the rights context.[15] Liberal democracy is not the setting against which rights have to be fought for in many parts of the world, and it is not always the aim that those who advocate more rights strive for. She recognises the usefulness of liberal democracy as a yardstick against which extremism is measured but not as the setting in which situations necessarily have to be interpreted.[16] From this viewpoint, the EU Charter may not be able to contribute to the global human rights discourse, as it is too clearly anchored in a specific setting.

In many European countries and thus also in European institutions, cases related to Islam have figured prominently when it comes to interpretation of rights and cultural sensitivities in such interpretation. It is not difficult to find support for the gut feeling that, in cases that are in some way related to Islam, the courts or other organs adjudicating have a sceptical starting point to this religion and presuppose that elements of it are incompatible with democracy and rule of law. In addition to political reasons for scepticism toward Islam, the fact that it contains a special legal system through the so-called Sharia law increases the possibility of legal conflicts. The status of Sharia in Muslim countries (apart from the expressly secular ones like Turkey) is nominally at the top of the hierarchy, but the real impact in daily life is weakened by concurrent secular legislation. The impact of Sharia is mainly felt in family law (and inheritance).[17] The scepticism it arouses reaches further than this, however.

In the *Refah party* case of the European Court on Human Rights (ECtHR),[18] it was permitted in Turkey to outlaw the party in question because it was in favour of Sharia, and this was seen to be incompatible with democracy and the rule of law. Finnis finds that the state does not have the competence to assume the legitimacy of religious beliefs, as this would be incompatible with the duty of neutrality and impartiality of state that is recognised in secular rule of law states, such as those in

---

[15] Malik (2009), p. 98.

[16] *Ibid.*

[17] Abiad (2008), pp. 51–52.

[18] Refah and others v. Turkey (2003).

Europe. Although the state appears not to have explicitly dealt with the legitimacy question in *Refah*, Finnis still feels that the court too readily found certain faith-based matters to be incompatible with the European Convention on Human Rights.[19]

The Charter makes no special concessions to differences in religion and culture but is based on the understanding that there is coherence between the Member States. Freedom of thought, conscience, and religion is recognised in Article 10 of the Charter with what has become standard language in human rights instruments. Article 21 bans discrimination based, among other things, on religion. From the drafting history of the Charter, the controversy over whether to mention the Christian heritage of European states in the preamble may be recalled.[20] No such reference was made, only a general one to spiritual and moral heritage, although there are those who find that in essence this can be seen as including faith.

3   Social and Economic Rights

Classical human rights discourse uses the image of three generations of rights: the first generation consists of civil and political rights; the second, of economic and social rights; and the third, of collective rights. Many authors still use this description as a handy pedagogical tool,[21] but others find it oversimplified.[22] In any case, traditionally the Western world, including European states, puts most emphasis on the first generation rights as fundamental rights of a special nature—capable of being truly universal. Economic and social rights normally entail a cost for the state and are thus linked to social and economic policy, making their enforcement more difficult and highlighting the limitations of the international legal system, in which it may be possible to hold states to account for abuses of rights (even if also this is limited) but is more or less impossible to, in any meaningful way, impose positive obligations on states to undertake specific social reforms or use their funds in certain ways.

In a more limited setting and especially if linked to a legal system with the tools to make demands on its Member States (such as the EU), the second generation rights, however, fit the European system very well, as this is a system construed around an understanding of a social state with responsibility for the well-being of its citizens. The European Social Charter from 1961 is one illustration, but specific EU

---

[19] Finnis (2009), p. 436.

[20] For example http://www.dw.de/merkel-wants-eu-charter-to-make-reference-to-christianity/a-2320266; http://www.religioustolerance.org/const_eu.htm.

[21] In varying ways and to a varying extent, see Freeman (2011), Moeckli et al. (2010), and Vincent (2010).

[22] One such sceptic is Anderson, who thinks that the talk of generations may distract from the responsibility to react to human suffering wherever it arises by instead focusing on theoretical differences between types of rights. Anderson (2011), p. 357.

law on social matters takes the common understanding of such rights even further. The Charter can be seen as following in the footsteps of a multitude of different initiatives; the Economic and Social Committee in an opinion from 2011 on the social dimension of the internal market gives expression to a not unusual view in the EU: that the development toward even more emphasis on social rights is only just starting. The Committee says that "In the longer term the European Union should strive to strengthen the social dimension and realise the full potential of the internal market. The Lisbon Treaty and the annexed Charter of Fundamental Rights have not yet had their full impact on the balance between fundamental rights and economic rights. Strengthening the social dimension requires that the fundamental social rights be strengthened and that any limitation of fundamental rights which includes social rights be very restrictive. A Treaty change could be pursued to achieve this objective".[23]

The social and economic rights that the Committee is looking for are, to a large extent, linked to the core principles of the EU, most specifically the free movements. They also reflect an understanding of rights that is specific for relatively like-minded countries. In the context of universality, social and economic rights pose many challenges, as they tend to be very influenced by economic conditions, income level of the state, tax policies, and other such matters external to the rights area. Whether one should draw the conclusion from this that such rights cannot be universal is another question. There may be a level of universality possible even regarding such rights, if there is some value to the right also after the externalities have been peeled away. It is not difficult to find such value: workers can have rights to decent working conditions and to take certain action to ensure such conditions at a low as well as high end of the scale, and education should be a right for all, even if the standards in which it is provided must differ as long as there are economic differences between countries. The problem with the Charter rights in this respect may be that they go for the more specific and that which needs a certain context in order to have value. Thus, the Charter may not be able to contribute much to the global development of rights—in any case not as anything more than an interesting example of what can be, once a certain level has been reached. But at the same time, it should not pose any danger to universality of economic and social rights up to the kind of level where such universality may be of relevance.

4 Rights Affected by Technology

Globalisation means that more and more people live for shorter or longer time in countries other than that in which they (or their parents) were born or where their ethic group is in majority. There is, however, another effect of globalisation that

---

[23] Opinion of the European Economic and Social Committee on 'The Social Dimension of the Internal Market' (own-initiative opinion) (2011/C 44/15), 11 February 2011, section 1.7.

may be seen as pulling in the opposite direction as far as universality of rights is concerned. Instead of complicating the issue, by bringing cultural differences even to the domestic arena, this other side of globalisation—elimination of borders through technology—supports universality. Technology has even led to a discussion on a fourth generation of rights: rights related to scientific and technological development.[24]

The protection of privacy is a right that is affected directly by modern technologies. There are new ways of communicating, reaching many more people in a very short time. Through this, new threats to privacy have arisen or the potential negative effects of violations have multiplied. Perhaps even more important than the technologies as such are the differences to culture of communications and perceptions of what is the private and the public sphere that have come about in the past decade or so (the post-Facebook era). The interpretation of the right to privacy is in a process of change, even in cases where legislation may not have changed, and there are various reforms of legislation going on. In this context, the Charter does not offer anything new. It does not include any novel provisions on privacy but repeats traditional words on respect for private and family life, home, and communications.[25] If this may appear disappointingly traditional, given the rapid technological developments that affect this right, it would be difficult to formulate new provisions without the risk of these becoming obsolete soon, so new technologies more suitably should be taken into consideration through interpretation. The preamble of the Charter mentions changes in society, social progress, and scientific and technological developments as reasons for making rights more visible in a Charter.[26]

Significantly for privacy and new technologies, the right of data protection is explicitly recognised in the Charter, including the right to access and rectify data about themselves and the need for control by an independent authority.[27] Data protection is not a right that is mentioned in most major human rights instruments. As an explicit right is relatively new, it was previously seen as an element of privacy, included through interpretation but thus also less specific.

The EU has dealt with aspects of privacy that are directly related to modern communications through instruments applicable specifically to technologies. This includes restriction of unsolicited communications in instruments of consumer protection and is related to telecommunications or electronic communication as the modern term is.[28] Such instruments that deal with protection of privacy both

---

[24] Ovey and White (2006), pp. 5–6. This concept is, however, much less widespread than the use of the other three generations.

[25] Charter of Fundamental Rights, Article 7.

[26] Charter of Fundamental Rights, Preamble (Paragraph 4).

[27] Charter of Fundamental Rights, Article 8.

[28] Like Directive 97/7/EC on the Protection of Consumers, Directive 97/66/EC concerning Processing of Personal Data and the Protection of Privacy in the Telecommunications Sector, Directive 2000/31/EC on Certain Legal Aspects of Information Society Services, and Directive 2002/58/EC concerning Processing of Personal Data and the Protection of Privacy in the Electronic Communications Sector.

from a more "classical" perspective and from the explicit data protection perspective show evidence of the importance the EU attaches to these rights. How to ensure that rights can be adequately protected also in light of new communications without stifling the development of such communications is a matter to which the EU legislator pays attention.[29]

Privacy protection is an area where a lack of common, universal understanding of the right can be seen. The difference may be more generational than cultural, but as the entire concept of privacy is changing, countries are reaching different conclusions when battling with the new realities the courts and other organs are faced with. The ECtHR case *von Hannover v. Germany*[30] illustrates the possibilities for different interpretation of privacy versus freedom of the press. The case, concerning Princess Caroline of Monaco, dealt with expectations of privacy. The German court said that privacy does not end at the walls of the house but extends also to public places, if there is a reasonable expectation of privacy. However, in the case at hand, there was no such expectation, given the public profile of the Princess. The verdict of the German court was overturned by ECtHR, which found that a spatial criterion for privacy is unsuitable and the criteria should be functional. In this court's view, only when the press exercises a proper watchdog function does freedom of the press take over from the privacy expectations of persons. Not only was the outcome of the two courts different, but Grimm finds that the reasoning was also very different with the court using fundamentally different interpretation of the meaning and function of the right.[31]

In this case, the difference is between two courts that form a part of the same system: the European system of human rights. In such a situation, there is likely to be a harmonisation of the interpretation following ECtHR cases overturning national verdict. On a global level, there is no such formal mechanism for harmonisation. Data protection is an area where the differences between the European view and that of the US is well known. Tensions arise between these systems, in particular, as there is so much exchange between these countries and consequently a need to exchange data. The EU concern for data protection clashes with the US practice of more extensive use by authorities of personal data, without independent control mechanisms.[32] Whether the mention of data protection as an explicit right in the Charter will change the dynamics of the debate between the EU and US remains to be seen. Most probably it will not add anything totally new and different, as most cases are anyhow negotiated and decided on a case-by-case basis, but the addition underlines the importance the EU attaches to data protection.

Another topic of interest in the context of global media is the difference of viewpoints, notably between the United States of America and most of the rest of

---

[29] Gonzales Fuster et al. (2010), pp. 107–109.

[30] Case von Hannover v. Germany, application 59320/00, European Court of Human Rights 24 June 2004.

[31] Grimm (2009), p. 20.

[32] For example, see Bellanova (2010).

the (democratic) world, on whether special types of speech—hate speech—should be banned by law. The US view based on the First Amendment to the US Constitution (as interpreted by the US Supreme Court[33]) means that all speech is essentially protected and content restrictions cannot be made. It is another matter that there may be restrictions in some situations, but the restrictions will be made because of the situation and not the content of the speech. This almost absolute protection of speech has meant that the US has made reservations, for example, when signing the 1965 Convention on Elimination of All Forms of Racial Discrimination,[34] which requires signatories to condemn all racist propaganda and promotion of racism.[35] It appears as if the trend in Europe is going rather in the direction of more restrictions on types of expressions, thus leading to more divergence with the US. In the Charter, Article 11 provides a traditional protection of freedom of expression, adding explicitly freedom and pluralism of the media.

Without a universal standard for free speech, the Internet and its ability to quickly and easily spread information across borders do pose challenges that are not yet resolved, but where cases go in different directions in different jurisdictions, the challenge is not just regarding what is allowed but also how jurisdiction should be determined.[36]

5 European Exceptionalism?

All the while international conventions on human rights have been developed, there still has been a widespread agreement that countries differ too much to apply exactly the same standards, even if they are parties to the same conventions. There are those who oppose international conventions because of this, but more commonly it is thought that interpretation must take into account such differences and the extent to which universality should even be striven for is limited. This does not prevent the view that it is possible in the human rights context for certain countries to propagate human rights in other parts of the world, using the basic universality as the explanation for this but, in reality, topping this up with the understanding that they have the "right" view of how rights should be applied. The Americans have been vociferous in claiming such a right to bring ideas to the world, but if there was ever any universally common view that the USA was a leader in human rights, this is likely to have totally eroded following the many torture scandals, events of prison abuse, and other events linked to the so-called war on

---

[33] Most importantly in the Brandenburg case, *Brandenburg v. Ohio* 395 US 444 (1969).

[34] International Convention on the Elimination of All Forms of Racial Discrimination, 21 December 1965, 660 UNTS 195 (1965).

[35] Rosenfeld (2012), p. 272.

[36] Kulesza (2012), p. 45.

terror in the 2000s.[37] This also erodes the corollary view that a country that is ahead enough to teach others can take some liberties on what it does itself—the American "exceptionalism".

Nonetheless, perhaps the Charter of Fundamental Rights indicates a European exceptionalism? Instead of using this to limit rights in universal human rights declaration (like the US approach to the death penalty, completely exceptional to democratic states), the European version consists of adding a new layer onto existing rights and interpreting the "old" rights through a new prism.

In the context of exceptionalism, it may be recalled that any such idea applied to human rights in fact goes against one of the very basic ideas (and ideals) of international human rights. The basic dogma of human rights has been called the first universal ideology to illustrate that certain rights should be devoid of any cultural or historical differences. The individual and her rights and freedoms should be at the centre of the human rights discourse, primarily protecting the rights of individuals against the state. This idea risks getting lost in a situation where the rights get all the more specific.[38] The kind of rights that are now referred to under the heading of human rights includes rights where the protection is not really focused on protection against abuses by the state, but the possible abuses as well as the ability to guarantee rights is rather for the private sector or at least mixed between the state, private sector, and other organisations. The idea of human rights and the responsibility the state has have always included the principle that the state must undertake measures to ensure that there are sanctions for human rights violators and measures to support respect for human rights by everyone, but with the kind of more concrete and specific rights that, for example, the Charter contains, there may be more of a need for active involvement by a variety of bodies if the rights are to have any real value. In addition to globalisation, there may be a trend of privatisation of rights.

The Charter is an example of a "Western" approach to rights, with specific rights suitable for a developed society with a certain living standard. At the same time, social and economic rights are involved on the same footing as political and civil rights, which departs from the classical "Western" approach. The question of rights as universal or as Western impositions via colonialism or neo-colonialism has been going on for at least 30 years, and is still ongoing, but has changed in focus lately, as more different states of different backgrounds take more active roles in world affairs. Some authors recently mention fundamental survival issues—the need to alleviate human suffering—as concepts that should enter the rights discourse.[39] Such suffering may be caused by environmental factors, war, political crises, and

---

[37] Europeans will not be the only ones to cringe at statements like that American exceptionalism exists as "the United States is a beacon of liberty, democracy and equality of opportunity to the rest of the world", said in a statement disputing the reference by a Supreme Court Justice to cases from the European Court of Human Rights, in the case anti-sodomy law case, Lawrence v. Texas. See Greene (2012), p. 109.

[38] Kerikmäe and Nyman-Metcalf (2012b).

[39] Anderson (2011), p. 356.

other factors. A novelty for human rights if such concepts are given a role is, according to Anderson, that in what he calls a Southern view on rights; the emphasis is on various rights outside the traditional institutional architecture of states or international protection mechanisms. The focus is alleviating suffering— the actual measure to do this is decided based on what causes the suffering, which can be very different things.[40]

If juxtaposing "Southern" and "Western" (or African or Asian and European) views on rights, what is then the European view? Is it more than the enumeration of rights, backed up by a specific philosophy that is more important than the listed rights as such, as it provides a framework in which to interpret any rights? Williams is somewhat sceptical as to the existence of a clear philosophy of EU law while still maintaining that there is a philosophy even if incomplete.[41] The problems of the incompleteness of the philosophy is seen not least in the fundamental rights field, where, in the words of Williams, such rights were grafted onto the EU institutional framework in an ill-defined and incoherent way.[42]

Another angle of European exceptionalism may be to stress the strong emphasis on individual human rights, overriding other concerns such as national security, at least if the threat to the rights of the individual is of a certain severity. Such an interpretation does not follow from the Charter as such, and it is yet too early to say whether the application of the Charter will lead to such a conclusion—there is not much case law on the Charter yet. However, this conclusion can be made from the *Kadi* case,[43] in which the European Court of Justice (changing on appeal the decision of the Court of First Instance) went against a UN instrument imposing sanctions on individuals suspected of terrorism activities because of the insufficient guarantees that the rights of the individuals were respected. For there to be such a principle of pre-eminence of rights that can actually be applied, there is a need for a set of values that is, if not explicitly listed, at least well known enough to be usable as a yardstick for interpretation.[44] The Charter can help in providing this set of values even if the concrete issues may not all be explicitly handled in the Charter. This is only provided that Member States of the EU, as well as EU institutions, will regard the Charter as an important instrument that not only will be applied in specific cases but also will be considered in lawmaking, in the public discourse on rights and as an interpretative tool. Such development could make European exceptionalism very positive from the human rights perspective—as that beacon of rights that the US rather hypocritically likes to present itself as. Unfortunately, also, Europe has a way to go before it could act as such a beacon.

---

[40] *Ibid.* p. 357.

[41] Williams (2009), p. 551.

[42] *Ibid.* p. 552.

[43] Joined Cases C-402/05P and C-415/02P *Kadi v. Council* (8 September 2008).

[44] Williams (2009), p. 563.

6   Some Concluding Reflections

The question that may be read into the title of this chapter is whether there is a future for the universality of rights, and as this is a book dealing with the Charter for Fundamental Rights of the EU, the influence this instrument has on the universality is understood as a sub-question. In a typically lawyerly fashion, one may respond to the question with a both yes and no, depending on how the question is phrased.

There are conflicting trends affecting universality of rights as has been shown. There is globalisation with people moving, travelling, and forming relationship over national borders at an increasing rate. There is globalisation through modern technologies that ignore national borders. The information flow means that we know much more, much more rapidly about what happens in other parts of the world. Abuses of rights are brought to the attention of the world through modern media almost in real time, even when regimes still try to supress information. Only the most reclusive regimes (and not even these) manage to maintain information embargos. These trends all speak in favour of universality of rights. We are part of a global community, and our rights should reflect this.

On the other hand, what is very relevant about communication mentioned as a trend supporting universality is that it also leads to meetings of different cultures and traditions on the micro-level at an increasing frequency. Different cultures and ensuing different interpretations of rights are much more likely to occur much more frequently than a bit more than half a century ago, when many human rights instruments were born. This highlights the different perceptions that colour how people interpret rights.

What, if anything, is the role of the Charter of Fundamental Rights in this development? It is an instrument of a regional organisation that, albeit consisting of many countries and peoples, is reasonably coherent. It may appear as if it does not need to worry about issues outside of this limited spectrum and, consequently, will have marginal influence outside its area of application. If taking a purely functional and instrumental view, this position can be accepted. However, in the human rights discourse, such limited views are not normally of great interest. The whole idea of rights, why we have them, and where they come from—natural law or positive law—is not conductive to being reduced to a narrow functional question. It is an ongoing debate where it is easy to forget in the midst of disappointment of even liberal democracies violating rights with reference to the "war on terror" that there has indeed been a great development toward respect for human rights, if compared to, for example, the situation prior to or just after the Second World War. The development is a step-by-step edifice where the understanding of rights is added by any new instruments and their interpretation. Here, the EU and the Charter may lead by example and provide new understandings of rights.

References

Books and Articles

Abiad N (2008) Sharia, Muslim States and International Human Rights Treaty Obligations: a comparative study. British Institute of International and Comparative Law, London

Anderson GW (2011) Human rights and the global south. In: Campbell T, Ewing KD, Tomkins A (eds) The legal protection of human rights. Sceptical essays. Oxford University Press, Oxford, pp 347–364 (Chapter 17)

Bellanova R (2010) The case of the 2008 German–US agreement on data exchange: an opportunity to reshape power relations. In: Gutwirth S, Poullet Y, de Hert P (eds) Data protection in a profiled world. Springer, London, pp 211–226

Bieber R (2009) The Lissbon Urteil: an association of Sovereign States. Eur Constitut Law Rev 5 (3):391–406

Finnis J (2009) Endorsing discrimination between faiths: a case of extreme speech? In: Hare I, Weinstein J (eds) Extreme speech and democracy. Oxford University Press, Oxford, pp 430–441

Freeman M (2011) Human rights: an interdisciplinary approach. Cambridge University Press, Cambridge

Gonzales Fuster G, Gutwirth S, de Hert P (2010) From unsolicited communications to unsolicited adjustments. In: Gutwirth G, Poullet Y, de Hert P (eds) Data protection in a profiled world. Springer, London, pp 105–117

Greene J (2012) Hate speech and the demos. In: Herz M, Molnar P (eds) The content and context of hate speech – rethinking regulation and responses. Cambridge University Press, Cambridge, pp 92–115

Grimm D (2009) Freedom of speech in a globalized world. In: Hare I, Weinstein J (eds) Extreme speech and democracy. Oxford University Press, Oxford, pp 11–22

Heinze E (2009) Cumulative jurisprudence and hate speech: sexual orientation and analogies to disability, age and obesity. In: Hare I, Weinstein J (eds) Extreme speech and democracy. Oxford University Press, Oxford, pp 265–285

Kerikmäe T, Nyman-Metcalf K (2012a) The European Union and Sovereignty: the sum is more than it's parts? Temas de Integracao, junho 5–16

Kerikmäe T, Nyman-Metcalf K (2012b) Less is more or more is more? Revisiting universality of human rights. Int Comp Law Rev 12(1):35–51

Krygier M (2011) Approaching the rule of law. In: Mason W (ed) The rule of law in Afghanistan. Cambridge University Press, Cambridge, pp 15–34

Kulesza J (2012) International Internet law. Routledge, London

Locke T (2009) Why the European Union is not a State: some critical remarks. Eur Constitut Law Rev 5(3):407–420

Malik M (2009) Extreme speech and Liberalism. In: Hare I, Weinstein J (eds) Extreme speech and democracy. Oxford University Press, Oxford, pp 96–120

Moeckli D, Shah S, Sivakumaran S (eds) (2010) International human rights law. Oxford University Press, Oxford

Molnar P (2012) Interview with Robert Post. In: Herz M, Molnar P (eds) The content and context of hate speech – rethinking regulation and responses. Cambridge University Press, Cambridge, pp 11–36

Ovey C, White RCA (2006) Jacobs and White: The European Convention on Human Rights, 4th edn. Oxford University Press, Oxford

Rosenfeld M (2012) Hate speech in contemporary jurisprudence in. In: Herz M, Molnar P (eds) The content and context of hate speech – rethinking regulation and responses. Cambridge University Press, Cambridge, pp 242–289

Vincent A (2010) The politics of human rights. Oxford University Press, Oxford

Williams AT (2009) Taking rights seriously: towards a philosophy of EU Law. Oxf J Leg Stud 29 (3):549–577

Official Material

International Convention on the Elimination of All Forms of Racial Discrimination, 21 December 1965, 660 UNTS 195 (1965)
Directive 97/7/EC on the Protection of Consumers
Directive 97/66/EC concerning Processing of Personal Data and the Protection of Privacy in the Telecommunications Sector
Directive 2000/31/EC on Certain Legal Aspects of Information Society Services
Directive 2002/58/EC concerning Processing of Personal Data and the Protection of Privacy in the Electronic Communications Sector
Opinion of the European Economic and Social Committee on 'The Social Dimension of the Internal Market' (own-initiative opinion) (2011/C 44/15), 11 February 2011

Case Law

European Court of Human Rights
Case *Refah and others v. Turkey*, applications 41340/98; 41342/98; 41343/98; 41344/98, European Court of Human Rights 13 February 2003
Case *von Hannover v. Germany*, application 59320/00, European Court of Human Rights 24 June 2004

European Court of Justice

Joined Cases C- 402/05P and C-415/02P *Kadi v. Council* (8 September 2008).

United States Supreme Court

Case *Brandenburg v. Ohio* 395 US 444 (1969

The Freedom to Conduct Business and the Right to Property: The EU Technology Transfer Block Exemption Regulation and the Relationship Between Intellectual Property and Competition Law

Katrin Nyman-Metcalf, Pawan Kumar Dutt, and Archil Chochia

1 Introduction

Although the European Union (EU) does not stipulate in detail the economic system of its Member States, it is a system based on market economies with a protection of private property and the right to conduct business. This has been explicitly stipulated in the Charter of Fundamental Rights. The Charter recognises the freedom to conduct business, Article 16, as well as the right to property, Article 17. The second paragraph of Article 17 states that intellectual property shall be protected. This short line includes interesting potential legal conflicts, as Intellectual Property Rights (IPR) may limit the free conduct of business or, otherwise put, the free competition. The history of the EU shows that competition law promoting especially competition across the EU is of primary concern. Furthermore, the EU promotes research and development (R&D), which leads to creation of new Intellectual Property. R&D includes creative work carried out on a systematic basis in order to increase the stock of knowledge of man, culture, and society and the use of this knowledge to devise new applications.[1] Such property can then be commercially exploited by its owner by means of production, distribution, sales and/or licensing. Since an IPR very often gives rise to a monopoly, its grant can run contrary to Competition laws and the anti-trust measures supported by such laws.

Intellectual property laws and Competition law have often been portrayed as each other's opposites. This is mainly because an IPR grants an artificial protection to companies and can sometimes give them an advantage over competitors, by way of dominance in a market or even a complete monopoly. On the other hand, Competition law works towards promoting and enhancing competition. It must be

---

[1] European Commission, Eurostat "Glossary".

K. Nyman-Metcalf (✉) • P.K. Dutt • A. Chochia
Tallinn Law School, Tallinn University of Technology, Akadeemia tee 3, 12618 Tallinn, Estonia
e-mail: katrin.nyman-metcalf@ttu.ee; Pawan.Dutt@ttu.ee; archil.chochia@ttu.ee

T. Kerikmäe (ed.), *Protecting Human Rights in the EU*,
DOI 10.1007/978-3-642-38902-3_4, © Springer-Verlag Berlin Heidelberg 2014

noted, however, that both have the same aim of enhancing consumer welfare, efficiently allocating resources, and promoting effective competition through innovation and investment in product development.[2] They thus both contribute to enjoying the right to conduct business and the protection of property.

In recent times, IPRs are increasingly deemed to be crucial to business performance. In this context, it is pertinent to note that a new term, Intellectual Capital, has also come into vogue. It is defined as all intangible resources that are available to an organisation that give a relative advantage and that, in combination, are able to produce future benefits. Further, Intellectual Capital is the product of interaction of three different classes of intangibles: human resources, organisational resources (which represent the "tangible" intangibles, i.e., everything of value that stays behind after the employees have left the organisation, like codified knowledge, procedures, processes, goodwill, patents, etc.), and relational resources.[3] Intellectual Capital is also defined by certain authors as the product of combining the products of R&D with the complementary assets that result in value creation.[4]

IPRs are beneficial to all sectors of the economy, and therefore the protection of such rights, once the Intellectual Property is created in any one country or region, is often made global through a crucial patchwork of bilateral and multilateral agreements. As increasing globalisation takes hold, firms manufacture and market their products worldwide. Therefore, licensing of the IPR they hold or need often proceeds on a global scale, and differences among nations' licensing rules have the potential to disrupt cross-border commerce. The United States (US), the European Union (EU), and Japan remain the three jurisdictions with the most comprehensive and up-to-date competition laws. The interplay of US, EU, Japan, and other international licensing regimes is important because the ability of firms to license IPRs internationally is one of the cornerstones in the foundation of a strong global economy. Surveys have shown how fear of weak IPR protection in other countries may act as a barrier to transfer of technologies even to subsidiaries in other countries.[5] Also important in this regard is accurate Intellectual Capital Reporting. This involves identifying, measuring, and reporting the Intellectual Capital of an enterprise, as well as constructing a coherent presentation of how the enterprise uses its knowledge resources. The main idea behind Intellectual Capital Reporting is that financial information tells something about the past performance of the enterprise but nothing about its future potential. The future potential of an enterprise lies, not within its financial capital, but in its Intellectual Capital.[6]

In this context, one must note that in the field of innovation, Europe lags behind her international competitors. In recent years, the structural difference in R&D funding between EU and its main competitors has drawn a lot of attention.

[2] Schmidt (2010), p. 224

[3] Stam and Andriessen (2008), pp. 489–500.

[4] RICARDIS REPORT 2006, p. 19.

[5] Odagiri et al. (2010), p. 11.

[6] RICARDIS REPORT 2006, p. 11.

Policymakers in EU have tried to increase R&D business expenditure, and R&D was at the heart of the strategy of the EU to become the most competitive and dynamically knowledge-based economy by 2010; one of the original goals set by the Lisbon Strategy was for the EU to increase its R&D expenditure to at least 3 % of GDP by 2010. In the Europe 2020 Strategy, adopted in 2010, the EU decided to maintain the 3 % objective for 2020.[7]

Research is recognised in the Charter of Fundamental Rights, in Article 13, from the viewpoint that research, as well as the arts, shall be free of constraints with respect for academic freedom. Attention is being devoted towards the concept of the European Research Area (ERA). This addresses the need to better exploit the intellectual potential of Europe, notably through the completion of the ERA by 2014. The ERA could be described in simple terms as a single market for knowledge, where ideas and those responsible for generating them circulate freely without legislative or economic barriers. It is hoped that ERA will help to remove obstacles to researcher mobility and to cross-border co-operation. The focus is on developing and using Europe's "intellectual capital" to pull Europe out of the current economic crisis and to build long-term sustainable growth.[8]

As part of the Innovation Union, the EU Commission has already introduced specific initiatives such as the unitary patent proposal, measures to improve standardisation, and launching of the pilot European Innovation Partnership on Active and Healthy Ageing. However, many other issues are also being tackled, such as improving of researchers' careers, better training and mobility, and modernisation of universities so that Europe can draw full benefit from its human capital.[9]

There is an ever-present need to create an environment in which innovation can flourish. Along with the above, the EU Commission's approach to governing technology transfer agreements must be considered in this context. Such rules must work twofold—firstly, they should provide the right basis for the diffusion of technology and, secondly, their interpretation and application need to take into account the short- to medium-term effects (i.e., the static effects on competition), as well as the long-run effects on the incentives to innovate (i.e., the dynamic effects on competition).[10]

---

[7] It should be noted that gross domestic expenditure on R & D (GERD) stood at EUR 245,673 million in the EU-27 in 2010, which was a 3.8 % increase from the 2009 GERD level, and was 43.5 % higher than ten years earlier (2000)—note that these rates of change are in current prices and so reflect price changes as well as real changes in the level of expenditure. In 2008, the level of expenditure on R & D in the EU-27 was 88.5 % of that recorded by the United States, although slightly more than double the level of expenditure in Japan and considerably above R & D expenditure levels in the emerging economies—for example, EU-27 expenditure was 5.3 times as high as in China. The EU-27's R & D expenditure relative to GDP remains well below the corresponding shares recorded in Japan (3.45 %) and the United States (2.79 %) in 2008; this pattern has existed for a lengthy period. European Commission, "R & D Expenditure" (2012).

[8] European Commission, "European Research Area" (2012).

[9] European Union, Press Release on the "Intellectual Capital" (2012).

[10] Bishop and Gore (2005).

Commission Regulation (EC) No 772/2004 of 27 April 2004 on the application of Article 101(3) of the Treaty on the Functioning of the European Union (the Treaty) to categories of technology transfer agreements, also known as the Technology Transfer Block Exemption Regulation (TTBER), was published on April 2004 and came into force on 1 May 2004. It was accompanied by the Guidelines for the assessment of technology transfer agreements, being the Guidelines on the application of Article 101 of the Treaty to technology transfer agreements (the guidelines).[11] The TTBER governs technology transfer arrangements, whereby the owner of a technology permits another party to exploit that technology for the production of goods and services. The accompanying guidelines cover agreements falling within the scope of the block exemption and also those falling outside.

This article focuses on the concrete application of the freedom to conduct business, the support for research, and the protection of property, including intellectual property, in that it analyses the TTBER and its accompanying guidelines, assessing to what extent it encourages innovation, and maintains effective competition and how it stands up against other like-minded pieces of legislation drafted across the world. The comparison will first show the similarities and then the differences between the approach herein that has been developed and followed in the EU, US, and Japan, among other countries. It will be analysed to what extent this approach towards IPR and Competition law is coherent and how things may possibly stand in the future in this regard. Finally, the authors will attempt to answer these questions: how meaningful and essential is this interface between IPR and competition law, and has the TTBER in particular served its purpose? Only if such practical measures work can it be said that the Charter protection for elements of the market economy is implemented?

The TTBER is due to be revised in 2014, which, together with the fact that the US Agencies have as recently as in 2007 conducted a review on antitrust enforcement and IPR, goes to show that this topic is very relevant to global trade and commerce. Further, the topic of the interface between IPR and Competition law will continue to stay in a state of flux as Intellectual Property continues to evolve. In this regard, it will serve us well to mark the following words: "Authorship and invention, the very acts to be rewarded by Intellectual Property law, may not be timeless concepts plucked from Heaven but may emerge in conjunction with - and be inextricably intertwined with - technology that makes them possible".[12]

2   Competition Laws and IPR

IPRs generally comprise trademarks, patents, copyrights, designs, and other legally protected rights. These are the intellectual property rights that Article 17 of the Charter affords explicit protection to. Article 1 (1) (g) of the TTBER provides, inter

---

[11] Official Journal C 101, 27.04.2004, pp. 2–42.

[12] Morris (2009), p. 218, wherein this quote by Palmer (1989), 273 is quoted.

alia, that "intellectual property rights" includes industrial property rights, know-how, copyright, and neighbouring rights. Grants of patents, trademarks, copyrights, and designs create monopolies concerning the specific property right for which they were granted. Intellectual Property laws confer exclusive rights on holders of the above-mentioned rights, like being permitted to prevent unauthorised use and to decide how to exploit the property, i.e., by licensing it. One limitation to this is the principle of Community exhaustion, which means that when a product incorporating an IPR has been put on the market inside the EU by the holder or with his consent, the IPR is exhausted.[13] Apart from having been set out in case law, this principle is also included in legislative acts like Article 7(1) of Directive 2008/95/ EC to approximate the laws of the Member States relating to trademarks.[14] "The principle of Community exhaustion is in line with the essential function of IPRs, which is to grant the holder the right to exclude others from exploiting his Intellectual Property without his consent."[15]

The above-mentioned grant to patent holders appears at a first glance to run contrary to Competition laws. In other words, what Intellectual Property law does is that it grants market power to its owners. On the other hand, Competition law reins in the market power and or potential abuse of it. It is this that creates the allegedly "great conflict" or "tension" between the two areas of law.[16]

It must be noted that such a conflict between IPR and Competition laws is not a new problem. It was pointed out by the US District Court that ever since a patent–antitrust conflict was considered by the English Court of King's Bench in 1602 in the first reported case on the subject (*Darcy v. Allein*), the issues arising in this field have yielded few clear or satisfying answers. The US District Court stated further, inter alia, that although economic arguments could be forwarded to the effect that the two statutes had a common goal of maximising wealth by means of facilitating the production of what the consumers desired at the lowest cost possible, whatever their economic congruency is, there was little doubt that these two sets of laws are judicially divergent.[17]

Most countries treat IPR as special exceptions to their general laws prohibiting monopolies in order to balance the interests of consumers and the state with the rights of IPR owners. Further, the IPRs held by patent, trademark, and copyright owners are strictly construed and limited to the narrow confines of the grant. Licensing arrangements involving statutory grants therefore should, accordingly, be limited to the rights contained in the grant. Any attempt to go beyond the scope of the grant— such as trying to license an expired patent, trademark, or copyright—is deemed to be a misuse of the grant and is treated as being either without effect or illegal.[18]

---

[13] Whish (2003), p. 765.

[14] OJ L 299, 8.11.2008, p. 25.

[15] Paragraph 6 of the guidelines.

[16] Morris (2009), p. 224.

[17] August 2002, p. 507, and case *SCM Corp. Vs. Xerox Corp* (1978) from which this quote is taken.

[18] *Ibid.*

It is necessary to also stress the complementary role of competition and
innovation policies, which both aim at promoting consumer welfare and an efficient
allocation of resources. The guidelines stress that innovation is an important
element of a competitive market economy, promoted by IPRs.[19] It is generally
agreed that the main objective of IPR laws is to promote technical progress, which
will likely lead to the ultimate benefit of the consumers or indeed of mankind, if the
right level of protection is found.[20] Competition policy aims at promoting consumer
welfare by protecting competition, making it the driving force of efficient markets
and innovation.[21] The relevant question is therefore not one of conflict but of
complementarity and possibly adjustment in the individual case.

On the question as to what extent should competition policy intervene and try to
improve the balance produced by IPR law, some general lines of agreement and
also some marked differences exist between different jurisdictions. For instance,
there is agreement on the small yet positive role that competition policy may play in
forming IPR law. Competition policy expertise comes handy in helping to decide
on issues like the correct scope and duration to be awarded under IPR law, i.e., in
deciding ex ante on the balance to be found in IPR law. An efficient competition
policy like an effective IPR policy is geared towards keeping the scope and duration
limited to the minimum necessary to elicit the inventors' efforts. Further, competition policy has to play its normal role where IPR is used to produce an anticompetitive effect beyond the exploitation of the IPR. For example, this can be seen in the
case of the conditioning of licensing on the purchase of a non-patented product
(tying) or on the imposition of a non-compete obligation (exclusive dealing), both
of which should be dealt with under Competition law.[22] There is also general
agreement that in such cases competition policy must take account of specific
IPR characteristics in order to properly protect dynamic efficiency. For instance,
a non-compete obligation may be required to protect the confidentiality of the
know-how transferred or to prevent the know-how benefiting competitors of the
licensor. There is, however, less agreement as to what extent there should be
interference by competition policy in respect of the exploitation of IPR. This is
seen to be true in the case of exploitation and licensing by both dominant and
non-dominant companies.[23]

The propriety of states adopting rules to regulate the anticompetitive aspects of
Intellectual Property licenses is now specifically recognised in International law.
Article 40, paragraph 1, of the Agreement on Trade-Related Aspects of Intellectual
Property Rights 1994 provides, inter alia, that the Members agree about the
possibility that some licensing practices or conditions pertaining to IPRs that

---

[19] Paragraph 7 of the guidelines.

[20] Brownsword and Goodwin (2012), p. 179. It is a delicate balance between protecting IPR and
allowing knowledge to be the common heritage of mankind. *Ibid.*

[21] Although this link is not uncontroversial. See Orbach (2011), pp. 133–164.

[22] Whish (2003), p. 203.

[23] Mehta and Peeperkorn (2002).

restrain competition may have adverse effects on trade. Further, the above may also impede the transfer and dissemination of technology. Accordingly, paragraph 2 provides, inter alia, that the World Trade Organisation members may specify in their national legislation licensing practices or conditions that may, in particular cases, constitute an abuse of IPRs having an adverse effect on competition in the relevant market. Thus, a member may adopt, consistently with the other provisions of this Agreement, appropriate measures to prevent or control such practices. The above practices are deemed to include, but are not limited to, exclusive grant-back conditions, conditions preventing challenges to validity, and coercive package licensing.[24]

Such competition rules are commonly found in long-standing anti-monopoly legislation. For example, in the US the Sherman Act of 1890 covers this area. Similarly, Articles 101 (formerly Article 81) and 102 (formerly Article 82) of the Treaty on the Functioning of the European Union stipulate various measures to prevent unfair competition.[25]

Article 101 of the Treaty prohibits cartels and other agreements that could disrupt free competition in the European Economic Area's common market. Article 101(1) applies only where the agreement has the object or effect of restricting competition. The "object" (purpose) of an agreement is determined by an objective assessment of its terms, not by the parties' subjective intent. In cases where it is not clear that the object of an agreement is to restrict competition, then it is necessary to consider its effects and whether such effects are necessary to achieve a legitimate pro-competitive business purpose.[26] Where the "effects" standard applies, Article 101(1) prohibits agreements containing restrictions on competition that have an "appreciable" impact on competition or on interstate trade.[27] This rule of appreciability is, in some respects, comparable to the rule of reason analysis under the United States Sherman Act. It was ruled by White CJ that a standard of reason had to be applied in order to determine whether a restraint was within the Sherman Act and that only undue or unreasonable restraints should be condemned.[28] According to Article 101(2), agreements that fall within the prohibition of Article 101(1) are automatically void.[29]

Under Article 101(3) of the Treaty, the Commission is empowered to exempt restrictive agreements from the prohibition of Article 101(1) if the agreement (or provision) at issue contributes to improving the production or distribution of the goods involved or to promoting technical or economic progress. Such contributions include savings in distribution costs, avoidance of duplicative development costs, promotion of technological innovation, and protection of the

---

[24] TRIPS Agreement 1994.

[25] Whish (2003), p. 427.

[26] Case C-234/89 *Delimitis v. Henninger Bräu AG* (1991) ECR 1-935.

[27] Case C-180/98 *Pavlov v. Stichting Pensionenfonds Medische Specialisten* (2000) ECR 1-6451.

[28] *Standard Oil v. US* 221 US 1 1911.

[29] Craig and De Burca (2008), pp. 969 and 976.

environment. Further, consumers must obtain a fair share of the resulting benefits. Consumers are recognised as a category worthy of protection also in the Charter, albeit briefly: Article 38 states that Union policy shall ensure a high level of consumer protection.

Article 102 of the Treaty is aimed at preventing undertakings that hold a dominant position in a market from abusing that position. Its core role is the regulation of monopolies, which restrict competition in private industry and produce worse outcomes for consumers and society. It is the second key provision, after Article 101, in EU Competition law. Whereas Article 101 is primarily directed at restrictive practices between two or more undertakings, Article 102 aims primarily at the conduct of one powerful undertaking. Market share is the primary test for determining whether a firm has a dominant position. The dominance must be assessed in relation to the product market, the geographical market, and the temporal factor, i.e., a firm may possess market power at a particular time of year, when competition from other products is low because of seasonal availability. Other factors the Commission may consider are the degree of vertical integration, economies of scale, technological advantages, the existence of a highly developed sales network, the absence of potential competition, and whether the relevant market is mature or rapidly changing. The mere holding of a dominant position is not unlawful. Article 102 does not prohibit market power per se. It proscribes the abuse of market power. Examples of abusive conduct include tying, predatory pricing, use of discriminatory trading conditions within the common market, and conduct aimed at preventing entry of new competitors into a market or eliminating existing competitors. Abusive conduct must, of course, be distinguished from aggressive competition on the merits, since the purpose of Article 102 is to protect consumers rather than particular competitors.[30]

Although the traditional view is that the exercise of an IPR cannot be prohibited by Article 102, there are cases where the exercise of IPR by dominant firms has been held to violate Article 102 and has therefore been enjoined.[31] In another case, the SACEM proceeding, the Commission held that it may be an abuse of dominant position under Article 102 for a copyright collection society to seek from its members royalties that a court deems to be "excessive".[32]

The last condition of Article 101(3), according to which the agreement must not afford the parties the possibility of eliminating competition in respect of a substantial part of the products concerned, presupposes an analysis of remaining

---

[30] *Ibid.*, pp. 1005, 1006, 1015, 1020 and 1037.

[31] In joined cases C-241/91 P and C-242/91P *Radio Telefis Eireann (RTE) and Independent Television Publications Ltd (ITP) v. Commission* p. I-00743, it was held that *The conduct of an undertaking in a dominant position, consisting of the exercise of a right classified by national law as "copyright", cannot, by virtue of that fact alone, be exempt from review in relation to Article 86 of the Treaty....However, the exercise of an exclusive right by a proprietor may, in exceptional circumstances, involve abusive conduct...*

[32] See paragraph 61 of Case T-114/92 *Bureau Européen des Médias de l'Industrie Musicale v. Commission.*

competitive pressures on the market and the impact of the agreement on such sources of competition. In the application of the last condition of Article 101(3), the relationship between Article 101(3) and Article 102 must be taken into account. Moreover, since Articles 101 and 102 both pursue the aim of maintaining effective competition on the market, consistency requires that Article 101(3) be interpreted as precluding any application of the exception rule to restrictive agreements that constitute an abuse of a dominant position.[33] According to settled case law, the application of Article 101(3) cannot prevent the application of Article 102 of the Treaty.[34]

3 The Development of Technology Transfer Regulation

The TTBER and the guidelines cover agreements for the transfer of technology. Article 1(1)(b) of TTBER defines "technology transfer agreement" as a patent licensing agreement, a know-how licensing agreement, a software copyright licensing agreement, or a mixed patent, know-how, or software copyright licensing agreement, including any such agreement containing provisions that relate to the sale and purchase of products or the licensing of other intellectual property rights or the assignment of intellectual property rights, provided that those provisions do not constitute the primary object of the agreement and are directly related to the production of the contract products, assignments of patents, know-how, software copyright, or a combination thereof where part of the risk associated with the exploitation of the technology remains with the assignor, in particular, where the sum payable in consideration of the assignment is dependent on the turnover obtained by the assignee in respect of products produced with the assigned technology, the quantity of such products produced, or the number of operations carried out employing the technology, shall also be deemed to be technology transfer agreements.[35]

Added to this exhaustive general definition, Article 1(1)(b) and (h) of the TTBER further stipulates that the concept of "technology" covers patents and patent applications, utility models, and applications for utility models, design rights, plant breeders rights, topographies of semiconductor products, supplementary protection certificates for medicinal products or other products for which such supplementary protection certificates may be obtained, software copyright, and know-how. Know-how is defined in Article 1(1)(i) of the TTBER as a package of

---

[33] Paragraph 151 of the guidelines.

[34] Footnote 62 of the guidelines. It states, inter alia, that the application of Article 101(3) does not prevent the application of the Treaty rules on the free movement of goods, services, persons, and capital. These provisions are in certain circumstances applicable to agreements, decisions, and concerted practices within the meaning of Article 101(1); see, to that effect, Case C-309/99 *Wouters.*

[35] Article 1(1)(b) of TTBER.

non-patented practical information, resulting from experience and testing, which is secret, substantial, and identified. The licensed technology should allow the licensee with or without other inputs to produce the contract products.[36] Know-how differs from IPR in that it is not seen as an IPR as such but rather as something protected under the law of obligations but still having many similar characteristics to IPR.[37] The Charter, as stated, mentions intellectual property without defining it or showing whether it takes a wider or a more restrictive view on how to interpret the term.

The concept of "transfer" implies that technology must flow from one undertaking to another. Such transfers normally take the form of licensing, whereby the licensor grants the licensee the right to use his technology against payment of royalties.[38] Licences can be sole or exclusive. Paragraph 162 of the guidelines provides that a licence is deemed to be exclusive if the licensee is the only one who is permitted to produce on the basis of the licensed technology within a given territory, even the whole world. Where the licensor undertakes only not to licence third parties to produce within a given territory, the licence is a sole licence. Often exclusive or sole licensing is accompanied by sales restrictions, and there may be rules on sub-licensing.[39]

The TTBER only applies to agreements that have as their primary object the transfer of technology, and it only covers the licensing of other types of Intellectual Property such as trademarks and copyright (other than software copyright) to the extent that they are directly related to the exploitation of the licensed technology and do not constitute the primary object of the agreement.[40]

Technology transfer agreements that concern the licensing of technology usually improve economic efficiency and are pro-competitive, as they can reduce duplication of research and development, strengthen the incentive for the initial R&D, spur incremental innovation, facilitate diffusion, and generate product market competition. Being thus efficiency enhancing and pro-competitive should outweigh any anticompetitive effects of the agreements.[41]

Licence agreements may have pro-competitive effects, as they introduce the IPR-protected technology into the market and entail efficiencies. At the same time, such agreements can lead to a reduction of inter-technology competition between companies, as well as of intra-technology competition between undertakings that

---

[36] Paragraph 46 of the guidelines.

[37] Whish (2003), p. 742.

[38] Where one person grants to another, or to a definite number of other persons, a right to do, or continue to do, in or upon the immovable property of the grantor something that would, in the absence of such right, be unlawful and such right does not amount to an easement or an interest in the property, the right is called a licence. This simple yet concise definition of licence (though applicable to immovable property) has been taken from Section 52 of the Indian Easements Act, 1882.

[39] Paragraph 48 of the guidelines.

[40] Paragraphs 49–50 of the guidelines.

[41] Recital 5–6 of TTBER.

produce products on the basis of the same technology.[42] The framework of Article 101(3), which contains an exception from the prohibition rule of Article 101(1), should be recalled. For this exception to be applicable, the licence agreement must produce objective economic benefits, the restrictions on competition must be indispensable to attain the efficiencies, consumers must receive a fair share of the efficiency gains, and the agreement must not afford the parties the possibility of eliminating competition in respect of a substantial part of the products concerned.[43] If this is to be linked to the aspects protection under the Charter, these are all considerations giving real meaning to freedom to conduct business.

It must be appreciated that licence agreements have the potential of bringing together complementary technologies and other assets allowing new or improved products to be put on the market or existing products to be produced at lower cost. Outside the context of hard-core cartels, licensing often occurs because it is more efficient for the licensor to licence the technology than to exploit it himself.[44] The guidelines give examples of efficiencies at the distribution stage that licensing agreements may give rise to, in the same way as vertical distribution agreements. This can be cost savings or the provision of valuable services to consumers. Pro-competitive licensing may also occur to ensure design freedom. In sectors where large numbers of IPRs exist and where individual products may infringe upon a number of existing and future property rights, licence agreements whereby the parties agree not to assert their property rights against each other are often pro-competitive because they allow the parties to develop their respective technologies without the risk of subsequent infringement claims.[45]

Even agreements that substantially reduce some dimension of competition do not necessarily entail that competition is eliminated within the meaning of Article 101(3). The guidelines recognise that a technology pool,[46] for instance, can result in an industry standard, leading to a situation in which there is little competition in terms of the technological format. Once the main players in the market adopt a certain format, network effects may make it very difficult for alternative formats to survive. This does not imply, however, that the creation of a de facto industry standard always eliminates competition. Within the standard, suppliers may compete on price, quality, and product features.[47] However, in order for the agreement to comply with Article 101(3), it must be ensured that the agreement does not unduly restrict competition or future innovation.[48]

---

[42] Whish (2003), p. 735. In the guidelines, especially paragraphs 141 and 146 reflect this.

[43] Article 101(3) Treaty on the Functioning of the European Union.

[44] Whish (2003), p. 735.

[45] Paragraph 148 of the guidelines.

[46] On this, see Armillotta (2010).

[47] Calderini and Giannaccari (2006), p. 549.

[48] Paragraph 152 of the guidelines. Whish (2003), p. 571 on what characterises standards. On the wider implications of related IPR, Odagiri et al. (2010), p. 15.

Originally, Regulation No 19/65/EEC empowered the Commission to apply Article 101(3) of the Treaty by Regulation to certain categories of technology transfer agreements and corresponding concerted practices. Pursuant to the above Regulation, the Commission had, in particular, adopted Regulation (EC) No 240/96 of 31 January 1996 on the application of Article 101(3) of the Treaty to certain categories of technology transfer agreements. It may be noted that under 240/96, where there was a risk that the agreement would have been caught by Article 101, the parties could apply for negative clearance or exemption from the Commission. A more usual course of action was to ensure that the terms of the agreement fall within the "block exemptions". Both the above regulations list "white" clauses, which are allowable, and "black clauses", which are definitely not and should be avoided.[49]

For a long period of time, the Commission did not regulate vertical agreements in accordance with sound economic principles. This was due to the market integration imperative, as had been set out in the important case law of *Consten and Grundig*,[50] and to the fact of the unduly extensive interpretation of the concepts of restrictions of competition in Article 101(1). Thus, few agreements were prohibited outright, and in other instances, the Commission forced parties to select between two routes to legality, either notification and a plea for an individual exemption or modification to the agreement so that it would fit within the range of Block Exemption Regulations that the Commission drafted.[51] It may be noted that although the notification route gave parties greater contractual freedom, it also had the undesirable feature of exposing them to extraordinary delays or the uncertainty of a comfort letter. Block Exemption Regulations provided something akin to a standard form contract, listing which clauses would gain exemption and which would not. Parties who structured their agreements so that they conformed to the Block Exemption were rewarded with automatic legality without the burden and delays of notification. However, the Block Exemption straitjacket removed any commercial flexibility for the parties. In 1996, after decades of criticism, the Commission responded by commencing a review of its policy. This resulted in an acknowledgment of the inadequacy of the policy that had been implemented until that time.[52] It has not benefited the right to conduct business.

On 20 December 2001, the Commission published an evaluation report on the transfer of technology block exemption Regulation (EC) No 240/96,[53] which generated a public debate with the response from Member States and third parties generally in favour of reform. The general consensus was that the new regulation should meet the two requirements of ensuring effective competition and providing adequate legal security for undertakings. The pursuit of those objectives should take

---

[49] Whish (2003), p. 169.

[50] Joined Cases 56/64 and 58/64, *Consten and Grundig*.

[51] Chalmers et al. (2006), p. 1015.

[52] *Ibid* at p. 1016.

[53] COM (2001) 786 final.

account of the need to simplify the regulatory framework and its application. It was deemed to be appropriate to move away from the approach of listing exempted clauses and to place greater emphasis on defining the categories of agreements that are exempted up to a certain level of market power and on specifying the restrictions or clauses that are not to be contained in such agreements. This was considered to be consistent with an economics-based approach, which assesses the impact of agreements on the relevant market. It was also considered to be consistent with such an approach to make a distinction between agreements between competitors and agreements between non-competitors. Thus was born the TTBER in its present form.[54]

TTBER treats agreements between competitors in a fundamentally different manner from agreements between non-competitors, and as has been seen in the case of other modern block exemption regulations, its application depends on the market shares of the parties involved and the absence of specific hard-core restrictions. The old formalistic white, grey, and blacklist rules have been abolished. The TTBER's scope will extend beyond patent and know-how licenses to include software copyright and design right licenses.[55]

4 The TTBER

The TTBER block exempts certain patent licensing agreements, know-how licensing agreements, software copyright licensing agreements, or mixed patent, know-how, or software copyright licensing agreements for the purposes of manufacture, use, and commercialisation. Technology transfer agreements that fulfil the conditions set out in the TTBER are block exempted from the prohibition rule contained in Article 101(1). Block exempted agreements are legally valid and enforceable. Such agreements can only be prohibited for the future and only upon withdrawal of the block exemption by the Commission or a Member State Competition Authority. Block exempted agreements cannot be prohibited under Article 101 by national courts in the context of private litigation.[56]

Block exemption of categories of technology transfer agreements is based on the presumption that such agreements fulfil the conditions in Article 101(3): the agreements give rise to economic efficiencies, the restrictions are indispensable, consumers receive a fair share of the efficiency gains, and the agreements are proportional, namely, they do not provide the possibility of eliminating competition

---

[54] Recitals 1, 2, 3, and 4 to the TTBER.

[55] Wilmer et al. (2003), p. 1.

[56] Communication from the Commission—Notice—Guidelines on the application of Article 81 (3) [now 101 (3)] of the Treaty, OJ C 101, 27.4.2004, pp. 97–118, paragraphs 35–37 and paragraph 34 of the guidelines.

in respect of a substantial part of the products in question.[57] The market share thresholds (Article 3), the hard-core list (Article 4) and the excluded restrictions (Article 5) set out in the TTBER aim at ensuring that only restrictive agreements that can reasonably be presumed to fulfil the four conditions of Article 101(3) are block exempted.[58]

The TTBER is quite clear in its understanding of the necessity of IPR protection, not explicitly making any allowance to the discussion gaining ground in recent years on whether knowledge should be restricted or should be common heritage of mankind.[59] TTBER builds on the understanding, explained in the guidelines, that creation of IPRs is often risky and entails substantial investment. To not reduce dynamic competition but rather maintain the incentive to innovate, the innovator must not be unduly restricted in the exploitation of IPRs that turn out to be valuable, especially for the period of time required to recoup the investment. It is relevant to note that there is no presumption that IPRs and licence agreements as such give rise to competition concerns.[60] TTBER has a positive attitude to IPRs, sees them as central, and does not emphasise the possible problems with them.

This attitude is reflected in the assessment of licence agreements. The Guidelines find that efficiencies at the level of the licensee often stem from a combination of the licensor's technology with the assets and technologies of the licensee, also removing obstacles to the development and exploitation of the licensee's own technology.[61] This description of the content of TTBER shows how the Regulation is based on a favourable view of licensing for technology transfer, and its aim is to provide a clear regulatory setting for specific agreements that form part of business practice in this sphere.

The TTBER is composed of three main elements[62]:

(i) Safe harbour—the TTBER creates a safe harbour for technology transfer agreements concluded by two undertakings. The safe harbour is circumscribed by market share thresholds of 20 % in the case of agreements between competitors and 30 % in the case of agreements between non-competitors. In limiting the scope of the safe harbour by market share thresholds, the TTBER follows the approach of the block exemption regulations in the fields of vertical restraints and horizontal cooperation agreements. These are Commission Regulation (EC) No 2658/2000 on the application of Article 101(3) of the Treaty to categories of specialisation agreements, Commission Regulation 2659/2000 on the application of Article 101(3) to categories of research and development agreements, and Commission Regulation (EC) No 2790/1999 on

---

[57] Article 101 Treaty on the Functioning of the European Union, see also above.

[58] Paragraph 35 of the guidelines.

[59] Brownsword and Goodwin (2012), p. 179. On the common heritage of mankind concept, see Nyman-Metcalf (2009).

[60] Paragraphs 8–9 of the guidelines.

[61] Paragraph 17 of the guidelines.

[62] Peeperkorn and Kjolbye (2005), p. 2.

the application of Article 101(3) of the Treaty to categories of vertical agreements and concerted practices.[63]

(ii) Hard-core restrictions—agreements containing hard-core restrictions fall outside the scope of the block exemption in their entirety. In the absence of hard-core restrictions, market analysis is required.

(iii) Excluded restrictions—the TTBER contains a limited list of excluded restrictions that are not block exempted. Such restrictions are subject to individual assessment.

The assessment of whether a licence agreement restricts competition must be made within the actual context in which competition would occur in the absence of the agreement.[64] It is necessary to take account of the likely impact of the agreement on inter-technology competition (i.e., competition between undertakings using competing technologies) and on intra-technology competition,[65] competition between the parties, and competition from third parties. For instance, where two undertakings established in different Member States cross-licence competing technologies and undertake not to sell products in each other's home markets, (potential) competition that existed prior to the agreement is restricted. Similarly, where a licensor imposes obligations on his licensees not to use competing technologies and these obligations foreclose third party technologies, actual or potential competition that would have existed in the absence of the agreement is restricted.

An agreement or contractual restraint is only prohibited by Article 101(1) if its object or effect is to restrict inter-technology competition and/or intra-technology competition.[66] These are restrictions that, in light of the objectives pursued by the Community competition rules, have such a high potential for negative effects on competition that it is not necessary for the purposes of applying Article 101(1) to demonstrate any actual effects on the market.[67] The assessment of whether or not an agreement has as its object a restriction of competition is based on factors such as the content of the agreement, the objective aims pursued by it, the context in which it is (to be) applied, the manner of implementation, or the actual conduct and behaviour of the parties on the market.[68]

Often, if an agreement is not restrictive of competition by object, it is necessary to examine whether it has restrictive effects on competition. Account must be taken of both actual and potential effects. The likely negative effects on competition must

---

[63] Paragraph 56 of the guidelines.

[64] See Case C-7/95P *John Deere*, paragraph 76.

[65] See, in this respect, Joined Cases 56/64 and 58/64, *Consten and Grundig*.

[66] Paragraph 13 of the guidelines.

[67] See, in this respect, Case C-49/92P *Anic Partecipazioni*, paragraph 99.

[68] See Compagnie Royale Asturienne des Mines SA and Rheinzink GmbH v Commission of the European Communities, Joined Cases 29/83 and 30/83, paragraph 26, and NV IAZ International Belgium and others v Commission of the European Communities, Joined Cases 96/102, 104, 105, 108, and 110/82 (ANSEAU-NAVEWA), paragraphs 23–25.

be appreciable. Guidance on the issue of appreciability can be found in Commission notice on agreements of minor importance, which do not appreciably restrict competition under Article 101(1) of the Treaty.[69] The notice defines appreciability in a negative way. Agreements, which fall outside the scope of the de minimis notice, do not necessarily have appreciable restrictive effects. An individual assessment is required.

Appreciable anticompetitive effects are likely to occur when at least one of the parties has or obtains some degree of market power and the agreement contributes to the creation, maintenance, or strengthening of that market power or allows the parties to exploit such market power. Market power is defined as the ability to maintain prices above competitive levels or to maintain output in terms of product quantities, product quality and variety, or innovation below competitive levels for a not insignificant period of time. The degree of market power normally required for a finding of an infringement under Article 101(1) is less than the degree of market power required for a finding of dominance under Article 102.[70]

For the purposes of assessing the competitive effects of licence agreements, it may be necessary to define relevant goods and service markets (product markets), as well as technology markets.[71] The term "product market" used in Article 3 of the TTBER refers to relevant goods and service markets in both their geographic and product dimension. As is clear from Article 1(1)(j) of the TTBER, the term is used merely to distinguish relevant goods and service markets from relevant technology markets.[72] TTBER and the guidelines are concerned with effects both on product markets for final products and on product markets for intermediate products. The relevant product market includes products that are regarded by the buyers as interchangeable with or substitutable for the contract products incorporating the licensed technology by reason of the products' characteristics, their prices, and their intended use. The Commission also acknowledges that at times it may be necessary to identify the innovation market. This may be the case where the licensing agreement will restrict the introduction of new or improved products. Innovation is thus seen as a form of potential competition, which naturally can have an impact on the market as well.[73]

---

[69] OJ C 368, 22.12.2001, p. 13.

[70] Paragraph 15 of the guidelines.

[71] As to these distinctions, see also Commission Guidelines on the applicability of Article 101 of the EC Treaty to horizontal cooperation agreements, paragraphs 44 to 52.

[72] Paragraph 20 of the guidelines.

[73] Paragraph 25 of the guidelines. See Schmidt (2010), p. 232. It may be noted that the US Intellectual Property Licensing Guidelines, 1995, similarly identify three different forms of markets: the product market, the technology market, and the innovation market under Sections 3.2.1, 3.2.2, and 3.2.3. US Department of Justice and the Federal Trade Commission, "Antitrust Guidelines for the Licensing of Intellectual Property" (1995).

5   Competitors and Non-competitors

In general, agreements between competitors pose a greater risk to competition than agreements between non-competitors. However, competition between undertakings that use the same technology (intra-technology competition between licensees) constitutes an important complement to competition between undertakings that use competing technologies (inter-technology competition). For instance, intra-technology competition may lead to lower prices for the products incorporating the technology in question, which may not only produce direct and immediate benefits for consumers of these products but also spur further competition between undertakings that use competing technologies.[74] In the context of licensing, it must also be taken into account that licensees are selling their own product. They are not reselling a product supplied by another undertaking. The guidelines emphasise that there may thus be greater scope for product differentiation and quality-based competition between licensees than in the case of vertical agreements for the resale of products.[75] It is possible that parties become competitors after the conclusion of the agreement because the licensee develops and starts exploiting a competing technology, in which case it is taken into account that the parties were non-competitors at the time of conclusion of the agreement and that the agreement was concluded in that context. The Commission will therefore mainly focus on the impact of the agreement on the licensee's ability to exploit his own (competing) technology.[76]

If the parties own technologies that are in a one-way or two-way blocking position, the parties are considered to be non-competitors on the technology market. A one-way blocking position exists when a technology cannot be exploited without infringing upon another technology. This is, for instance, the case where one patent covers an improvement of a technology covered by another patent. In that case, the exploitation of the improvement patent presupposes that the holder obtains a licence to the basic patent. A two-way blocking position exists where neither technology can be exploited without infringing upon the other technology and where the holders thus need to obtain a licence or a waiver from each other. In assessing whether a blocking position exists, the Commission will rely on objective factors as opposed to the subjective views of the parties.[77]

The TTBER applies to licence agreements for the production of contract products[78] whereby the licensee is also permitted to sub-license the licensed technology to third parties provided, however, that the production of contract

---

[74] Calderini and Giannaccari (2006), p. 543.

[75] Paragraph 26 of the guidelines.

[76] Paragraph 31 of the guidelines.

[77] Calderini and Giannaccari (2006), p. 549. Paragraph 32 of the guidelines.

[78] The term "contract products" encompasses goods and services produced with the licensed technology. This is the case both where the licensed technology is used in the production process and where it is incorporated into the product itself. Paragraph 43 of the guidelines.

products constitutes the primary object of the agreement and to so-called non-assertion agreements and settlement agreements whereby the licensor permits the licensee to produce within the scope of the patent.[79] The TTBER also covers "subcontracting", whereby the licensor licenses technology to the licensee who undertakes to produce certain products on the basis thereof exclusively for the licensor, possibly involving the supply of equipment by the licensor to be used in the production of the goods and services covered by the agreement.

The framework of the TTBER and the guidelines is based on the premise that there is a direct link between the licensed technology and an identified contract product. In cases where no such link exists, the main object of the agreement is R&D as opposed to bringing a particular product to the market; in that case, the analytical framework of the TTBER and the guidelines may not be appropriate.[80]

6 Application of Article 101(1) and 101(3) Outside the Scope of the TTBER

Agreements that fall outside the block exemption, for example because the market share thresholds are exceeded or the agreement involves more than two parties, are subject to individual assessment. Agreements that either do not restrict competition within the meaning of Article 101(1) or fulfil the conditions of Article 101(3) are valid and enforceable. It is recalled that there is no presumption of illegality of agreements that fall outside the scope of the block exemption provided that they do not contain hard-core restrictions of competition. In the application of Article 101 to individual cases, it is necessary to take due account of the way in which competition operates on the market in question. Factors such as the nature of the agreement, the market position of the parties and of competitors, the market position of buyers of the licensed products, the entry barriers, and the maturity of the market are particularly relevant in this respect.[81]

The importance of individual factors may vary from case to case and depends on all other factors, and the guideline sets out that firm rules on individual factors cannot be given.[82] For instance, a high market share of the parties is usually a good indicator of market power, but in the case of low entry barriers it may not be.[83] Technology transfer agreements can take many shapes and forms and need to be examined beyond the express terms of the agreement. The existence of implicit restraints may be derived from the way in which the agreement has been

---

[79] Paragraphs 42–43 of the guidelines.

[80] Paragraph 45 of the guidelines.

[81] Whish (2003), p. 755.

[82] Paragraph 132 of the guidelines.

[83] Whish (2003), p. 24.

implemented by the parties and the incentives that they face.[84] The guidelines are very important in explaining the application of the law in specific described instances. The guidelines explain in detail the manner of application of Article 101 in respect of individual assessment of various types of licensing restraints, like royalty obligations, exclusive licenses, sales restrictions, output restrictions, field of use restrictions, captive use restrictions, tying and bundling, exclusive dealing, settlements, licensing of future developments, and technology pools.

It must be noted that the guidelines use the term significant degree of market power to indicate the threshold where competition concerns will normally arise, whereas the term substantial market power appears to be used to indicate dominance. However, no attempt is made to quantify these terms, since market power is often a question of degree.

7 Analysis of the Global Legal Situation for Technology Transfer

The EU is an important player on the global market, and by supporting research, innovation, and business also as fundamental rights, it wants to create a beneficial situation for maintaining and strengthening this role. TTBER and the guidelines are believed to represent an important improvement compared to the previous Regulation in terms of clarity and scope and economic approach. While providing more freedom to companies to draw up licence agreements according to their commercial needs, they also enhance the protection of competition and therewith innovation. Further, authors stress that the new rules bring about an important degree of convergence between the application of the competition policy to licence agreements in the EU and US.[85]

In the US, there are several case laws that govern application of the Sherman Act to Intellectual Property licensing. Further, the Department of Justice and the Federal Trade Commission has sought to clarify their enforcement positions by issuing guidelines. In 2007, the Report on Antitrust Enforcement and Intellectual Property Rights was issued by the US Department of Justice Antitrust Division and the US Federal Trade Commission.[86] This was in addition to the US Anti Trust Guidelines for the Licensing of Intellectual Property, published in 1995.

Japan also has several precedents applying its Antimonopoly Act to Intellectual Property affairs. In 2007, the Japan Fair Trade Commission issued the Guidelines for the Use of Intellectual Property under the Antimonopoly Act, which superseded

---

[84] Paragraph 133 of the guidelines.

[85] Peeperkorn and Kjolbye (2005), p. 1.

[86] US Department of Justice and the Federal Trade Commission, "Antitrust Enforcement and Intellectual Property Rights: Promoting Innovation and Competition" (2007).

the Patent and Know-How Licensing Guidelines of 1999 and supplement the Guidelines on Standardization and Patent Pool Arrangements, published in 2005.[87]

The above are similar to the EU's TTBER and the guidelines thereto and point to a convergence of views in this area. In particular, the above sources state that with the exception of certain practices that are deemed likely to harm competition, restrictions in Intellectual Property license agreements generally will be reviewed under a rule of reason-type analysis. The potential pro-competitive benefits of restraints contained in Intellectual Property licensing agreements are what the courts and competition authorities try to identify. Further, in most cases, a violation would arise only if actual harm to competition outweighed the pro-competitive benefits of the restraint or if conduct ancillary to the license had an exclusionary effect by virtue of the dominant market position of the licensor. However, important differences remain, which can cause serious risks if ignored. For instance, treatment of royalty rates, customer or territorial restraints, restraints affecting multiple licensees, and package or bundled licensing are examples of restraints that might be analysed differently under the Competition laws of different jurisdictions.[88] More importantly, under EU law, there is considerable reliance on classification of restraints by type. Further, certain types of restraints are categorised as hard core. Thus, application of EU law may depend on categorisation of an agreement in terms of the share of the relevant market affected and whether it involves competitors or non-competitors, provides for one-way or reciprocal licensing, and conveys exclusive or non-exclusive rights. While these factors are likely to be relevant in other jurisdictions as well, the analysis is likely to be more flexible (especially in the United States).[89]

The interplay of US, EU, Japan, and other international licensing regimes is important because the ability of firms to license IPRs internationally is one of the cornerstones in the foundation of a strong global economy.[90] In today's world, whether firms are creators or consumers, IPRs are crucial to performance. IPRs are beneficial to all sectors of the economy, and therefore the protection of such rights, once the Intellectual Property is created in any one country or region, is often made global through a crucial patchwork of bilateral and multilateral agreements. As firms manufacture and market their products globally, licensing of the IPRs they hold or need often proceeds on a global scale, and differences among nations' licensing rules have the potential to disrupt cross-border commerce.[91]

There is famous case law on EU application of Competition law to non-EU companies. Generally, under EU competition law, a "mere" refusal to license does not constitute a violation. Nevertheless, as was laid down in the Microsoft case law,

---

[87] Japan Fair Trade Commission, the English translation of "the Guidelines for the Use of Intellectual Property under the Antimonopoly Act" (2007).

[88] Odagiri et al. (2010), p. 11.

[89] Evrard et al. (2009), p. 2.

[90] Odagiri et al. (2010), p. 11.

[91] Delrahim (2004).

EU law may regard a refusal to license IPRs as an abuse of a dominant position in violation of Article 102. This would arise if (1) the would-be licensor is dominant in the relevant market, (2) the refusal relates to IPRs that are indispensable to exercise a particular activity in a neighbouring or downstream market, (3) the refusal to license excludes any effective competition in that neighbouring or downstream market, (4) the would-be licensee would, if it were granted a license, offer new products or services not being offered by the would-be licensor, for which there is a potential consumer demand, and (5) the refusal to license is not objectively justified.[92]

In the US, the general rule is that the Sherman Act does not restrict the right of a company to freely exercise its own independent discretion as to parties with which it will deal. Thus there is a strong presumption that an unconditional unilateral refusal to license does not violate the antitrust laws.[93] The US Agencies thus recognise the traditional understanding that a unilateral right to decline the grant of a license is a core part of the patent grant.[94] However, the US Agencies acknowledge that tension can exist between the right to exclude under the patent laws and the prospect that a unilateral refusal to license to a particular company could give rise to antitrust liability.

We believe that in future years, the global landscape in this field is likely to become more complicated. For instance, a number of countries have been fairly active in applying their Competition laws and are likely to start facing issues at the intersection of Competition and Intellectual Property laws more frequently.

Recognising that intellectual property licensing is generally pro-competitive, many foreign jurisdictions have followed the US lead in creating transparency in this area by adopting their own intellectual property guidelines. Countries like Canada, South Korea, Singapore, and Taiwan are in this growing list.[95]

---

[92] Case T-201/04 *Microsoft*, 331–332.

[93] See *Verizon Communications v. Law Offices of Curtis V. Trinko*, 540 U.S. 398, 408 (2004), where the court also stated, *inter alia*, that enforced sharing also requires antitrust courts to act as central planners, identifying the proper price, quantity, and other terms of dealing—a role for which they are ill-suited. Moreover, compelling negotiation between competitors may facilitate the supreme evil of antitrust: collusion.

[94] The Unites States Department of Justice, "Report on Antitrust Enforcement and Intellectual Property Rights" (2007): 30.

[95] For example:

1. Competition Bureau, Government of Canada, "Intellectual Property Enforcement Guidelines" (2000)
2. Korea Fair Trade Commission, "Guidelines of Reviewing Undue Exercise of Intellectual Property Rights" (2000)
3. Competition Commission of Singapore, "Guidelines on the Treatment of Intellectual Property Rights" (2007)
4. Taiwan Fair Trade Commission, "Fair Trade Commission Disposal Directions (Guidelines) on Technology Licensing Arrangements"

Further, China and India have also begun to implement Competition laws.[96] Article 55 of the China Antimonopoly Act 2007 provides, *inter alia*, that this law shall not apply to undertakings' conducts that are exercising their IPRs in accordance with the provisions of laws and administrative regulations relating to IPRs. However, this law shall apply to undertakings' conducts that eliminate or restrict competition by abusing their IPRs. What needs to be noted is that it does not define what constitutes an "abuse".[97]

Section 3 of the Indian Competition Act 2002 defines and prohibits anticompetitive agreements. Section 3(5) states, *inter alia*, that nothing contained in this section shall restrict the right of any person to restrain any infringement of, or to impose reasonable conditions, as may be necessary for protecting any of his rights that have been or may be conferred upon him under the Copyright Act, the Patents Act, the Trade Marks Act, the Geographical Indications of Goods (Registration and Protection) Act, the Designs Act, or the Semi-conductor Integrated Circuits Layout-Design Act. Once again, what is "reasonable" is not defined and is thus open to interpretation.[98]

In Russia and neighbouring fast-growing economies, the following can be deduced after a careful reading of their laws (which are mostly available in domestic languages, namely Russian, Georgian, etc.):

Article 10.4 of the Competition Law of Russia (2006) provides that the rules on abuse of dominant position do not apply to the acts of use of exclusive rights to the results of intellectual activity, as well as IPRs. However, any unlawful use of the results of IPR by putting a commodity into circulation in the market is prohibited as unfair competition and is subject to penalties under the appropriate administrative, civil, and criminal laws.[99]

Article 2.2 of the Law of the Republic of Armenia on Protection of Economic Competition (2000) provides that this Law shall not apply to relations connected with intellectual property rights, except for cases when these rights are used for the purpose of preventing, restricting, or prohibiting the economic competition.[100]

In Ukraine, the government-appointed Antimonopoly Committee has recently proposed alterations to some legislative acts of Ukraine, including alterations to the Law of Ukraine "On protection from unfair competition" and Code of Ukraine on Administrative Delinquencies. The Committee states that the proposed changes are caused due to the necessity to take into account the experience of the competition legislation application by the Antimonopoly Committee of Ukraine and juridical authorities. The above takes into consideration the changes in the conditions of the economic activity, which took place in Ukraine, especially in the context of Article 4 of the Law of Ukraine "On protection from unfair competition", which provides for "Non-legal use of other's trademarks, advertising materials, packing".[101]

---

[96] Wang (2008), pp. 88–98.

[97] American Bar Association (2007), p. 14.

[98] The Indian Competition Act (2002).

[99] The Competition Law of Russia (2006).

[100] The Law of the Republic of Armenia on Protection of Economic Competition (2000).

[101] Draft laws in the field of Competition (Ukraine).

In Georgia, it has been proposed to draw up a suitable Competition law, and the drafting process is continuing. The report on Competition Policy and Practice of Market Regulation (2012) provides at page 24 that the proposed Competition law will not apply to IPR.[102]

It remains to be seen how all these countries will apply their respective laws to Intellectual Property licensing issues. The increasing complexity of this area of law makes it all the more important for Intellectual Property holders to consider potential implications in all relevant jurisdictions at the time Intellectual Property licenses are being planned.

8 Analysis of the Effectiveness of the TTBER

The remaining sections of this paper mainly contain the evaluation and analysis by the authors. The TTBER was introduced in an attempt to address technical and economic developments by regulating IPRs that had been neglected by the previous acts. It has in a way succeeded in taking the balance between IPRs and Competition law to the next level. Its scope is much wider than the previous block exemption and applies to more IPRs (but not to all). Extending the scope to include software copyright licensing is very important since software is a major part of today's technological development. The EU is taking concrete measures to ensure protection of both intellectual property and competition (freedom to conduct business).

The most important feature of the TTBER is its flexibility, together with its more economically oriented framework. It blacklists only certain clauses, and thus it imports a certain degree of flexibility to the evaluation of the competitive effects of technology licensing agreements.[103] Thus, the TTBER has replaced the 'straitjacket' of the previous regulation—the exhaustive list of exempted and whitelisted clauses—and by doing so, it allows firms to formulate their licensing agreements according to their commercial and business needs. It would be pessimistic to state that the TTBER eliminated the list of permitted licensing practices in the old technology transfer block exemption regulation and that all practices are now suspect for arrangements that exceed the market share thresholds. The guidelines provide a very useful foundation for the TTBER and inform businessmen and practitioners alike about the types of transactions that could possibly raise antitrust concerns in the EU. The guidelines also provide an analytical methodology that covers certain licensing arrangements that are omitted by the TTBER, for example, multilateral cross-licensing and technology pools.[104]

---

[102] Centre for Economic Problems Research, Georgia, "The report on Competition Policy and Practice of Market Regulation" (2012).

[103] Aristidou (2010).

[104] Gilbert (2004), p. 15.

However, there are some criticisms reserved for the TTBER.[105] It has been stated that the blacklisted practices and the market share thresholds of the TTBER cause it to be rigid. This can unfortunately have the consequence (though unintentional) of impeding the parties to a distribution agreement from organising distribution as efficiently as possible. This in turn deprives consumers of the benefits that can follow from a more efficient, more consumer responsive distribution system. Although great care is exercised in the TTBER to not reduce intra-brand competition, however, the strict imposition of uniform rules may in turn have the consequence of impeding inter-brand competition. This will ultimately be to the disadvantage of consumers.

On the one hand, there is the need to grant some degree of certainty to firms; on the other hand, there arises the need to introduce a (limited) block exemption to vertical restraints entered into by undertakings that may not enjoy market power. Thus, the market share ceilings are a middle ground between the above two extremes. It is thus a compromise (although not a very optimal one) between a more economic approach *vis-à-vis* the usual (and very often persistent) tendency prevalent in the EU institutions to over-regulate competition policy while doggedly pursuing the policy of integration of the internal market through the application of Article 101.

Although this may appear to be justified in light of the decentralisation of the application of EU competition policy and the need to ensure rules applicable to all Member States and since many of the new entrants do not have a tradition of competition law and enforcement, nonetheless, one cannot ignore the unintended negative economic consequences that may thus result.

It has been observed that market share does not always mirror the market power of a firm.[106] Further, with such low market share thresholds, the Commission should have provided broader exemptions for most forms of vertical restraint. Assessment of market shares is a difficult and costly process, and it is often impossible to be precise, even for an experienced observer. In such an event, the consequence may be legal uncertainty for the undertakings, which are then called on to bear the onerous burden to prove the correctness of their assessments.

Further, the market shares of the firms may deviate from the original determinations and estimates after the conclusion of a long-term distribution agreement. In the event that the market share rises after the date of conclusion of the agreement, the TTBER continues to apply for a period of one or two consecutive years after the relevant threshold is first exceeded (within certain limits). This causes the parties to the agreement to have to constantly monitor and constrain their sales to ensure the market share is not exceeded, since such an increase would result in the heightened risk of them losing the protection awarded by the TTBER. This constant monitoring and adjustment is a difficult and problematic issue for most parties. Such a regulatory framework that might potentially constrain an

---

[105] Incardona (2005).
[106] Whish (2003), p. 23.

undertaking from succeeding is clearly inconsistent with the goal of promoting a thriving economy.[107]

Further, as we have seen above, the market share is difficult to determine. Thus, mere inability to determine the market share might already pose a hurdle for IPR owners to benefit from the TTBER.

Another objection to the TTBER is that the permissible market shares are considered to be low. Where R&D are expensive, then to make the process commercially viable, it could be required that a large part of the market be suppliers. Consequently, many technology markets are concentrated. Hence, it is feared that in certain industries, for example, the pharmaceutical industry, these limitations to the safe harbour of the Regulation will result in these firms carrying on R&D and productions outside EU and in turn supplying EU by export. This could in turn lead to the evaporation of good quality jobs in the common market.[108] Reference has been made in the recent past to the rapid growth in the market and research environment in emerging economies outside EU, leading to a migration of research activities outside of EU to these fast-growing markets.[109]

It is to the credit of the TTBER that the hard-core restrictions grant legal certainty to undertakings. Thus, they now know what not to include in their agreements in order to ensure that they are exempted under the TTBER. Nevertheless, while the above-mentioned restrictions serve as a guide to the lawyers who draft a distribution agreement, they also have a significant drawback. It should not be forgotten that these restrictions constrain parties to limit their actions to exempted provisions and those that avoid blacklisted elements. All of this is done at the expense of non-consideration of alternatives that might work better for their market, their product, and their customers. This is contrary to what one sees in the US, where the emphasis is on a more economic approach, including fewer hard-core restrictions. There, the emphasis is on more principles and less regulation.

The hard-core restrictions were originally intended to reduce uncertainty. However, they state a general prohibition but then confuse the application of the prohibition by allowing many specified exceptions. The current authors find that this very often results in the situation that they are not 'user-friendly'. It would be desirable to have rules that specify clearly what is prohibited, instead of the current approach that leans towards fixing rules and then goes on to list confusing exceptions to the mentioned rules.

It is nonetheless true that a case-by-case analysis is not an optimal approach. Such analysis usually tends to be expensive, time-consuming, and riddled with uncertainties. Such an analysis can also be very demanding for both undertakings and competition authorities, in terms of available resources and allotted manpower. Since the old system required advance approval that was seen as very complicating, it may well have led regulators to adopt the new TTBER with its preordained set of

---

[107] Incardona (2005), p. 35.

[108] *Ibid.* p. 36.

[109] European Federation of Pharmaceutical Industries and Associations (2011).

internal, rigid rules that (possibly in the view of the Commission) simplifies their case-by-case review efforts. It also has the added advantage of ensuring that their approvals are granted in a visibly consistent manner.

It should also not be forgotten that by practising such a set of rigid standards, the regulators are freed from the responsibility of having to make true case-by-case judgments. Thus, a mechanised, robot-like approach helps regulators to avoid criticism. They are also afforded the opportunity to justify their actions on the grounds that they have merely followed the rules, in true bureaucratic form. Perhaps the regulators simply released their internal rules to the outside world in the form of TTBERs as a response to the call arising from undertakings to be able to predict in advance the likely results of the regulatory approval process. This has the added advantage for the regulators of simplifying their own work processes by placing the onus on undertakings to self-evaluate their degrees of compliance. Although this approach seems simple enough, the fact is that the rule of reason type of analysis cannot be completely abandoned by the regulators. The conclusion that can be thus deduced is that the approach of the regulators may have been necessary initially (when the TTBER was introduced); however, what is required today is an adoption of the US approach that actually helps to optimise economic and business development. The existing regulatory structure, as it stands today, makes it difficult for an experienced observer to state with certainty as to who is the intended beneficiary of EU Competition law, be it the consumers, competition, competitors, or market integration.[110]

There is visibly a clear need to focus on two primary aspects—the protection of competition and consumer welfare. It can be hoped that in doing so the trickle down effects will be the natural consequence thereof when it comes to the efficient allocation of resources, the protection of (efficient) competitors, and market integration.

In this regard, other authors have offered some more criticisms. One potential problem that can foreseeably arise is in the context of a new product or technology that may potentially create a new market. Such a product or technology could be a potential "game-changer". In such a case, the IPR owner would account for a market share of 100 %. Under these circumstances, if he wished to exploit his IPR by licensing it, then his monopoly would from the very beginning have the unfortunate consequence of excluding him from the benefits of the TTBER.[111]

More importantly, the TTBER in its present form provides for a shift of the burden of proof. This in turn is contrary to Intellectual Property laws. Generally, under Intellectual Property laws, the burden of proof to establish invalidity, unenforceability, or other improper conduct is upon the party that seeks to challenge its validity in the first place. However, under the TTBER, the table is turned by the Commission, since it puts the onus of proof (and a rather heavy one at that)

---

[110] Incardona (2005), p. 37, and footnote 127 on the same page where the author attempts an interesting, although brief, review of the existing literature on this subject. Also Orbach (2011).

[111] Schindler (2008), p. 62.

required by Article 101(3) on the party that seeks to claim that the agreement is legal. The IPR owner now has to bear the burden of proving the legality of the contents of the proposed agreement. He would also have to analyse (at his expense) the relevant markets and, furthermore, to deduce correctly the market shares of all market participants in the relevant market. This is difficult, as has been noted above. Therefore, such a shift in the burden of proof might possibly deter the owner of Intellectual Property from actually exploiting his rights commercially by licensing them. This in turn could potentially stifle licensing. Such a chain reaction would continue further, potentially affecting the effective dissemination of technology, which in turn would defeat the very purpose of the TTBER. Moreover, the burden of proof listed above has a consequential effect on heightened costs for the IPR owner. Market analysis can be expensive and time-consuming, especially in the case of new technologies. Thus, the Commission's approach of imposing the onus of pre-exploitation assessment of legality on the IPR owner can potentially counteract national Intellectual Property legislation by effectively limiting the reward an IPR owner can reasonably expect to obtain.[112]

Moreover, the TTBER may have to be amended to include more IPRs and more Intellectual Property-related agreements that could affect Competition law. For instance, trademark licensing and merchandise agreements that were left outside the scope of the TTBER are capable of creating anticompetitive effects.

With the entry into force in December 2009 of the so-called Lisbon Agreement, the Treaty on the European Union, and the Treaty on the Functioning of the European Union (TFEU), the position of intellectual property rights in EU law was strengthened through Article 118 TFEU, which provides explicit competence for EU legislation in this area as opposed to the earlier situation when such rights were dealt with in relation to free movements or competition law as an element that may justify restrictions to other rights.[113] This may lead to more EU-level IPR rules, which may also affect the relationship in the EU between competition (antitrust) and IPR legislation.

9   Future Trends

It is important to consider that Intellectual Property legislation does not regulate Competition law issues. The role of IPR is to protect innovation. IPR is concerned particularly with the protection of the exclusive right of the owner to enjoy the financial rewards of the said innovation. Consequently, there arises a necessity to regulate the relationship between IPR and Competition law. Since IPR is intimately related to both innovation and high technology, as further development of technology results in the creation of more complex systems, new IPR can possibly be

---

[112] *Ibid* at pp. 63–64.

[113] Heinemann (2011), p. 304.

created. It is impossible to accurately predict how these new rights will be exercised and exploited. This naturally gives rise to concerns regarding Competition law. Consequently, the EU has a duty to keep abreast with new technological developments and to regularly update the relevant legislation so that the newly developed IPR do not have any anticompetitive effects.[114]

As regards things that stand at present, certain proposals have already been made with respect to the proposed amendment of the TTBER in the near future. These deal essentially with issues related to cross-licensing agreements, which are perceived as being potentially disadvantageous to smaller firms for which barter is a more prominent form of exchange. It is felt in certain quarters that cross-licensing agreements can potentially allow large or dominant firms to take unfair advantage of their size or dominance to gain a further advantage in the market at the expense of rivals with smaller patent portfolios and thus deserve closer scrutiny. It is also suggested to reserve the safe harbour provisions only for essential patents. What are essential patents is, however, open to debate and could prove to be a contentious issue in itself. Another key area of concern is that related with mergers of companies that make the distribution of Intellectual Property less symmetric. Also of relevance are mergers involving vertically integrated parties where Intellectual Property issues are prominent. It is proposed that all the above areas should be covered adequately by a revised version of the TTBER in more detail.[115]

However, some experts generally question the approach taken by US and EU in this regard. It is alleged that regulation of Intellectual Property licenses based on antitrust considerations might be flawed as follows—firstly, because it might block the view on legitimate interests of IPR owners and, secondly, it might fall short of a proper confinement of IPRs. Further, it is suggested that a Competition law-driven evaluation (which is primarily economical in nature) might unbalance the Intellectual Property system.[116] The authors do not agree with such an assumption and feel that the present Competition law approach is correct because along with IPR owners, the interests of consumers must also be taken into account. This is also shown by the brief but important references in the Charter of Fundamental Rights in support of innovation and business.

As we are aware, Article 11 of the TTBER states, inter alia, that it shall expire on 30 April 2014. Since it is apparent that new technologies will be developed that will considerably change the scope of IPR, any legislation that deals with the interface between IPR and Competition law will not only have to anticipate such changes but also have to be ready to counterbalance any adverse impact that they may have on this interface.

An indicator of the EU attitude is readily apparent in another vertical agreement that came to an end recently. The current Block Exemption Regulation on vertical

---

[114] Aristidou (2010).

[115] "Assessment of potential anticompetitive conduct in the field of intellectual property rights and assessment of the interplay between competition policy and IPR protection," 2011: 95.

[116] Schindler (2008), p. 77.

restraints expired in May 2010. When it and its associated guidelines were adopted more than 10 years ago, the aim was to considerably reduce the regulatory burden on firms, in particular firms with no market power, and to introduce an effects-based approach to the assessment of vertical restraints. In the Commission's assessment, these objectives and concerns remain valid. Further, they have stated that two major developments have marked the 10-year period following the adoption of the current rules: an increase in large distributors' market power and the evolution of sales on the Internet.

According to the Commission, the proposed regime does not intend to significantly alter the current regulation. Of particular interest are the changes proposed in relation to the interaction between selective distribution and online commerce. While maintaining the distinction between active and passive sales, in the Draft Guidelines, the Commission proposes to consider hard-core restrictions and, therefore, to presume illegal as an infringement of Article 101(1) certain restrictions to Internet commerce, which are considered to amount to barriers to the common market.[117]

What Intellectual Property law does is that it grants market power to its owners. On the other hand, Competition law reins in the market power and/or potential abuse of it. It is this that creates the allegedly "great conflict" or "tension" between the two areas of law.[118] It is necessary to balance the interests of consumers and the state with the rights of Intellectual Property owners. The interface between IPR laws and Competition laws is of crucial importance in today's globalised economy. Since IPR are related both to innovation and to high technology, as technology develops and becomes more complex, new IPR can possibly be created. This in turn will lead to greater challenges, as the EU strives to fulfil the four conditions laid down in Article 101(3), namely that the agreements give rise to economic efficiencies, that the restrictions contained in the agreements are indispensable to the attainment of these efficiencies, that consumers within the affected markets receive a fair share of the efficiency gains, and that the agreements do not afford the undertakings concerned the possibility of eliminating competition in respect of a substantial part of the products in question.

The area of law covering the interface between Intellectual Property laws and Competition laws is not very lucid. There are large-scale possibilities for confusion, misgivings, and mistrust. However, given the nature of technological advancements, on one hand, and the growing globalisation of world trade, on the other, it has become imperative that this interface remains in focus. The knowledge-driven economy, which the developed world (and the developing world) quests for, depends on the right balancing act between IPR and Competition laws. Given the constraints that the EU works under, namely the need to develop and keep open the Common Market and also to integrate the economies of all the Member States, however disparate their scales of economies or their legal processes may be, the

---

[117] *Ibid.*

[118] Morris (2009), p. 224.

TTBER has managed to do its job well for the last several years. EU still remains an important global player in the economic market, and EU is still in the race for greater technological prowess.

Developing IPR is only the beginning. Maintaining a lead in this field is very often a daily challenge. And to commercially exploit this IPR requires effective licensing tools. Where the scientists stop, the lawyers take over. Very often, as they say, the devil is in the fine print. Within the EU, the TTBER defines the broad outlines of the Technology Transfer Licence Agreement regime. The EU approach to this subject is very detailed, which probably reflects the traditions of a code-based system of law. The US instead sets forth broader policy statements with fewer details, which reflects its tradition of developing specific precedent through a common law, case-based system. Either way, the developed world knows that time is not in its favour, and nations of the developing world are relentlessly reducing the technological gap that exists between the haves and the have nots.[119]

Whether technology transfers can someday benefit the whole of humanity is a question that one dares not ask. If technology transfers can give rise to economic efficiencies, increase innovation, benefit consumers, and encourage competition, then they should suffice for now.

References

Books and Articles

Armillotta M (2010) Technology pooling licensing agreements: promoting patent access through collaborative IP mechanisms. Nomos, Munich

August R (2002) International business law, 4th edn. Pearson Prentice Hall, New Jersey

Bishop S, Gore D (2005) Black and white to enlightenment? An economic view of the reform of EC competition rules on technology transfer. In: Ehlermann C-D, Atanasiu I (eds) European competition law annual. The interaction between competition law and intellectual property law. Hart, Oxford

Brownsword R, Goodwin M (2012) Law and the technologies of the twenty-first century. Cambridge University Press, Cambridge

Calderini M, Giannaccari A (2006) Standardisation in the ICT sector: the (complex) interface between antitrust and intellectual property. Econ Innovat New Technol 15(6):543–567

Chalmers D, Hadjiemmanuil C, Monti G, Tomkins A (2006) European Union Law. Cambridge Publishers, Cambridge

Craig P, De Burca G (2008) EU law: text, cases and materials, 4th edn. Oxford University Press, Oxford

Delrahim M (2004) US and EU approaches to the antitrust analysis of intellectual property licensing: observations from the enforcement perspective. US Department of Justice. http://www.justice.gov/atr/public/speeches/203228.htm

---

[119] Brownsword and Goodwin (2012), pp. 219–220.

Democritos Aristidou & Co., Cyprus (2010) The EU has/has not achieved a proper balance between competition law and intellectual property. http://www.mondaq.com/article.asp?articleid=83430#twitter

Evrard SJ, Harris SH Jr, Oliver GD, Watanabe S, Zöttl J (2009) International licensing of intellectual property rights: issues arising under U.S., European, and Japanese Competition Law. Intellectual Property Counselor 148:1, at 2. http://www.jonesday.com/files/Publication/7cae02fc-33d4-422e-900a-8413007b318b/Presentation/PublicationAttachment/ccc4abcf-f450-4c92-b06c-9742e2a6d34a/~3261069.pdf

Gilbert R (2004) Converging doctrines? US and EU antitrust policy for the licensing of intellectual property. Competition Policy Center, University of California Berkeley. http://escholarship.org/uc/item/7j60d3r2

Heinemann A (2011) Intellectual property rights and market integration. In: Anderman S, Ezrachi A (eds) Intellectual Property and Competition Law. Oxford University Press, Oxford, pp 303–322

Incardona R (2005) Distribution Agreements under EC Competition Law. http://brunoleonimedia.servingfreedom.net/WP/051007_Mises_WP_Incardona.pdf

Mehta K, Peeperkorn L (2002) Licensing of intellectual property under EU competition rules: the review of the technology transfer block exemption regulation. http://www.ftc.gov/opp/intellect/020522mehtadoc.pdf

Morris PS (2009) Patent licensing and no-challenge clauses: a thin line between article 81 EC treaty and the new technology transfer block exemption regulation. Intellect Property Q 2:217

Nyman-Metcalf K (2009) Space for the benefit of mankind? New developments and old problems. Annals of Air and Space Law, XXXIV, pp 621–644

Odagiri H, Goto A, Sunami A, Nelson RR (2010) Introduction. In: Odagiri H, Goto A, Sunami A, Nelson RR (eds) Intellectual property rights, development, and catch-up. Oxford University Press, Oxford

Orbach BY (2011) The antitrust consumer welfare paradox. J Compet Law Econ 7(1):133–164

Palmer TG (1989) Intellectual property: a non-Posnerian law and economics approach. Hamline Law Rev 12(2):261

Peeperkorn L, Kjolbye L (2005) (DG Competition, European Commission) The new technology transfer block exemption regulation and guidelines, 2. http://www.eui.eu/RSCAS/Research/Competition/2005/200510-CompPeeperkorn&Kjolbye.pdf

Schindler G (2008) Wagging the dog? Reconsidering anti-trust based regulation of IP licensing. Marquette Intellectual Property Law Rev 12:49

Schmidt HKS (2010) The influence of IP rights on product definition in competition law – the curious case of tying. Int Company Commercial Law Rev 21(6):224

Stam C, Andriessen D (2008) Intellectual capital of the European Union 2008: measuring the Lisbon strategy for growth and jobs. Electron J Knowl Manage 7(4):489–500, http://www.ejkm com

Wang X (2008) Anti-monopoly law in the compulsory licensing of intellectual property. Soc Sci China 29(1):88–98

Whish R (2003) Competition law, 5th edn. Lexis Nexis Butterworths, London

Wilmer, Cutler and Pickering (2003) The European Commission proposes new competition rules for technology licensing. http://www.wilmerhale.com/files/Publication/cf99fe97-2f8d-4760-bb0b-ff8ef3766e15/Presentation/PublicationAttachment/6fea9515-65cb-4745-b5c0-cfee368fd8bf/News_215243279180219011515101300.pdf

Legal Acts and Official Material

a) EU:

Regulation No 19/65/EEC empowering the Commission to apply Article 101(3) of the Treaty by Regulation to certain categories of technology transfer agreements and corresponding concerted practices to which only two undertakings were party and which fell within Article 101(1)

Directive 104/89/EEC to approximate the laws of the Member States relating to trade marks (OJ L 40, 11.2.1989)

Regulation (EC) No 240/96 of 31 January 1996 on the application of Article 101(3) of the Treaty to certain categories of technology transfer agreements

Commission notice on the definition of the relevant market for the purposes of Community competition law (OJ C 372, 9.12.1997)

Commission Regulation (EC) No 2790/1999 on the application of Article 101(3) of the Treaty to categories of vertical agreements and concerted practices

Commission Regulation (EC) No 2658/2000 on the application of Article 101(3) of the Treaty to categories of specialisation agreements

Commission Regulation 2659/2000 on the application of Article 101(3) to categories of research and development agreements

Guidelines on vertical restraints (2000/C 291/01)

Commission Guidelines on the applicability of Article 101 of the EC Treaty to horizontal cooperation agreements (OJ C 3, 6.1.2001)

Commission notice on agreements of minor importance which do not appreciably restrict competition under Article 101(1) of the Treaty (OJ C 368, 22.12.2001)

Commission Regulation (EC) No 772/2004 of 27 April 2004 on the application of Article 101 (3) of the Treaty to categories of technology transfer agreements ("the TTBER")

The guidelines on the application of Article 101 of the Treaty to technology transfer agreements (2004/C 101/02)

The Treaty on the Functioning of the European Union, 2008

b) Non - EU:

Indian Easements Act (1882)

The Sherman Act (1890)

The Agreement on Trade-Related Aspects of Intellectual Property Rights (1994)

The US Anti trust guidelines for the licensing of IP (1995)

Japan Patent and Know-How Licensing Guidelines (1999)

Canada Intellectual Property Enforcement Guidelines (2000)

Korea Guidelines of Reviewing Undue Exercise of Intellectual Property Rights (2000)

U.S. Department of Justice & Federal Trade Commission, Antitrust Guidelines for Collaborations Among Competitors (2000)

Taiwan Rules for Review of Technology Licensing Arrangement Cases (2001)

The Indian Competition Act (2002)

Japan Guidelines on Standardization and Patent Pool Arrangements (2005)

Singapore Guidelines on the Treatment of Intellectual Property Rights (2005)

The US Report on Antitrust Enforcement and Intellectual Property Rights (2007)

Japan Guidelines for the Use of Intellectual Property under the Antimonopoly Act (2007)

China Antimonopoly Act (2007)

The Competition Law of Russia (2006)

The Law of the Republic of Armenia on Protection of Economic Competition (2000)

Report of the Anti Monopoly Committee of Ukraine

The report on Competition Policy and Practice of Market Regulation of Georgia

Table of Cases

a) EU:
Darcy v. Allein, English Court of King's Bench, English Reports, vol.77, p.1260 (1602)
Joined Cases 56/64 and 58/64, Consten and Grundig, [1966] ECR 429
Case 26/76, Metro (I), [1977] ECR 1875
Case 258/78, Nungesser, [1982] ECR 2015
Joined Cases 96/102, 104, 105, 108 and 110/82, NV IAZ International Belgium and others v Commission of the European Communities, (ANSEAU-NAVEWA), [1983] ECR 3369
Joined Cases 29/83 and 30/83, CRAM and Rheinzink, [1984] ECR 1679
Case 193/83, Windsurfing International, [1986] ECR 611
Case 65/86, Bayer v. Süllhofer, [1988] ECR 5249
Case C-234/89 Delimitis v. Henninger Bräu AG (1991) ECR 1-935
Radio Telefis Eireann (RTE) and Independent Television Publications Ltd (ITP) v Commission of the European Communities. - Joined cases C-241/91 P and C-242/91 P. European Court reports 1995 Page I-00743
Bureau Européen des Médias de l'Industrie Musicale v. Commission of the European Communities.Case T-114/92. ECR 1995 Page II-00147
Case C-7/95 P, John Deere, [1998] ECR I-3111
Case C-49/92 P, Anic Partecipazioni, [1999] ECR I-4125
Case C-180/98 Pavlov v. Stichting Pensioenfonds Medische Specialisten (2000) ECR 1-6451
Case C-309/99, Wouters, [2002] ECR I-1577
Court of First Instance, Case T-201/04, Microsoft v. Commission
Commission Decision of February 27, 2008, COMP/C-3/37.792 Microsoft
Knorr-Bremse Systems for Commercial Vehicles Ltd v. Haldex Brake Products GmbH [2008] EWHC 156 (Pat)
b) Non - EU:
Standard Oil v. US 221 US 1 (1911).
Ethyl Gasoline Corp. v. U.S., 309 U.S. 436, US Supreme Court, 456 - 457 (1940)
Brulotte v. Thys Co., 379 U.S. 29, Supreme Court, 33 (1964)
SCM Corp. v. Xerox Corp., District of Connecticut, United States District Court, District of Colombia (1978) Federal Supplement, vol. 463
Verizon Communications v. Law Offices of Curtis V. Trinko, 540 U.S. 398, 408 (2004)
U.S. Philips Corp. v. International Trade Commission, United States Court of Appeals, Federal Circuit, 424 F.3d 1179 (Fed. Cir. 2005)

Other Sources

R & D Expenditure Statistics Report http://epp.eurostat.ec.europa.eu/statistics_explained/index.php/R_&_D_expenditure#Further_Eurostat_information
The EU Industrial R & D Investment Scoreboard reproduced online at http://iri.jrc.ec.europa.eu/research/docs/2009/JRC54920.pdf
The Report to the Commission of the High Level Expert Group on Reporting Intellectual Capital to Augment Research, Development and Innovation in SMEs, 2006 (RICARDIS REPORT). The report is reproduced online at http://ec.europa.eu/invest-in-research/pdf/download_en/2006-2977_web1.pdf
The MEMO/09/503 being 2009 "EU Industrial R&D Investment Scoreboard" - Questions & Answers, dated the 16th November, 2009 reproduced online at http://europa.eu/rapid/pressReleasesAction.do?reference=MEMO/09/503&format=HTML&aged=0&language=EN&guiLanguage=en
EU spends more on research, Science and technology - 16/11/2009. Information reproduced online at http://ec.europa.eu/news/science/091116_en.htm

The Public Consultations for the Review of the competition rules applicable to vertical agreements reproduced online at – http://ec.europa.eu/competition/consultations/2009_vertical_agreements/index.html

The report on the Pharmaceutical Industry in Figures, 2011 produced by the European Federation of Pharmaceutical Industries and Associations (EFPIA)which represents over 2000 pharmaceutical companies in Europe. The report is reproduced online at http://www.efpia.eu/Content/Default.asp?PageID=559&DocID=11586

The Contribution of the European Charter of Human Rights to the Right to Legal Aid

Edita Gruodytė and Stefan Kirchner

The life of the society depends on the individual rights.
(Herbert Spencer)[1]

1 Introduction

In many countries, legal aid is an indispensable tool in order to ensure that everybody has access to the judicial system. Effective access to the judicial system is necessary in order to enliven fair trial guarantees. The rule of law requires not only that all are under, that is, bound by, the law but also that all can take refuge under the law in order to protect their rights. The high cost of legal services as compared to the average income in many countries, though, often provides a barrier that prevents those who require legal services from actually obtaining them. While insurance schemes[2] can provide a way to offset some of these costs, many potential clients decide against such forms of insurance because attorney fees are seen as a low-probability risk. From the perspective of the client, it is unlikely that one will be in need of an attorney. If this risk is then realized in the form of a legal dispute for which expert advice or even representation in the courtroom is required, the low-probability risk turns into a high-cost expense. This can lead to those who actually have a valid claim to forgo it for want of the funding that would be necessary to pursue the claim in the first place. This problem can be solved not only through voluntary *pro bono* services but more effectively through granting

---

[1] Quote taken from Pasca (2011), p. 1 *et seq.*, at p. 1.

[2] On the importance to insurance schemes for the access to court, see also Regan (2003), p. 49 *et seq.*; van Velthoven and Klein Haarhuis (2011), p. 587 *et seq.*

E. Gruodytė (✉) • S. Kirchner
Law Faculty, Vytautas Magnus University, E.Ožeškienės st.18, Kaunas LT-44254, Lithuania
e-mail: e.gruodyte@tf.vdu.lt; kirchnerlaw@yahoo.com

T. Kerikmäe (ed.), *Protecting Human Rights in the EU*,
DOI 10.1007/978-3-642-38902-3_5, © Springer-Verlag Berlin Heidelberg 2014

legal aid.[3] While it might at first sight seem unfair that society at large should cover the expenses of a private pursuit, in particular if insurance services are available, it has to be kept in mind that the losing party will usually be required to pay the costs incurred by the victor. If the party to a court dispute that has received legal aid wins the case, the opponent effectively will have to cover the costs that were initially borne by the state, hence turning legal aid into a kind of credit that is paid back not by the initial beneficiary but by the other party in the dispute. This course of events can be made more likely by screening cases prior to a decision as to whether or not legal aid is granted.[4] Just like a state has to provide a base investment in order to establish and maintain a functioning judicial system, for example, by paying for the maintenance of court buildings or the salaries of judges and other employees, the state will be required to spend money on the establishment and permanent maintenance of an effective judicial system in which everybody can participate without discrimination regarding their financial means. The rule of law and legal certainty are fundamental elements of an environment that is conductive not only to a harmonious co-existence within a society and the protection of individual rights. Their importance for the conduct of business transactions and as a fertile ground for economic development can hardly be overestimated. States therefore have an interest in a functioning judicial system that goes beyond their fair trial obligations. In other words, a functioning judicial system pays off—and providing legal aid can make sense from an economic perspective as well. (It has to be noted, though, that in order to be effective, a legal system does not necessarily have to allow for a nearly unlimited number of lawsuits through which individuals can permanently block important development measures—although any generalization in this regard appears dangerous as it might lead to the neglect of rights in individual cases.)

In Europe, despite the pride of place that is rightly given to the European Convention on Human Rights,[5] human rights guarantees are found also within EU law. EU human rights have long been known to be relevant in the context of fair trial guarantees in general, for example, as they pertain to European Criminal law.[6] But while legal aid makes sense from the perspective of the state and is important for many persons who are involved in legal disputes, the question needs to be asked whether, and if so, how, the European Charter of Human Rights contributes to strengthening the right to legal aid?

The European Court of Justice has been developing the idea of human rights in Community (and later Union) law since the late 1960s.[7] This approach was necessary because the human rights contained in the Convention did not bind the

---

[3] On the comparative degrees of effectiveness of *pro bono* services and legal aid, see Gruodytė and Kirchner (2012), p. 43 *et seq.*

[4] The allocation of costs described here mirrors the current legal situation with regard to cases in civil and administrative laws in Germany.

[5] European Treaty Series No. 5, http://conventions.coe.int/treaty/en/treaties/html/005.htm.

[6] See Kirchner (2003), p. 127 *et seq.*

[7] Klein and Scherer (2002), p. 2.

Community directly and because Community and Union laws take precedence[8] over the laws of the member states.[9] Unlike the European Convention on Human Rights, the European Charter of Human Rights does not primarily apply to states but rather to the EU itself[10] and to EU member states when they implement EU law.[11] It has entered into force only on 1 December 2009 with the Treaty of Lisbon.[12] The Charter rights were already included in the failed draft Constitution and stand in the tradition of the human rights that have been developed in the jurisprudence[13] of the European Court of Justice over the last decades. In Europe's multilevel system of governance, the European Charter of Human Rights does not stand alone but has to be seen in the context of not only the human rights that are guaranteed by national constitutions but also the European Convention on Human Rights.[14] In fact, both the Convention and the Charter are to be interpreted in identical ways:

> In early 2011, the presidents of the ECtHR and the EU's European Court of Justice signed a joint declaration to the effect that the human rights contained in the EU's Charter of Fundamental Rights[[15]] and in the ECHR are to be interpreted in parallel.[[16]] This parallel interpretation serves to prepare the eventual accession of the European Union to the ECHR.[17]

This parallel interpretation is a direct consequence of Article 6 (2) of the EU Treaty,[18] according to which

> [t]he [European] Union shall respect fundamental rights, as guaranteed by the European Convention for the Protection of Human Rights and Fundamental Freedoms signed in Rome on 4 November 1950 and as they result from the constitutional traditions common to the Member States, as general principles of Community law.[19]

---

[8] European Court of Justices, *Costa v E.N.E.L.*, Case 6/64, Judgment of 15 July 1964.

[9] Klein and Scherer, p. 2.

[10] Klein and Scherer, p. 6.

[11] Klein and Scherer, p. 6; see also Frenz (2009), p. 138.

[12] Official Journal 2007 C 306, p. 1 *et seq.*

[13] For example, European Court of Justice, *Nold v Commission*, Case 4/73, Judgment of 14 May 1974; European Court of Justice, *Internationale Handelsgesellschaft mbH v Einfuhr- und Vorratsstelle für Getreide und Futtermittel*, Case 11/70, Judgment of 17 December 1970.

[14] On the relationship between human rights under EU law and human rights under the ECHR, see Peters (2003), p. 27 *et seq.*; Grabenwarter (2008), p. 26 *et seq.*

[15] EU Charter of Fundamental Rights, Official Journal of the European Union 2000 C 364, p. 1 *et seq.*

[16] *Joint communication from Presidents Costa and Skouris*, Strasbourg and Luxembourg, 24 January 2011, available online at http://curia.europa.eu/jcms/upload/docs/application/pdf/2011-02/cedh_cjue_english.pdf.

[17] Kirchner (2012), p. 147, footnotes renumbered and reformatted.

[18] A consolidated version is published in Official Journal 2012 C 326, p. 13 et seq.

[19] Art. 6 (2) EU Treaty.

That the jurisprudence of the European Court of Human Rights has to be taken into account in the interpretation of Article 47 of the Charter has already been decided by the European Court of Justice in *DEB Deutsche Energiehandels- und Beratungsgesellschaft mbH v Germany*.[20]

In this text, we will attempt to answer this question by looking at the topic from the perspective of both practicing attorneys and academicians. Based on our practical experience, we will begin with the need of poor clients for legal aid, as well as the regulation of legal aid in different states. Afterwards, we will look at the right to a fair trial as it pertains to legal aid, paying attention to legal aid in different cases before answering the question of the EU Charter's impact on legal aid.

2   Legal Aid

2.1   The Need for Legal Aid

Historically, the beginning of legal aid in Europe is related to the Age of Enlightenment[21] in which equality before the law and equal rights were established with the basic aim of creating equal opportunities for individuals to obtain justice.[22] Legal aid was initially known as the law for the underprivileged,[23] which was actively introduced in European countries, together with ideas regarding the reduction of costs.[24] Some sources indicate that already in the fifteenth century first legislation regarding the provision of legal aid has been enacted.[25] For example, in Scotland the right to defense counsel had become common by the 1520s at the latest; in the Holy Roman Empire, the *Codex Carolinus* of 1532 recognized the right to a defense counsel,[26] while in such EU countries as France and England legal acts prohibited the usage of defense counsel (with certain exceptions[27]) for persons

---

[20] European Court of Justice, *DEB Deutsche Energiehandels- und Beratungsgesellschaft mbH v Bundesrepublik Deutschland*, Case C-279/09, Judgment of 22 December 2010, para. 37.

[21] Usually, the concept of public support for those who are facing legal proceedings is associated with the seventeenth and eighteenth centuries, Age of Enlightenment, in: New World Encyclopedia, http://www.newworldencyclopedia.org/entry/Age_of_Enlightenment; Hackett (1992).

[22] Kiraly (2010), pp. 57–74 *et seq.*, at p. 59.

[23] Which aim to ensure possibility of participation in a legal procedure notwithstanding the financial abilities of an individual in order not to be just privilege of the wealthy, Kiraly (2010), pp. 57–74 *et seq.*, at p. 57.

[24] Cited in Kiraly (2010), pp. 57–74 *et seq.*, at p. 57.

[25] The Act was drafted in England, Regan (1999–2000), pp. 383–404 et seq., at p. 386.

[26] Wasser (2005), p. 186 *et seq.*, at p. 189.

[27] In both countries, the judge was empowered to make exceptions and assign counsel to the accused, Wasser (2005), p. 186 *et seq.*, at p. 189.

accused of crimes.[28] However, before the emergence of the state legal aid, such an assistance usually consisted of various forms of "charity" or *pro bono* work by legal professionals, i.e., providing services to the poor at little or no cost.[29] This in turn is a reminder of the fact that in ancient Greece, the provision of legal advice by those who had knowledge of the law was supposed to be free of charge.[30]

Only in the eighteenth and nineteenth centuries the rules of underprivileged law became a social duty of the state as the previous rules were unable to help the poor effectively. For example, in Hungary legal aid developed from underprivileged law to a social responsibility of a State only in the later nineteenth century.[31] In Finland, legal aid was provided by attorneys as late as 1896.[32] The most significant developments of state legal aid happened after World War II as many governments established state legal aid schemes, thereby allowing equal justice becoming more attainable for people.[33]

Nowadays, States should guarantee access to justice as a human right that requires the state to take a positive action, a *status positivus* obligation. In order to have a functioning judicial system, it has to be accessible *de facto*,[34] as

> the equality principle underpinning the rule of law places the state under an obligation to formalize the theoretical right of access to justice into a substantive citizen right to both civil and criminal legal aid.[35]

In a democratic society, everybody is entitled to the right to justice and to choose the various available kinds of legal services. The efforts of citizens themselves while trying to implement their rights and to protect them are insufficient; therefore, the state is obliged to help them to exercise their rights and, in a case of an infringement, to defend them.[36] *The availability of legal defense principle both in national and international level is treated as one of the most fundamental legal principles, requiring each state to create such a mechanism of legal defense which could ensure real and effective protection of violated rights and interests of the individual concerned,*[37] which indicates that in cases when this right is depending on the financial status of the individual, the state has a positive obligation to provide state-supported legal aid. However, this State obligation could not so easily be

---

[28] In France, article 162 of the 1539 Criminal Code forbade the use of defense counsel to any person accused of a crime; the same regulation was reinforced by the next major code in 1670, while in England defense counsel was normally denied to people accused of felonies, Wasser (2005), p. 186 *et seq.*, at p. 187.

[29] Regan (1999–2000), pp. 383–404 et seq., at p. 386.

[30] Bers and Lanni (2003), p. 3.

[31] Kiraly (2010), pp. 57–74 *et seq.*, at p. 60.

[32] Vendidinen (2008), pp. 135–146 et seq., at p. 137.

[33] Regan (1999–2000), pp. 383–404 et seq., at p. 387.

[34] Gruodytė and Kirchner (2012), p. 43 *et seq.*

[35] Sommerlad (2004), pp. 345–368 *et seq.*, at p. 351.

[36] Vaišvila (2000), p. 383.

[37] Krolienė (2010), pp. 116–135 *et seq.*, at pp. 116–117.

implemented in practice if an individual is indigent because he/she cannot afford lawyers (especially the best ones) or to bear the costs of the legal procedure.

If the State is not able to ensure the right to legal aid, human rights, including the right to a fair trial, become worthless and people will distrust in democracy and its values. But legal aid that is provided by the state must be balanced because "*tax payers in the end have to finance state aid [. . .] but State resources are limited*"[38] and it is necessary for states to make choices.

2.2 Legal Aid in Selected EU Member States

The EU Commission indicated that "despite the fact that the law and criminal procedures of all Member States are subject to ECHR standards and must comply with the EU Charter when applying EU Law, there are still doubts about the way in which standards are upheld across the EU".[39]

In the course of European integration, the matters related to criminal issues (which are closely related to the principle of fair trial and the right to defense counsel) developed gradually,[40] and now the principle of mutual trust[41] dominates in the area of freedom, security, and justice, which is treated as a cornerstone of judicial cooperation in civil and criminal matters because only in such cases that the necessary approximation of legislation, cooperation between competent authorities, and protection of individual rights may be guaranteed.[42] The principle of mutual trust is seen as an important instrument for protection of individual rights, and this issue is stressed in various EU documents,[43] and the importance afforded to this principle appears to be only natural as the trust in the legal systems of other EU

---

[38] Commission of the European Communities, State Aid Action Plan "Less and better targeted state aid: a roadmap for state aid reform 2005–2009" (Consultation document), Brussels, 7.6.2005, COM (2005) 107 final, section 8.

[39] EU Commission Green Paper "Strengthening mutual trust in the European judicial area – A Green Paper on the application of EU criminal justice legislation in the field of detention". Brussels, 14.6.2011, COM (2011) 327 final, p. 3.

[40] Gruodytė and Kairienė (2009), p. 32 *et seq.*

[41] Because of the introduction of the mutual trust principle as a leading one, criminal law cooperation has been systematically biased towards law enforcement, Wolfgang (2011), art. 3.

[42] Directive 2010/64/EU of the European Parliament and of the Council of 20 October 2010 on the Right to Interpretation and Translation in Criminal Proceedings, Official Journal 2010 L 280, section (1), 26.10.2010.

[43] For example, the Programme of measures to implement the principle of mutual recognition of decisions in criminal Matters (2001/C 12/02), Official Journal 2001 C 12, 15.1.2001, p. 10; Directive 2010/64/EU of the European Parliament and of the Council of 20 October 2010 on the Right to Interpretation and Translation in Criminal Proceedings, Official Journal 2010 L 280, section (1), 26.10.2010.

countries is based on the shared respect for human rights and freedoms and on the principles of freedom and democracy. Notwithstanding recent progress in the EU[44]

> many Member States still do not offer sufficient fundamental rights protections for suspects and defendants, and without an enforceable right to access a lawyer, the basis for mutual trust is lacking.[45]

In European countries, access to justice and legal aid (especially in criminal cases) is usually guaranteed by the Constitution and statutory laws,[46] but evaluating if the state legal aid is ensured just in criminal cases or if provisions are more general, the states show that the cases at hand may be divided in two big groups. For example, Article 24 of the Constitution of the Italian Republic[47] declares that "Defense is an inviolable right at every stage and instance of legal proceedings" and that "the poor are entitled by law to proper means for action or defense in all Courts"; in Finland, the right to legal help regardless of one's economic situation is guaranteed by section 21 of the Finnish Constitution,[48] which means that the legal aid for indigent people is guaranteed without difference between civil or criminal matters. The Belgian Constitution contains a rather general norm that states that "Everyone has the right to lead a life in keeping with human dignity",[49] and the right to legal aid is identified in the Belgian Constitution together with other rights as a one constituent of human dignity.[50] In other states, for example, Cyprus, Spain, or Lithuania, the right to legal aid is declared expressly in the Constitution—but only as far as criminal cases are concerned.[51]

In scientific literature,[52] State legal aid services are divided into two groups: "inside" litigation, i.e., helping people to defend their rights in courts (including legal representation, legal advice, and duty solicitor services), and "outside" litigation (such as legal advice and information; minor assistance with documents,

---

[44] For example, the proposal for a Directive of the European Parliament and of the Council on the right of access to a lawyer in criminal proceedings and on the right to communicate upon arrest, COM (2011) 326 final.

[45] Fair Trials International (2012), p. 2.

[46] Bolocan (2002), p. 64.

[47] Constitution of the Italian Republic, Article 24, http://www.senato.it/documenti/repository/istituzione/costituzione_inglese.pdf.

[48] Kosonen and Tolvanen (2010), pp. 233–256 *et seq.*, at p. 244.

[49] The Belgian Constitution, Article 23, http://legislationline.org/documents/section/constitutions.

[50] The Belgian Constitution, Article 23, http://legislationline.org/documents/section/constitutions.

[51] The Constitution of Cyprus states that in case of the arrest of a person, he or she shall be allowed to have the services of a lawyer of his or her own choosing, Constitution of the Republic of Cyprus, Article 11, http://www.kypros.org/Constitution/English/appendix_d_part_ii.html; the Constitution of Lithuania guarantees the right to the defense only in criminal matters from the moment of the detention or first interrogation, Constitution of the Republic of Lithuania, Adopted by citizens of the Republic of Lithuania in the Referendum of 25 October 1992, Valstybės žinios [Official Gazette], 1992-11-30, Nr. 33-1014, article 34. An analogous right is guaranteed in Spain, Bolocan (2002), p. 64.

[52] Regan (1999–2000), pp. 383–404 et seq., at pp. 385–386.

letters, telephone calls; public education and training), i.e., assistance not related to litigation.[53] In our opinion, the provision of both types of services is necessary in order to ensure equal justice. Therefore, both types of legal aid should be provided. This is the case, for example, in Lithuania and Germany. In both states, two kinds of legal aid are provided: primary legal aid (legal advice and drafting of some small documents) and secondary legal aid (representation in courts and preparation of court documents). The organization of how legal aid is provided differs somewhat between those two jurisdictions: in a majority of Germany's 16 federal states legal aid is provided by attorneys, while in remaining states by court employees.[54] In Lithuania, it is an institution that makes a decision if a person is unable to pay and needs legal aid; in Germany, it is the local court of the applicant's place of residence in Germany. While in Lithuania the primary legal aid is organized and provided by municipal institutions, every person is entitled to it regardless of his/her income or property. The secondary legal aid is given by attorneys selected by the State[55] through State legal aid services established in five biggest cities in Lithuania. In Germany, every attorney is obliged to provide legal aid (with some exceptions) if a person gets a special document from the court (*Beratungshilfeschein*). In Lithuania, the State legal aid service is provided by the institution, which evaluates if a person is entitled to secondary legal aid and provides him/her with an attorney, i.e., if the person is not able to get any attorney he/she wishes, he/she may just choose from the ones who are on the list. In Germany,[56] as in many EU countries (example Sweden, Netherlands, Austria), but not Lithuania, legal aid insurance (Legal Expenses Insurance, LEI) is widely developed, but it has limitations particularly with regard to advice (instead of representation) and in the fields of criminal and family laws, while legal aid is usually *"available for all areas of litigation and for representation in criminal cases, subject to a means and merits test"*.[57]

In Sweden, up till 1997, the state legal aid model, introduced in 1970, was comprehensive and generous, as legal aid was provided for most legal problems. It also was universal because it was available to most of the population.[58] As Bernard Michael Ortwein indicated, *"Through a combination of public legal aid and private legal insurance, it seems that no citizen in Sweden is denied access to legal assistance due to an inability to pay"*.[59] In 1980–1990 because of difficult economic situation in Sweden, as in other Nordic societies, less finances were foreseen for welfare programs, including legal aid; thus, there was an increase in charges for legal aid, increase in contributions from the clients for litigation, and tightening of eligibility. criteria.[60] While after reform in 1997 the scheme of State legal aid in

---

[53] Regan (1999–2000), pp. 383–404 et seq., at pp. 385–386.

[54] Gruodytė and Kirchner (2012), p. 43 *et seq.*, at p. 54.

[55] The details may be found in the article Gruodytė and Kirchner (2012), p. 43 *et seq.*, at p. 50.

[56] On Legal Expenses Insurance in Germany, see Buschbell (2007), p. 63 *et seq.*

[57] Kilian and Regan (2004), pp. 233–255 *et seq.*, at p. 237.

[58] Regan (2003), No. 1, pp. 49–65 *et seq.*, at p. 52.

[59] Ortwein (2003), pp. 405–446 *et seq.*, at p. 425.

[60] Regan (2003), pp. 49–65 *et seq.*, at p. 53.

Sweden in civil cases was reformed and shifted from public to private as in certain specified cases (such as most civil and family court cases), Sweden must rely on their Legal Expense Insurance policy that restricts state legal aid.[61] As a consequence of the reform, many public law offices were closed,[62] but the criminal legal aid was not touched and remains the most generous in Europe.[63] An accused individual in criminal cases is entitled to a public defense counsel (advocate) appointed by the court and, additionally, to compensation for the costs of preparing a defense (usually such as production of evidence, traveling expenses, and subsistence).[64]

In the Netherlands, state legal aid was introduced by law in 1958, followed by the establishment of Legal Aid Bureaus 1974, after various reforms (in 1994 and 2005/2006) replaced by the Legal Services Counters.[65] The model partially resembles earlier analyzed approaches because legal aid consists of primary and secondary legal aid. Every individual is entitled to free primary legal aid, which is provided by the Legal Services counters and is basically related to provision of general information about rules, regulations, legal procedures; clarification of the nature of the problem; giving of advice in simple legal matters; and reference of clients to private lawyers and mediators. On the other hand, the secondary legal aid consists of extended consultation (more than one hour) and actual legal aid and is provided by private lawyers only. The main difference of this from the Lithuanian model is that the client may contact a lawyer by himself or may be referred by the legal aid services counter. But a lawyer willing to provide such services must be registered with the legal aid board.[66] However, during the aforementioned reforms, the previously more generous state legal aid scheme gradually became more limited as they are being provided only to poorer people[67] and is subject to a private contribution depending on the level of income and wealth.[68] Another difference from the Lithuanian model is that, like in Sweden, the State legal aid model is combined with the legal expenses insurance, which is steadily growing while the

---

[61] After the legal reform under LEI policies, legal advice (which previously was 2 h) is not offered and usually Swedes should pay at least some costs of legal services for court cases and are discouraged from seeking advice, Regan (2003), pp. 49–65 et seq., at p. 62.

[62] Regan (2003), pp. 49–65 et seq., at p. 50.

[63] The defense counsel is offered to all criminals free of charge for serious crimes, not taking into account income or property issues of a criminal, Regan (2003), pp. 49–65 et seq., at pp. 62–63.

[64] Ortwein (2003), pp. 405–446 et seq., at p. 425.

[65] Poor citizens depending on their property and income were entitled to receive free of charge or by paying a small price the assistance of lawyer reimbursed by the State, van Velthoven and Klein Haarhuis (2011), pp. 587–612 et seq., at p. 589.

[66] Legal Aid Board (2013), p. 3 et seq.

[67] The person is eligible if the maximum income per family per year is 34,400 euros, and 24,000 euros for single, van Velthoven and Klein Haarhuis (2011), pp. 587–612 et seq., at p. 589.

[68] The private contribution is divided into five classes, ranging from 100 euros up to 750 euros per one assignment; court fees for less-well-endowed individuals are reduced by 50 or 75 %, but a losing party, even poor, must compensate the legal expenses of the winning party, van Velthoven and Klein Haarhuis (2011), pp. 587–612 et seq., at p. 590.

importance of legal aid is receding as a result of budget cuts.[69] The LEI usually covers legal disputes related to housing, medical errors, fiscal affairs, work and income, asset management, and motor vehicle accident policies. But it is controversial as it has some clear disadvantages for low-income citizens, though the disadvantages are compensated by some advantages (improvement of the process of problem resolution; as more disputes are solved by settlement, the procedure is cheaper as at first the problem is dealt by the staff of the insurer and only if not solved is the client able to choose the lawyer).[70]

In Finland, the Law on General Legal Aid and the Law on Free Trials were passed in 1973, vesting legal aid in the hands of municipalities. From 1998, legal aid was transferred from municipalities to the state.[71] Usually a private counsel is paid his fees and expenses from public funds when acting by virtue of the Criminal Procedure Code as a public defense counsel or counsel of the complainant because the defendant has a right to choose his own counsel or when acting by virtue of the Legal Aid Law as a trial counsel.[72] The Finnish model is really generous in its provision of legal assistance in litigation, while less opportunities are given for dealing with legal problems of everyday life.[73]

It may be concluded *"that legal aid and access to the courts are fully available in many countries although in some they are accessible only to the poorest"*,[74] the newest tendencies being diversification of legal aid and constant search for better and cheaper solutions.

3   The Right to a Fair Trial as the Legal Basis for Legal Aid

3.1   *Legal Aid as an Essential Element of a Fair Trial*

> *It is better that ten guilty persons escape than that one*
> *innocent suffer*
> -Sir William Blackstone (1765)[75]

In 2011, over 11 % of the clients of the non-governmental organization Fair Trials International reported being denied access to a lawyer during their police interview in the EU.[76] The concept of fair trial is rather complex, incorporating many

---

[69] van Velthoven and Klein Haarhuis (2011), pp. 587–612 *et seq.*, at pp. 591, 604.

[70] van Velthoven and Klein Haarhuis (2011), pp. 587–612 *et seq.*, at pp. 591, 606.

[71] Vendidinen (2008), pp. 135–146 et seq., at p. 137.

[72] Vendidinen (2008), pp. 135–146 et seq., at p. 137.

[73] Vendidinen (2008), pp. 135–146 et seq., at p. 137.

[74] Kiraly (2010), pp. 57–74 *et seq.*, at p. 64.

[75] William Blackstone. *Commentaries on the Laws of England*, 1765, http://www.lonang.com/exlibris/blackstone/index.html.

[76] Fair Trials International (2012), p. 1.

components, such as free access to justice; examination of the case in a fair, public trial and within a reasonable time; examination of the case by an independent, impartial court; and publicity of the sentencing.[77] But for the purposes of this article, we are examining only legal aid (the defense right) as an essential element of a fair trial, i.e., the right of the parties to be assisted by a lawyer chosen by them or an appointed lawyer. In a fair trial, nobody *"should be deprived of freedom at the hands of the state without first having the opportunity to test the allegations and supporting evidence in a court of law, and then only after being found guilty"*.[78]

The defense right may be treated as a positive procedural (opposite to substantial) obligation of the State because a State must take necessary actions in order to ensure that the usage of this right would be effective.[79] The principle of effectiveness could be used to measure identification of positive right and in establishing its limits—effective protection of human rights and freedoms requires the state to take actions in order for the usage of respective right or freedom to be effective.[80]

If an individual is not guaranteed the right to legal advice and representation, it may be the case that a person does not understand his or her legal rights and therefore will not be able to exercise them properly. *Not only are individuals suffering serious injustices, as our cases demonstrate, but time and costs are also being wasted due to subsequent appeals and delayed proceedings, when suspects are not provided with legal advice and representation sufficiently early in the case.*[81]

3.2 The Right to a Fair Trial Under the European Convention on Human Rights and the EU Charter

Article 6 of the European Convention for the Protection of Human Rights and Fundamental Freedoms (hereinafter the ECHR) and Article 47 of the Charter of Fundamental Rights of the European Union (hereinafter the Charter) enshrine the right to a fair trial. The issue of legal aid under Art. 6 ECHR was already decided in the 1979 case of *Airey v. Ireland*,[82] in which

> it was held that, although the right of access to court does not imply an automatic right to free legal aid in civil proceedings, it may imply the obligation on the part of the State to provide for the assistance of a lawyer to persons in financial need. This is the case when legal aid proves indispensable for an effective access to court, either because legal

---

[77] Pasca (2011), p. 1 *et seq.*, at p. 1.

[78] Ardrill (2000), pp. 3–8 *et seq.*, at p. 3.

[79] Urbaitė (2009), pp. 123–144 *et seq.*, at p. 126.

[80] Urbaitė (2009), pp. 123–144 *et seq.*

[81] Fair Trials International (2012), p. 5.

[82] European Court of Human Rights, *Airey v. Ireland*, Application no. 6289/73, Judgment of 9 October 1979, para. 24 *et seq.*

representation is rendered compulsory of by reason of the procedural complexity of the case. The State may also, if appropriate and possible, opt for abolition of compulsory representation and simplification of procedure to the effect that effective access to the court no longer requires a lawyer's assistance.[83] Moreover, an certain financial threshold for the legal costs to be incurred may be acceptable.[84] In the *Aerts* Case the Court adopted the opinion that legal aid may not be refused by the competent authority on the sole basis of the latter's assessment of the prospects of success of the review, unless the assessment is made by a court.[85] In the *Gnahore* Case the Court specified this by stating that the fact that representation by a lawyer was obligatory, had been decisive. It accepted the refusal of legal aid for reason of lack of any serious cassation ground in a case where legal representation was not required and the procedure of selection offered several guarantees.[86] The same position was adopted in the *Essaadi* and *Del Sol* Cases.[87] If an *ex gratia* offer has been made, but is refused by the applicant, the latter cannot complain about lack of effective access.[88,89]

This jurisprudence of the European Court will have to be taken into account when interpreting the Charter. But when we compare Article 47 of the Charter and Art. 6 of the Convention,[90] we will see that the Charter actually goes one step further than the Convention and includes a right to legal aid *expressis verbis*. Article 6 of the European Convention on Human Rights reads as follows:

Article 6 Right to a fair trial

1. In the determination of his civil rights and obligations or of any criminal charge against him, everyone is entitled to a fair and public hearing within a reasonable time by an independent and impartial tribunal established by law. Judgment shall be pronounced publicly but the press and public may be excluded from all or part of the trial in the interests of morals, public order or national security in a democratic society, where the interests of juveniles or the protection of the private life of the parties so require, or to the extent strictly necessary in the opinion of the court in special circumstances where publicity would prejudice the interests of justice.
2. Everyone charged with a criminal offence shall be presumed innocent until proved guilty according to law.
3. Everyone charged with a criminal offence has the following minimum rights:

---

[83] European Court of Human Rights, *Airey v. Ireland*, Application no. 6289/73, Judgment of 9 October 1979, para. 24 *et seq.*

[84] European Court of Human Rights, *Glaser v. the United Kingdom*, Application no. 32346/96, Judgment of 19 September 2000, para. 99.

[85] European Court of Human Rights, *Aerts v. Belgium*, Application no. 25357/94, Judgment of 30 July 1998, para. 60.

[86] European Court of Human Rights, *Gnahore v. France*, Application no. 40031/98, Judgment of 19 September 2000, para. 40 *et seq.*

[87] European Court of Human Rights, *Essaadi v. France*, Application no. 49384/99, Judgment of 26 February 2000, para. 33 *et seq.*, and European Court of Human Rights, *Del Sol v. France*, Application no. 46800/99, Judgment of 26 February 2000, para. 23 *et seq.*

[88] European Court of Human Rights, *Andronicou and Contantinou v. Cyprus*, Application 86/1996/705/897, Judgment of 9 October 1997, para. 200.

[89] van Dijk et al. (2006), p. 562. Footnotes edited and renumbered.

[90] On Art. 6 ECHR see in more detail Janis et al. (2008), p. 718 *et seq.*

(a) to be informed promptly, in a language which he understands and in detail, of the nature and cause of the accusation against him;

(b) to have adequate time and facilities for the preparation of his defence;

(c) to defend himself in person or through legal assistance of his own choosing or, if he has not sufficient means to pay for legal assistance, to be given it free when the interests of justice so require;

(d) to examine or have examined witnesses against him and to obtain the attendance and examination of witnesses on his behalf under the same conditions as witnesses against him;

(e) to have the free assistance of an interpreter if he cannot understand or speak the language used in court.

Article 47 of the Charter of Fundamental Rights of the European Union has the following text:

> Article 47 Right to an effective remedy and to a fair trial
> Everyone whose rights and freedoms guaranteed by the law of the Union are violated has the right to an effective remedy before a tribunal in compliance with the conditions laid down in this Article. Everyone is entitled to a fair and public hearing within a reasonable time by an independent and impartial tribunal previously established by law. Everyone shall have the possibility of being advised, defended and represented.
> *Legal aid shall be made available to those who lack sufficient resources in so far as such aid is necessary to ensure effective access to justice.*[91]

One might wonder why the right to legal aid is expressively included in the Charter but not in the Convention. To begin with, the Convention does not only provide a simple rule requiring the right to a fair trial, but it is already fairly detailed. The right to a fair trial under Article 6 ECHR includes a right to access to court.[92] Why then was legal aid not expressly included in the wording of Article 6 ECHR? In the jurisprudence outlined earlier, we have seen that the right to access to court was not thought to include a right to legal aid *per se*[93] but that this particular aspect of the right to a fair trial was developed over time. The Charter of Fundamental Rights of the European Union obviously is a much later document than the European Convention on Human Rights, and one possible conclusion is that the right to legal aid was included in Article 47 of the Charter because by the time this norm was drafted the right to legal aid—and its connection to access to justice, which is reflected in the wording of Article 47 of the Charter—had become clearer. But such a conclusion would miss part of the picture because the conditions of the time when the European Convention on Human Rights was drafted have to be taken into account as well. Back then, the drafters were still under the influence not only of the impression the horrors of the Shoa and World War II had left on Europe but also of the beginning Cold War. The Convention was a Western European project,

---

[91] Emphasis added.

[92] European Court of Human Rights, *Golder v. the United Kingdom*, Application no. 4451/70, Judgment of 21 February 1975, para. 34 *et seq.*; see also Ovey and White (2006), p. 170; Reid (2007), p. 85 *et seq.*

[93] European Court of Human Rights, *Glaser v. the United Kingdom*, Application no. 32346/96, Judgment of 19 September 2000, para. 99.

and it does not require much in terms of imagination that virtually everything that smelled of socialism was suspect at this time. That can explain why the right to property did not make it into the Convention. Given its importance, that right was to become codified with Article 1 of the Protocol No. 1 to the Convention.[94] Likewise, the fair trial guarantees under the Convention were broadened[95] with Protocol No. 7 to the Convention.[96] Protocol No. 7 dates back to 1984,[97] well after the aforementioned 1979 decision in *Airey*, indicating an unwillingness of the states that were involved in the drafting of Protocol No. 7 to include a right to legal aid.

This comes as no surprise because the right to legal aid is not only a political but also a social right, to use the parlance of human rights lawyers. Political rights are those that have an element of freedom, such as free speech, freedom of assembly, freedom of religion, etc. Usually the obligation incumbent on states in this context is a negative one, meaning that states have to refrain from infringing upon these rights. The right to property, on the other hand, is a social right. Social (or economic, as well as cultural) rights[98] are considered second generation rights even though, for example, for John Locke the right to property was the starting point for discourses on rights.[99] The right to access to court and the right to a fair trial are classical examples of political rights. The moment one adds a financial dimension, though, things change dramatically: the right to legal aid is not only a political but also a social right—and as such might have been suspect also during these coldest times of the Cold War in the early 1980s.

If now the Charter and the Convention are to be interpreted in parallel, the fact that one of these documents recognizes the hybrid right that is the object of our investigation while the other one does not mention it at all is bound to raise questions. One question is whether the inclusion of the right to legal aid in the Charter merely provides the fundament on top of which the conclusions of the jurisprudence of both the European Court of Human Rights and the European Court of Justice are added or whether Article 47 of the Charter is the point of departure for an entirely new development. This question can be answered by looking at the specific jurisprudence of the European Union's courts with regard to the right to legal aid under Article 47 of the Charter. In other words, the question is does the Charter provide anything new to our understanding of the right to legal aid?

---

[94] A consolidated version is available online at http://conventions.coe.int/Treaty/en/Treaties/Html/009.htm.

[95] But some problems remain: see Kirchner (2011), p. 4 *et seq.*

[96] Available online at http://conventions.coe.int/Treaty/en/Treaties/Html/117.htm.

[97] Protocol No. 7, http://conventions.coe.int/Treaty/en/Treaties/Html/117.htm.

[98] On social and cultural rights as a category of legal theory, see Steiner et al. (2007), p. 263 *et seq.*; Ssenyonjo (2010), p. 49 *et seq.*

[99] Kirchner (2008), p. 35.

3.3   Case Law on the Issue of Legal Aid Under Article 47 of the Charter

At the time of writing,[100] there are a number of cases that involve legal aid issues, but only a few of them are truly relevant for our purposes. The European Court of First Instance has been asked to provide legal aid[101] [which does not come as a surprise: after all, it is directly bound by Article 47 (3) of the Charter], but these decisions were made on the basis of the rules of procedure rather than the Charter. The interpretation of Article 47 (3) of the Charter therefore is not as easy at it might seem to be at first sight.

Rather, Article 47 (3) of the Charter appears to provide a significant challenge: recently, the Tribunale de Tivoli has asked the European Court of Justice in two cases: "Does Article 130 of Presidential Decree No 115 of 30 May 2002 on legal aid in Italian law - insofar as it stipulates that amounts payable to the defending council, the auxiliary to the judge and the court legal assessor are to be reduced by half - comply with Article 47(3) of the Charter of Fundamental Rights of the European Union, which stipulates that legal aid is to be made available to those who lack sufficient resources insofar as such aid is necessary to ensure effective access to justice?",[102] but the ECJ decided on 22 March 2013 that it had no jurisdiction to answer this matter.[103] The question should have been phrased differently because under Article 267[104] of the Treaty on the Functioning of the European Union,[105] the ECJ can only interpret EU, not national, law. The Tribunale de Tivoli should have asked how to interpret Article 47 (3) of the Charter.

The key case in which the European Court of Justice has dealt with the issue of legal aid has been the 2010 judgment in *DEB Deutsche Energiehandels- und Beratungsgesellschaft mbH v Germany*.[106] This case came before the ECJ by way

---

[100] This chapter is up to date as of 22 March 2013.

[101] See, for example, European Court of First Instance, *Egan and Hackett v Parliament*, Case T-190/10, Order of 10 May 2011. In this case, legal aid was granted for one applicant and denied for the other.

[102] European Court of Justice, *Elisabetta Gentile v Ufficio Finanziario della Direzione Ufficio Territoriale di Tivoli and Others*, Case C-499/12, Reference for a preliminary ruling from the Tribunale di Tivoli (Italy) lodged on 7 November 2012; European Court of Justice, *Antonella Pedone v Maria Adele Corrao*, Case C-498/12, Reference for a preliminary ruling from the Tribunale di Tivoli (Italy) lodged on 7 November 2012.

[103] European Court of Justice, *Elisabetta Gentile v Ufficio Finanziario della Direzione Ufficio Territoriale di Tivoli and Others*, Case C-499/12, Order of 7 February 2013; European Court of Justice, *Antonella Pedone v Maria Adele Corrao*, Case C-498/12, Order of 7 February 2013.

[104] On the procedure, see already Neville Brown and Kennedy (2000), p. 204 *et seq.*; Oppermann et al. (2009), p. 269.

[105] Official Journal 2008 C 115, p. 47 *et seq.*

[106] European Court of Justice, *DEB Deutsche Energiehandels- und Beratungsgesellschaft mbH v Bundesrepublik Deutschland*, Case C-279/09, Judgment of 22 December 2010.

of a reference from the Kammergericht (Court of Appeals) in Berlin.[107] It concerned the issue of legal aid for legal, rather than natural, persons.[108] It is noteworthy, though, that the Court's starting point was not Article 47 (3) of the Charter (which it dealt with at a later stage of the judgment[109]) but recitals 5 and 11 in the preamble to Council Directive 2003/8/EC,[110] which the Court quoted in the judgment.[111] It was specified that "[l]egal aid should cover pre-litigation advice with a view to reaching a settlement prior to bringing legal proceedings, legal assistance in bringing a case before a court and representation in court and assistance with or exemption from the cost of proceedings".[112] In its decision in *DEB v Germany*, the European Court of Justice relied on the precedent of the European Court of Human Rights in *Airey v. Ireland*.[113]

4 Conclusions

The right to legal aid is essential to the full realization of the right to a fair trial—not only in criminal law cases but also in the contexts of civil and public laws. Under the European Convention on Human Rights, the right to legal aid has been recognized decades ago. The contribution of the Charter, though, is less than spectacular. In particular, from the—very limited—jurisprudence of the European Court of Justice, it can be concluded that Article 47 (3) of the Charter clarifies and codifies the right to legal aid that, although not mentioned expressly in Article 6 of the Convention, is already part and parcel of the fair trial guarantees under the European Convention on Human Rights. In particular, in light of the parallel interpretation of the Convention and the Charter and the potential accession of the European Union to the Convention,[114] it can be concluded that despite the wording of Article 47 (3) of the Charter, legislative value of the norm is rather limited. In the aforementioned case of DEB v Germany, the ECJ held that "[t]he generally recognized right to access to justice is also *reaffirmed* by Article 47 of the

---

[107] European Court of Justice, *DEB Deutsche Energiehandels- und Beratungsgesellschaft mbH v Bundesrepublik Deutschland*, Case C-279/09, Judgment of 22 December 2010.

[108] European Court of Justice, *DEB Deutsche Energiehandels- und Beratungsgesellschaft mbH v Bundesrepublik Deutschland*, Case C-279/09, Judgment of 22 December 2010, para. 1.

[109] European Court of Justice, *DEB Deutsche Energiehandels- und Beratungsgesellschaft mbH v Bundesrepublik Deutschland*, Case C-279/09, Judgment of 22 December 2010, para. 36 *et seq.*

[110] Official Journal 2003 L 26, p. 41 *et seq.*

[111] European Court of Justice, *DEB Deutsche Energiehandels- und Beratungsgesellschaft mbH v Bundesrepublik Deutschland*, Case C-279/09, Judgment of 22 December 2010, para. 3.

[112] European Court of Justice, *DEB Deutsche Energiehandels- und Beratungsgesellschaft mbH v Bundesrepublik Deutschland*, Case C-279/09, Judgment of 22 December 2010, para. 3.

[113] European Court of Justice, *DEB Deutsche Energiehandels- und Beratungsgesellschaft mbH v Bundesrepublik Deutschland*, Case C-279/09, Judgment of 22 December 2010, para. 36.

[114] See Grabenwarter (2008), p. 33 *et seq.*

Charter of Fundamental Rights of the European Union".[115] This choice of words best describes the role of Article 47 of the Charter.

Acknowledgment This research was funded by a grant (No. MIP-020/2012) from the Research Council of Lithuania.

References

Books and Articles

Ardrill A (2000) The right to a fair trail. Alternative Law J 25(1):3–8
Bers V, Lanni A (2003) An introduction to the Athenian legal system. http://www.stoa.org/projects/demos/intro_legal_system.pdf
Bolocan MG (ed) (2002) Professional legal ethics: a comparative perspective. Central European and Eurasian Law Initiative (CEELI), Washington
Buschbell H (2007) Rechtsschutzversicherung und Prozessfinanzierung. In: Büchting H-U, Heussen B (eds) Beck'sches Rechtsanwalts-Handbuch, 9th edn. Verlag C.H. Beck, Munich
Fair Trials International (2012) Towards an EU law guaranteeing the right to a lawyer and to communicate with consular staff and others on arrest. Summary Report, August 2012. http://www.fairtrials.net/publications/defence-rights-in-europe-towards-a-law-guaranteeing-the-right-to-a-lawyer-and-to-communicate-with-consular-staff-and-others-on-arrest
Frenz W (2009) Handbuch Europarecht, Band 4: Europäische Grundrechte, 1st edn. Springer, Heidelberg
Grabenwarter C (2008) Europäische Menschenrechtskonvention, 3rd edn. Verlag C.H. Beck, Munich
Gruodytė E, Kairienė I (2009) The impact of EU law to the criminal law of the member states. Administrativa un Kriminala Justicija 2(47):32–40
Gruodytė E, Kirchner S (2012) *Pro bono* work vs. Legal Aid: approaches to ensuring access to justice and the social responsibility of the Attorney. Baltic J Law Polit 5(2):43–64
Hackett L (1992) The European dream of progress and enlightenment. http://history-world.org/age_of_enlightenment.htm
Janis MW, Kay RS, Bradley AM (2008) European human rights law – text and materials, 3rd edn. Oxford University Press, Oxford
Kilian M, Regan F (2004) Legal expenses insurance and legal aid—two sides of the same coin? The experience from Germany and Sweden. Int J Leg Profession 11(3):233–255
Kiraly L (2010) Legal services in European Union. Studia Juridica Auctoritate Ulegal niversitatis Pecs 57: 57–74
Kirchner S (2003) Strafrechtliche Prinzipiengewährleistung durch die Verfassung für Europa. In: Böllmann F, Hemme S, Korkmaz Ö, Kühn F, Sinn A (eds) Die Menschenrechte als Grundlage für eine gesamteuropäische Rechtsentwicklung und ihr Einfluss auf das Strafrecht, das Öffentliche Recht und das Zivilrecht – Tüm Avrupa'daki Hukuksal Gelişmelerin Dayanağı Olarak İnsan Hakları ve Bunun Ceza Hukuku, Kamu Hukuku ve Özel Hukuktaki Etkileri – Ausgewählte Vorträge und Referate der Sommerakademie in Foça/Izmir/Türkei vom 18.–30. Sept. 2005 und der Sommerakademie in Kemer/Antalya/Türkei vom 15.–28. Sept. 2003,

---

[115] European Court of Justice, *DEB Deutsche Energiehandels- und Beratungsgesellschaft mbH v Bundesrepublik Deutschland*, Case C-279/09, Judgment of 22 December 2010, para. 3, emphasis added.

Deutsch-Türkische Rechtsstudien, Band 5, 1. Auflage. BWV Berliner Wissenschafts-Verlag, Berlin, p 127

Kirchner S (2008) Freiheit und Revolution, 1st edn. Grin Verlag, München

Kirchner S (2011) The right to fair trial under Article 6 of the European Convention on human rights in Immigration Law Cases in Germany, the Netherlands, Belgium, the United Kingdom and Turkey, 1st edn. Grin Verlag, Munich

Kirchner S (2012) The pre-natal personal scope of Article 2 Section 1 Sentence 1 of the European Convention on Human Rights. Kaunas University Press, Kaunas

Klein M, Scherer F. Die (2002) "Allgemeinen Bestimmungen" der EU – Grundrechtecharta (v.a. Art. 52 – Tragweite der garantierten Rechte). http://www.jurawelt.com/sunrise/media/mediafiles/14132/grundrechtecharta-text.pdf

Kosonen H, Tolvanen M (2010) Balancing between effective realization of criminal liability and effective defence rights: the tasks and the roles of prosecutor and Defence Lawyer in Finnish Criminal Procedure. Jurisprudencija (Jurisprudence) 120(2): 233–256

Krolienė I (2010) Valstybės garantuojama teisinė pagalba kaip teisės į teisinę gynybą užtikrinimo priemonė [State guaranteed legal aid as a mean of right to the judicial defense. The right to judicial protection in the context of the reform of civil procedure] Collection of Scientific Articles. (Mykolo Romerio universiteto Leidybos centras, Vilnius 2010) pp 116–135

Legal Aid Board (2013) Legal Aid in the Netherlands, A broad outline. http://www.rvr.org/nl/brochures_en_publicaties

Neville Brown N, Kennedy T (2000) Brown & Jacobs: The Court of Justice of the European Communities, 5th edn. Sweet & Maxwell, London

Oppermann T, Classen CD, Nettesheim M (2009) Europarecht – Ein Studienbuch, 4th edn. Verlag C.H. Beck, Munich

Ortwein BM II (2003) The Swedish Legal System: an introduction. Indiana Int Comp Law Rev 13 (2):405–446

Ovey C, White RCA (2006) Jacobs & White: The European Convention on human rights, 4th edn. Oxford University Press, Oxford

Pasca MA (2011) Aspects regarding the right to a fair trial. Agora Int J Juridical Sci 2:1–4

Peters A (2003) Einführung in die Europäische Menschenrechtskonvention, 1st edn. Verlag C.H. Beck, Munich

Regan F (1999–2000) Legal aid without the State: assessing the rise of pro bono schemes. UBC Law Rev 33(383):383–404

Regan F (2003) The Swedish Legal Services Policy Remix: the shift from public legal aid to private legal expense insurance. J Law Soc 30(1):49–65

Reid K (2007) A practitioner's guide to the European Convention on human rights, 3rd edn. Sweet & Maxwell, London

Sommerlad H (2004) Some reflections on the relationship between citizenship, access to justice, and the reform of legal aid. J Law Soc 3(31):345–368

Ssenyonjo M (2010) Economic, social and cultural rights. In: Baderin MA, Ssenyonjo M (eds) International Human Rights Law: six decades after the UDHR and beyond, 1st edn. Ashgate, Surrey, p 49 et seq.

Steiner HJ, Alston P, Goodman R (2007) International human rights in context, 3rd edn. Oxford University Press, Oxford

Urbaitė L (2009) Assessment of the state's positive obligations in the cases of the European Court of Human Rights against Lithuania. Socialinių mokslų studijos – Soc Sci Stud 3(3):123–144

Vaišvila A (2000) Teisės teorija [Legal theory]. Justitia, Vilnius

van Dijk P, van Hoof F, van Rijn A, Zwaak L (eds) (2006) Theory and practice of the European Convention on human rights, 4th edn. Intersentia, Antwerp

van Velthoven BCJ, Klein Haarhuis CM (2011) Legal aid and legal expenses insurance, complements or substitutes? The case of the Netherlands. J Empir Leg Stud 8(3):587–612

Vendidinen M (2008) Russia adapts the model of the Finnish Legal Aid System. Rev Cent East Eur Law 33:135–146

Wasser M (2005) Defense Counsel in Early Modern Scotland: a study based on the High Court of Justiciary. J Leg Hist 26(2):183–201
Wolfgang W (2011) Negative and positive integration in EU criminal law co-operation. Eur Integrat online Papers 15. http://eiop.or.at/eiop/texte/2011-003a.htm

Official Material

Age of Enlightenment. New World Encyclopedia. Available online at http://www.newworldency-clopedia.org/entry/Age_of_Enlightenment
Commission of the European Communities State Aid Action Plan "Less and better targeted state aid: a roadmap for state aid reform 2005–2009" (Consultation document), Brussels, 7.6.2005, COM(2005) 107 final
Constitution of the Italian Republic. Available online at http://www.senato.it/documenti/reposi-tory/istituzione/costituzione_inglese.pdf
Constitution of the Republic of Cyprus. Available online at http://www.kypros.org/Constitution/ English/appendix_d_part_ii.html
Constitution of the Republic of Lithuania, Adopted by citizens of the Republic of Lithuania in the Referendum of 25 October 1992, *Valstybės žinios* [Official Gazette], 1992-11-30, Nr. 33–1014
Directive 2010/64/EU of the European Parliament and of the Council of 20 October 2010 on the Right to Interpretation and Translation in Criminal Proceedings. Official Journal of the European Union L 280, section (1), 26.10.2010
EU Commission Green Paper "Strengthening mutual trust in the European judicial area – A Green Paper on the application of EU criminal justice legislation in the field of detention". Brussels, 14.6.2011, COM (2011) 327 final
European Treaty Series No. 5. Available online at http://conventions.coe.int/treaty/en/treaties/ html/005.htm
EU Charter of Fundamental Rights, Official Journal of the European Union 2000 C 364/01
Joint communication from Presidents Costa and Skouris, Strasbourg and Luxembourg, 24 January 2011. Available online at http://curia.europa.eu/jcms/upload/docs/application/pdf/2011-02/ cedh_cjue_english.pdf
Official Journal 2003 L 26, pp. 41 *et seq.*
with these 2 sources from the official journal we might want to provide more information, depending on what is deemed necessary by the editors
Official Journal 2008 C 115, pp 47 *et seq.*
Programme of measures to implement the principle of mutual recognition of decisions in criminal Matters (2001/C 12/02), OJ C 12, 15.1.2001
Proposal for a Directive of the European Parliament and of the Council on the right of access to a lawyer in criminal proceedings and on the right to communicate upon arrest, COM(2011) 326 final
The Belgian Constitution, Article 23 // http://legislationline.org/documents/section/constitutions
The Treaty of Lisbon. Official Journal 2007 C 306

Case Law

European Court of Human Rights
Case *Aerts v. Belgium*, application no. 25357/94, European Court of Human Rights 30 July 1998
Case *Airey v. Ireland*, application no. 6289/73, European Court of Human Rights 9 October 1979

Case *Andronicou and Contantinou v. Cyprus*, application 86/1996/705/897, European Court of Human Rights 9 October 1997
Case *Del Sol v. France*, application no. 46800/99, European Court of Human Rights 26 February 2000
Case *Essaadi v. France*, application no. 49384/99, European Court of Human Rights 26 February 2000
Case *Glaser v. the United Kingdom*, application no. 32346/96, European Court of Human Rights 19 September 2000
Case *Gnahore v. France*, application no. 40031/98, European Court of Human Rights 19 September 2000

European Court of Justice
Case C-498/12 *Antonella Pedone v Maria Adele Corrao* (7 February 2013)
Case C-279/09 *DEB Deutsche Energiehandels- und Beratungsgesellschaft mbH v Bundesrepublik Deutschland* (22 December 2010)
Case T-190/10 *Egan and Hackett v Parliament* (10 May 2011)
Case C-499/12 *Elisabetta Gentile v Ufficio Finanziario della Direzione Ufficio Territoriale di Tivoli and Others* (7 November 2012)
Case 4/73 *Nold v Commission* (14 May 1974).
Case 11/70 *Internationale Handelsgesellschaft mbH v Einfuhr- und Vorratsstelle für Getreide und Futtermittel*, Case (17 December 1970)

Gender as an Impediment of Marriage, Free Movement of Citizens, and EU Charter of Fundamental Rights

Kristi Joamets

1 Introduction

The Estonian authority refuses to issue a marriage impediment certificate to an Estonian man who wants to marry a man in Sweden. The Estonian man turns to the Estonian court to sue the state who violated his rights for free movement. The court decides[1] referring to the decision of Schalk and Kopf v Austria[2] of the European Convention of Human Rights (ECHR) that the state acted legally and free movements as such has not been violated. A same-sex couple married in the Netherlands presents to Estonian authority their marriage certificate to enter the data of their marriage into Estonian Population Register. The state refuses to accept such document referring to the fact that Estonia does not recognise same-sex marriages. A same-sex couple married in England wants to divorce in Estonia, but the state authority refuses because according to Estonian law they are not married at all, as such marriage is not recognised in Estonia. An Estonian resident has a same-sex marriage in the Netherlands; now he wants to marry in Estonia with a person of the opposite sex. According to Estonian law, this is allowed. Now such person is double-married—Estonia recognises the one contracted here and the Netherlands, the one in the Netherlands as the first one.

These are examples familiar not only to Estonia but also to other member states. It is evident that vivid regulations of marriage in different member states cause

---

[1] Case 3-12-1446 Estonian Administrative court (18 October 2012).

[2] Case of *Schalk and Kopf v. Austria* ECtHR (June 2010).

K. Joamets (✉)
Tallinn Law School, Tallinn University of Technology, Akadeemia tee 3, 12618 Tallinn, Estonia
e-mail: joametskristi@gmail.com

T. Kerikmäe (ed.), *Protecting Human Rights in the EU*,
DOI 10.1007/978-3-642-38902-3_6, © Springer-Verlag Berlin Heidelberg 2014

problems when a citizen granted some rights in one member state wants to move or live or work in another member state where the same legal relation is regulated differently. Is, in these examples, the free movement of the citizen restricted? Can they also breach human rights? There have been questions in Estonian practice about these problems in the examples: do they arise from the fact that Estonian law does not follow the principles of human rights, or is it a normal situation that people just have to accept and has no relations to human rights at all? Marriage is a complicated issue,[3] in which the state interests and the interests of the individual collide with each other; the interests are mixed, and it is difficult to find balance between the right of choice of the individual and the obligation of the state to ensure the minimum protection to the same individual and society in general. Gender as an impediment for marriage has, in recent years, got more attention than other obstacles for marriage. Also, court decisions related to marriage impediments are mostly related to questions of gender. This is the character of our society today— quick changes in society have put policymakers and implementers of law in a rather difficult situation—would it be useful to follow the states that have legalised same-sex marriages, accept partnerships, or deny the possibility to recognise such relations at all? However, based on the annual Congresses of European Registrars,[4] there is a clear movement towards tolerance in same-sex marriages.

A question of conflict of law related to marriage (impediments) has been reflected to be mostly about same-sex marriages, but the same question can be raised related to other impediments that differ from state to state (age, kinship, health, etc.)—these impediments can be analysed analogously with question of gender, as they are also matters that can reach to the restriction of free movement.[5]

Marriage, family, and family life, discrimination, and free movement of citizens are the rights protected by the Charter. In Estonian practice, it is not clear how to apply EU law, as well as the provisions of the Charter in case of marriages. There are many theoretical gaps or misleading understandings and interpretations in applying the Charter in this question. Application is complicated also because the Charter is a living being, which means that the content of the principles provided

---

[3] Concept of marriage itself needs clarification. Ivic points out that in Europe there is a big gap between the theory and praxis, culture and legislation. The concepts of "marriage" and "family" are needed to be reopened and redefined. These concepts are not fixed (Ivic 2009, p. 288).

[4] http://www.evs-eu.org/.

[5] Ethnic, religious, or class divisions in society may be exacerbated rather than channelled into democratic debate, sowing seeds of conflict and undermining pluralism and respect for human rights. This especially applies to discriminated groups/people in vulnerable situations such as women, children, indigenous peoples, migrants and asylum seekers, minorities, LGBT persons, and persons with disabilities [European Instrument for Democracy and Human Rights (EIDHR) Strategy Paper 2011–2013 C (2010) 2432 21 April 2010, p. 7].

and protected by it are changing with the changes in the society. It seems that the institutions, including the European Court of Justice (ECJ), try to refrain from giving an evident statement which that be used as a certain understanding. Besides the fact that those statements seem unfinished, they also always include reference to the fact that the ECHR (also the Charter) is a living instrument. As also marriage has been changed and probably will change also in the future, an applicant of the law has difficulties making the decision of a member state, as he/she does not know how the appeal against his/her decision by the court would be solved.

In this article, the legal understanding in application of the Charter in case of marriage impediment in the context of free movement in EU is discussed by using empirical methods and based on the statements and opinions of legal scientists, practitioners, institutions of EU, legal acts, and also ECJ and ECtHR court practice.

2 Marriage and Free Movement

Marriage law has usually been treated in EU sphere as an area that belongs to the shared competence of member state as a branch of civil law. Common reference is to the traditions of member states that are supposed to be different because of the different cultures of member states. Related to family law, the EU more and more abandons this difference and has shown convergence also in family law, including marriage. It is evident that cross-border family relations are closely related to the principles of EU law, including the right of a person of free movement. Secondary law does not regulate family law directly, but certain cases and directives play a role.[6] Related to primary law, the EU Charter is an important act providing the general principles that can be part of EU law in case of marriage.

In 2011, in its report the Commission pursued a rigorous enforcement policy with a view to achieving the full and correct transposition and application of EU free movement rules across the EU, because intra-EU mobility of persons is a key factor for economic growth in a Europe with a declining population and a significant unbalance between supply and demand on a labour market in different parts of

---

[6] For example, mutual Recognition and Enforcement of Family Law Decisions throughout the EU: Council Regulation (EC) No 1347/2000 of 29 May 2000 (Brussels II); Council Directive 2003/86/EC of 22 September 2003 on the right to family reunification, OJ L 251 of 3.10.2003; Directive 2004/38/EC of the European Parliament and of the Council of 29 April 2004 on the right of citizens of the Union and their family members to move and reside freely within the territory of the member states amending Regulation (EEC) No 1612/68 and repealing Directives 64/221/EEC, 68/360/EEC, 72/194/EEC, 73/148/EEC, 75/34/EEC, 75/35/EEC, 90/364/EEC, 90/365/EEC and 93796/EEC.

the EU. At the same time, the free movement of students, tourists, workers, and their families between member states is a key European achievement and a practical expression of mutual respect, openness, and tolerance as core EU values.[7]

Free movement of persons is a principle derived from the beginning of the foundation of the EC, from the Treaty of European Union (TEU), the Lisbon Treaty, and also included into the Charter. The Charter's entry into force adds a third legal source on fundamental rights, an addition that may need to be clarified and communicated. According to Article 6 of the TEU, the three sources of fundamental rights law are the Charter, the general principles of EU law as established by the ECJ, and the European Convention on Human Rights (ECHR).[8] After the Lisbon Treaty, the free movement of persons as one of the main rights of persons got even more important meaning, supporting several important developments in this context related to family law. Emphasising more than earlier the area of freedom, security, and justice without internal frontiers for EU citizens, also families and their rights moving from one member state to another are considered more strongly in new developments of the EU. State acts hindering free movement, either on the basis of legally established or judicially admitted grounds, are bound by EU and constitutional rights at the same time. Due to the overarching nature of the EU freedoms of movement, almost any state act could be regarded as somewhat constraining free movement. Therefore, there is potential for expanding the scope of application of EU fundamental rights against the states.[9]

Free movement as a right of EU Law is also a fundamental right in the Charter. According to Article 45, every citizen of the Union has the right to move and reside freely within the territory of the member states.

As at the beginning of creation of EC free movement served the interests of economy, after introducing the institution of European citizenship the content of free movement was changed and related more to the person itself and not any more so significantly to work. Migration for work has been replaced by the migration of families. This has been considered also in the policies of EU and in the development or even in the interpretation of EU law. One part of this new process is family events, and EU attempt to harmonise family law to the extent it would promote free movement of citizens and avoid obstacles derived from the fact that states do not recognise all family events taking place in another member state.[10]

---

[7] Report from the Commission to the European Parliament, the Council, the European Economic and Social Committee and the Committee of the Regions. 2011. Report on the Application of the EU Charter of Fundamental Rights. COM(2012) 169 final.EC 16.4.2012. SWD(2012) 84final, SWD(2012) 85final, p. 10.

[8] Bringing the Charter to life—opportunities and challenges of putting the EU Charter of Fundamental Rights into practice. Copenhagen Seminar Report. 15–16 March 2012. Danish Presidency of the Council of the EU and EU Agency for Fundamental Rights, p. 5.

[9] Peréz (2009).

[10] See Green Paper—Less bureaucracy for citizens: promoting free movement of public documents and recognition of the effects of civil status records. European Commission. Green Paper. COM(2010)747final.14. December 2010.

However, EU developments show clearly that family law of member states does not have today such a subsidiarity as it has had before. Convergence of family law is evident in an example of change of values related to marriage impediments—especially same-sex marriages.[11] Though according to the Commentary of the Charter, the ECJ has, so far, privileged heterosexual marriage in its case law, thereby excluding relationships within the protective frame of the Community law to other forms of family life,[12] it can be argued if this statement is still contemporary, as the Charter does not have the reference to the different sexes of spouses any more. Cornides and Brussels conclude that either Article 9 of the Charter is interpreted in line with Article 12 of the ECHR (which would exclude same-sex marriages) or it is openly acknowledged that Article 9 of the Charter is in contradiction to Article 12 of the ECHR (which, in turn, would be impossible to reconcile with the Preamble of the Charter)[13]; Commentaries of the Charter explain that in Netherlands v. Reed, the Court held that a "spouse" for the purpose of granting free movement rights to family members is to be limited to married persons and does therefore not include cohabitees (heterosexual and homosexual).[14] On the other hand, the equal treatment of *de facto* couples and married couples and their children has been recognised in the Council Directive 2003/86/EC on the right to family reunification of 22 September 2003 [Article 4(3)].[15] One of the progressive elements of the Directive is the wide, modernised[16] concept of family, which comprises also registered partners for the purpose of family reunification [Article 4(3)].[17] The ECJ stressed in D. and the Kingdom of Sweden v. Council,[18] by advocating the generally accepted and traditional view of marriage,

---

[11] Ivic notes that the Charter should be revised in order to move towards the postmodernist political liberalism that does not base its concepts on metaphysical and moral assumptions but on political and constructivist approach, which emphasizes heterogeneity and multiple identities. Ivic refers to Taylor, explaining that political liberalism is neutral and does not include notions such as "common values", "moral heritage", "inherent", and so forth (Ivic 2009, p. 281).

[12] Case C-249/96, *Lisa Jacqueline Grant v. South West Trains Ltd.*(17 February 1998) and Case C-122/99 P and C-125/99 P, and the *Kingdom of Sweden v Council of the European Union* (31 May 2001).

[13] Cornides and Brussels (2010), pp. 2–3.

[14] Case C-59/85, *State of Netherlands v Ann Florence Reed* (17 April 1986).

[15] Council Directive 2003/86/EC of 22 September 2003 on the right to family reunification, OJ L 251 of 3.10.2003, p. 12.

[16] According to the "Legal Explanations" (drafted by the members of the ECHR that drafted the Charter), the wording of Article 9 has been "modernised" to cover cases in which national legislation recognises arrangements other than marriage for founding a family. This article neither prohibits nor imposes the unions between people of the same sex. This right is thus to that afforded by the ECHR, but its scope may be wider when national legislation so provides (Cornides and Brussels 2010, pp. 2–3).

[17] Commentary of the Charter of Fundamental Rights of the European Union, p. 87.

[18] Case C-122/99 P and C-125/99 P, *D and the Kingdom of Sweden v. Council*, ECHR I-4319 (31 May 2001).

that "Community notions of marriage and partnership exclusively address a relationship founded on civil marriage in the traditional sense of term".[19]

In the context of free movement, there can be raised an issue that norm should be
applied in case of conflict of laws, as it is not easy to decide which law prevails: the
ECHR, the Charter, or national law. According to Laffranque, despite duplication or
even triplication of legal protection by the national and supranational legal orders and
instruments, even with all these instruments there may be legal gaps, and when such
gaps will match, then there can be areas that should be fulfilled by the court practice.[20]
But the truth is that also courts have been very careful in forming their opinion.

Directive 2004/38/EU provides for the free movement a meaning that
connects this fundamental right to the application of Charter as EU secondary
law. The only question is to which extent. Same-sex partners are provided in this
directive as family members and have a significant right for free movement and
residence in 13 member states, in which registered partner is considered as
family member. Although the directive plays a more important role for the
third country family members than for EU citizens, it also comprises general
principles member states should follow, and it is not only the question of
travelling from one member state to another but also the avoidance of obstacles
related to administrative and legal deeds. If marriage contracted in one member
state is not recognised in another, there can be obstacles to reside in a member
state under equal conditions compared to other citizens. The aim of the directive
is to minimise formalities EU citizens and their family members have to follow
by using their rights to live in another member state. As a member state applies
here EU law, also the Charter is applicable.

3   Application of the EU Charter

The EU Charter states in its preamble, in its first recital, that the Union "places the
individual at the heart of its activities, by establishing the citizenship of the Union
and by creating the area of freedom, security and justice". Although the Charter has
no formal legal status within EU law, it has had a profound influence on the
institutions since it was adapted. According to Article 51, paragraph 1, the Charter
applies to the member states only when they are implementing Union law. This
means that the member states are only bound by the Charter when they act as agents
for the Union, e.g., when they execute an EU decision, when they apply an EU
Regulation at national level, or when they implement an EU Directive. When
member states act on their own initiative, there is no need to bind them to the
Charter, as in these cases, they are subject to their national law.

---

[19] Commentary of the Charter of Fundamental Rights of the European Union, p. 102.
[20] Laffranque (2006), p. 328.

There is still lack of clarity on the question how much a member state is obliged to follow the Charter as though Article 51(1) addresses the "institutions and bodies of the Union with due regard to the principle of subsidiarity" and member states "when they are implementing Union law". Article 51(2) provides that the Charter "does not establish any new power or task for the [...] Union, or modify powers and tasks defined by the Treaties". The latter refers to EU member states being bound by Union law when they "act in the scope" of it. This seems to follow ECJ case law and suggests that EU member states are also bound by the Charter when they invoke certain exceptions in the Treaties.[21] Accordingly, when EU member states apply exceptions to the internal market freedoms, they still need to comply with fundamental rights standards.[22] Such understanding can lead to the different court practice of national courts from the ECJ. The Charter does not replace national constitutions but merely complements them.[23]

Applying the Charter, it is often unclear which concrete aspects of fundamental rights are covered under EU law. This lack of clarity is especially felt by the holders of rights and also by those bodies and authorities that, at the national and international levels, are responsible for ensuring implementation.[24] This is evident in case of marriage, as seen in the discussion in the next chapter.

4 Principles of Marriage in the EU Charter

Article 9 of the Charter provides that the right to marry and to found a family shall be guaranteed in accordance with the national laws governing the exercise of these rights. As the reference to the man and woman in the ECHR, Article 12, has been replaced by "person" formulating the right to marry in a gender neutral manner, there are disputes on the meaning of this provision today.

Viviane Reding states that such wording provides more extensive protection than other human rights instruments. The scope of Article 9 may thus be extended to comprise other forms of marriage than the traditional, if these are established by national legislation. Domestic laws have consequently a crucial role under Article 9, and the national legislature is offered broad latitude in the elaboration of the domestic rules on marriage in accordance with the respective social and cultural concepts. On the other hand, the fact that the right to marry is included in the central

---

[21] Bringing the Charter to life—opportunities and challenges of putting the EU Charter of Fundamental Rights into practice. Copenhagen Seminar Report. Danish Presidency of the Council of the EU and EU Agency for Fundamental Rights. 15–16 March 2012, p. 6.

[22] Ibid., p. 7.

[23] Reding (2012).

[24] Ibid., p. 13.

human rights instruments[25] supports the idea that the exercise of the right cannot be wholly governed by national law.[26,27] Such interpretation makes the content of the provision indistinct again and raises a question if the aim of the Charter was to clarify Article 12 of the ECHR or change it. Cornides and Brussels argue that the Charter must be interpreted in the light of the ECHR: "marriage" (art 9) must be given the same meaning as in the ECHR (art 12) guaranteeing the access to a marriage of two persons of different sex. As Article 21 of the Charter and Article 14 of the ECHR do not have reference to the "sexual orientation", it can be concluded that the Charter does not entail an obligation for member states to foresee specific institutions for homosexuals such as "registered partnership".[28]

On the other hand, the ECtHR itself has interpreted Article 12 in the light of Article 9 of the Charter.[29]

Commentaries to the Charter explain that as a living instrument, the ECHR should be interpreted in the light of present-day conditions; it may be inferred that

---

[25] Commentaries refer to the Article 23(2) of the ICCPR, Article 10(1) of the ICESCR, Article 16 (2) of the CEDAW, and Article 5d(iv) of the CERD.

[26] The ECHR established in, e.g., F. V. Switzerland that a state may not restrict or reduce the right to marry in such a way or to such an extent that the very essence of the right is impaired (Case of *F. v. Switzerland*, 18 December 1987). The court has, furthermore, indicated that restrictions on marriage within European societies relate only to the aspects of marriage, which deal with procedures, the legal capacity or consent to marry (Commentary of the Charter of Fundamental Rights of the European Union, p. 98). In that sense, Article 9 of the Charter contains particularly dynamic and variable concepts. Different societies have dissimilar views regarding marriage, the family, and its functions. "(M)atrimony is so closely bound up with the cultural and historical traditions of each society and its deep-rooted ideas about family unit" (Case of *F. v. Switzerland*, 18 December 1987, para. 33). The EU Council has, in addition, expressed the view that family law is "Very heavily influenced by the culture and tradition of national (or even religious) legal systems, which could create a number of difficulties in the context of harmonisation". Council report on the need to approximate Member States' legislation in civil matters of 16 November 2001 (13017/01 justciv 129) (Commentary of the Charter of Fundamental Rights of the European Union, p. 98). See also the analysis about the meaning of marriage, Joamets (2012), pp. 97–115.

[27] Pull discusses if the right to marry is a fundamental right at all. He concludes that the notion of fundamental rights implies firm privileges that the state cannot deny, define, or disrespect, but marriage boundaries (the legal rules establishing who is eligible to marry whom, what formalities are required for marriage, and the legal ramification of marriage) in the United States have always been subject to almost plenary state control that denies some marriages and refuses to give legal effect to others. The word "marriage" has several different meanings that are related to each other but conceptually distinct. The fundamental right to marry conundrum arises in part from the conflation of these various meanings. Moreover, the history of Western marriage regulation— particularly the contemporary rejection of the traditional beliefs about sexuality and marriage that once provided principled boundaries for a right to marry—explains why the various meanings of marriage often are confeated today, and it suggests how the law can escape the "fundamental right to marry" comendrum (Pull 2006, p. 1).

[28] Cornides and Brussels (2010), pp. 2–3.

[29] See Case *Schalk and Kopf v. Austria* (Appl. No. 3014104 24) (June 2010), para. 60.

the family as an instrument is in a state of transition in structure, functions, and values.[30] This is a very important statement showing that the decision made by a state today can be wrong tomorrow and the Charter should be interpreted within the ECHR. However, it is still too precarious to state that the change in the wording of the ECHR replacing the "man and a woman" with the "person"[31] means that it is up to the member state to decide if the marriage between the same-sex persons is allowed or not, because also article 12 of the ECHR contains the part of the provision "according to the national laws governing the exercise of this right". The change was in the provision by this that the reference to the sex and age was left out. Also, the ECtHR has referred to the ECHR as a living instrument—this means that the meaning of "marriage" is changing. It is also important to note that though the aim of the Charter is to explain more exactly the ECHR, the Charter itself can be interpreted not by the ECtHR, but interpretation of the Charter falls into the competence of the ECJ.[32]

Such a strong reference to the social and cultural differences of member states, on the one side, and changing society, on the other, leads to the difficulties to choose the right position in this question. Thinking about EU as a common and trustable legal area raises a question that maybe marriage in a European context is an institute, which needs flexibility in a common, trustable legal area. Are the values of society of every member state so important in the context of marriage capacity that it is useful, reasonable, and rational to accept the conflict of laws and the obstacle to the free movement of citizens knowing that sooner or later these obstacles are annulled anyway? Looking at history, one can see that only in the beginning of the twentieth century in Denmark was unmarried cohabitation a criminal offence. At the same time, homosexuality was decriminalised and not seen as jeopardising society.[33] And today, Denmark is a society that abolished same-sex partnership in 2012 and legalised same-sex marriage. In Sweden, there were religious elements in Swedish Marriage Code still in the late 1960s. Restrictions on marital capacity, which included degrees of affinity, and provisions for annulment, which distinguished an invalid marriage from one ending in divorce, reflected religious values.[34] But already in 1970s it was clear that legal rules and the norms no longer reinforced traditional values.[35] If the principal determinant for marital capacity is whether a man and a woman can live together, a religious code as the foundation for the institution of marriage became irrelevant. The Swedish

---

[30] Commentary of the Charter of Fundamental Rights of the European Union, p. 98.

[31] Actually, the reference to anybody is missing completely.

[32] Cornides and Brussels (2010), p. 5.

[33] Bradley (1996), p. 49.

[34] Ibid., p. 65.

[35] Ibid., p. 66.

marriage and divorce law of 1973 pared restrictions on marriage between relatives to an absolute minimum.[36,37] A government commission subsequently recommended measures to improve the social status of homosexuals but rejected same-sex marriage. The basis for this was an assessment of contemporary public opinion rather than any direct commitment to religious values.[38]

Article 9 of the Charter does not enumerate any permissible restrictions on the right to marry. This does not suggest that the right as such is absolute in the sense that every couple, when they wish, may claim the right from the authorities responsible for the celebration of marriage to be married immediately without fulfilling any legal requirements at all.[39] It is generally agreed that if states establish restrictions on the right to marry, they should be based only on rational, reasonable, and non-arbitrary grounds (public interests). In the decisions (both in ECtHR and ECJ), there is no exact explanation what exactly in this certain state has been violated. Thinking about private life protection and the grounds that allow restricting private life [the interests of national security, public safety, or the economic well being of the country; prevention of disorder or crime; protection of health or morals; protection of the rights and freedoms of others (ECHR art 8)], it needs a lot of fantasy to find an example of how same-sex marriage violates any of them.

Some restrictions are universal; others are atypical. Legal restrictions in domestic laws that have been considered generally accepted in international law relate, among other things, to the marriageable age and requirement to uphold monogamy.[40] According to the Commentary of the Charter, the drafters of those international

---

[36] Ibid., p. 67.

[37] Direct lineal ascendants could not marry, and neither could full siblings. However, marriage between half-brother and half-sister was possible. Objections on genetic grounds were considered insufficient. Only the consent of the government was required (Bradley 1996, p. 67).

[38] Bradley (1996), p. 68.

[39] Commentary of the Charter of Fundamental Rights of the European Union, p. 99.

[40] However, according to international law, domestic laws must not prohibit or discriminate against marriage across racial, religious, or national border: for example, there should be no restrictions on interreligious marriages, inter-racial marriages, or marriages between a national of a country and a foreigner. Furthermore, a change has been brought about in the jurisprudence of the European Court through an alteration in the understanding of who can marry, i.e., post-operative transsexuals have a right to marry in their new sex. Case of *Christine Goodwin v. United Kingdom* (11 July 2002). Departing from its earlier decisions in Case of *Rees v. United Kingdom* (17 October 1986), Case of *Cossey v. UK* (27 September 1990), and Case of *Sheffield and Horsham v. UK* (30 July 1998) and invoking the living instrument doctrine, the Court acknowledged that the rights of transsexuals ought to be viewed in the light of medical progress and social changes in the attitudes towards transsexual person. According to the Court "the stress and alienation arising from a discordiance between the position in society assumed by a post-operative transsexual and the status imposed by law which refuses to recognize the change of gender, cannot be regarded as a minor inconvenience arising from a formality", in other words, a conflict between social and any other illegal coercion or domination of the will of one of the intending spouses. One can ask if the same-sex couples do not have the stress and alienation as well as social conflict (Commentary of the Charter of Fundamental Rights of the European Union, p. 99).

instruments meant the concept "marriage" to imply a heterosexual character to the relationship. Modern trends and developments in the domestic laws in a number of countries lead towards greater openness and acceptance of same-sex couples.[41] At present, there is a very limited legal recognition of same-sex relationships in the sense that marriage is not available to same-sex couples. The domestic laws of the majority of states presuppose, in other words, that the intending spouses are of different sexes. Nevertheless, in a few countries, e.g., in the Netherlands and in Belgium, marriage between people of the same-sex is legally recognised. Others, like the Nordic countries, have endorsed a registered partnership legislation, which implies, among other things, that most provisions concerning marriage, i.e., its legal consequences such as property distribution, rights of inheritance, etc., are also applicable to these unions.[42] Commentaries point out that the term "registered partnership" has intentionally been chosen, not to confuse it with marriage, and it has been established as an alternative method of recognising personal relationship. This new institution is, consequently, as a rule only accessible to couples who cannot marry, and the same-sex partnership does not have the same status and the same benefits as marriage.[43] There is no doubt that same-sex cohabitation is 'family life' and is protected as one, but it does not give the right to marry a spouse of the same gender.[44]

International courts and committees have so far hesitated to extend the application of the right to marry to same-sex couples.[45] The ECJ stressed in D. and the Kingdom of Sweden v. Council,[46] by advocating the generally accepted and traditional view of marriage, that "Community notions of marriage and partnership exclusively address a relationship founded on civil marriage in the traditional sense of term".[47]

These explanations in the Commentaries seem uncertain; they sound like justifying something that is not secure any more. A question "What is protected in reality?" can be raised. In a legal sense, legal relation as a collection of relations with certain character should be regulated similarly. Comparing marriage and registered partnership, one can ask: what are the differences between the two except the name? When registered partnership was found to give the not-married couples the same rights as the married couples have, then what is protected by the state—the name "marriage" and not the content? It is also important to note that in the question of same-sex marriages, the boards of judges have no unanimous

---

[41] Case of *Sheffield and Horsham v. United Kingdom* (30 July 1998).

[42] Commentary of the Charter of Fundamental Rights of the European Union, p. 102.

[43] Ibid., p. 102.

[44] Case of *Emonet and others v. Switzerland* (13 December), paras 33, 34, and Case of *Schalk and Kopf v. Austria* (24 June 2010), para. 92.

[45] Commentary of the Charter of Fundamental Rights of the European Union, p. 102.

[46] Case C-122/99 P and C-125/99 P, *D. and the Kingdom of Sweden v. Council*. 2001 ECR I-4319 (31 May 2001).

[47] Commentary of the Charter of Fundamental Rights of the European Union, p. 102.

understandings.[48] How is it possible to regulate a relation that has different content in every member state? Is this morals or something else that states protect by non-recognition of same-sex marriages?

The developments of EU member states since the beginning of the twentieth century show clearly that step by step they are approaching the acceptance of same-sex cohabitation form. In the context of free movement, this will probably lead to the recognition of same-sex relationships and, in turn, to the situation where it is not reasonable any more to have such marriage impediment as different sex and most of the EU member states would legalise also same-sex relations. Though there is a common acceptance and understanding that every member state decides itself if same-sex marriage is in accordance with their public interests or not, a practical and reasonable decision would be at least to recognise the marriage contracted abroad even if the member state itself does not contract such marriages.

5 Conclusion

Family status is a feature related closely to a person's identity, and when moving from one state to another it plays an important role granting certain status and social benefits. Recognition of family status avoids new legal relations, which can cause additional vagueness and illegitimacy.

The ECtHR has pointed out that it is of crucial importance that the Convention is interpreted and applied in a manner that renders its rights practical and effective, not theoretical and illusory.[49] Such statement supports recognition of marriages with the same sex contracted in another member state.

The ECJ has stated in its decision[50] that national legislation that places the nationals of the Member State concerned at a disadvantage simply because they have exercised their freedom to move and to reside in another member state is a restriction on the freedoms of every citizen of the Union.[51] The Court also states that "Although, as Community law stands at present, the rules governing a person's surname are matters coming within the competence of the member states, the latter must none the less, when exercising that competence, comply with Community law unless what is involved is an internal situation which has no link with Community law".[52] Collating this statement to the situation, where same-sex persons have

---

[48] See, for example, Joint Dissenting Opinion of Judges Rozakis, Spielman, and Jebens and of Judge Malinverni Concurring Opinion in Case of *Schalk and Kopf v. Austria* (http://hudoc.echr. coe.int/...).

[49] Case of *I. v. The United Kingdom* (11 July 2002), para. 54.

[50] Case C-353/06 *Grunkin and Paul v. Niebüll* (14 October 2008), para. 21.

[51] See Case C-406/04 *De Cuyper* (18 July 2006), para. 39, and Case C-499/06 *Nerkowska* (22 May 2008), para. 32.

[52] See Case C-148/02 *Garcia Avello* (20 October 2003), paras 25 and 26, and the case law cited (Case C-353/06 *Grunkin and Paul v. Niebüll* (14 October 2008), para. 16). See also Case C-148/02

contracted marriage in one member state and when moving to live in another member state their marriage is not recognised, the question arises in what sense a name of the person is less related and protected by the culture and traditions the court has referred to than cases of marriage.[53]

Similar to non-recognition of name, the non-recognition of family status can cause inconveniences for a citizen. How can a person use his/her right of free movement when the member state he/she moves to does not recognise his/her civil status? For example, if same-sex married couple comes to live and work in Estonia, these spouses are considered as family members according to the laws regulating social benefits to some extent, but their marriage as civil status is not recognised. This non-recognition means that marriage will not be entered into the Estonian Population Register. Every state authority uses only the data of marital status from Population Register. In case of deciding some benefit deriving from the marriage/ family unit, there can be problems. Even worse, such person can succeed to be granted some benefit by the state based on the fact that he/she has a family, can marry someone else (from a different sex) as he/she is single according to the Population Register if the marriage is not recognised and not entered in the Population Register. Even when the administrative body in the process of confirming the marriage does know that one of the future spouses has had same-sex marriage abroad, it cannot refuse confirming the marriage, as the previous marriage is not recognised and, hence, is not an obstacle for marriage. Does not the member state here restrict an important value of the state instead?

As seen from the ECtHR, the main disputes have been related to gender as an obstacle of marriage; other impediments are not handled[54]; hence, these are also the facts that derive from the culture and traditions of certain member state.

As ECtHR has emphasised in its decisions repeatedly that the ECHR (as living instrument) and marriage and society are changing, the decision of ECtHR are difficult to use in solving the cases of same-sex marriage or marriage impediment today—maybe society has been changed now and the statements of the court are outdated. Examples in Sweden and Denmark show coherently how quickly society changes, and there has not been any special reference to culture or traditions—it just has been the suitable time to follow the practical and effective measures regulating legal relations between people—especially in the context of legalising "partnership". On the one hand, the member state protects marriage but does not know any more what "marriage" is; on the other hand, it establishes a legal relation with the same or almost the same content, destroying the "marriage" by itself.

Carlos Carcia Avello v État Belge (20 October 2003), para. 72. Opinion of Advocate General Jacobs, delivered on 22 May 2003. http://curia.europa.eu 11.01.2013 para. 25.

[53] See *Schalk and Kopf v. Austria* (24 June 2010), para. 53: "...this reflects their own vision of the role of marriage in their societies...", para. 62 "...that marriage has deep-rooted social and cultural connotations which may differ largely from one society to another..."

[54] There is one decision about divorce as an impediment; see ECtHR Case of *Aresti Charalambous v. Cyprus*, Appl. 43151/04, (19 July 2007).

As the Charter is applicable only in case EU law is implemented, there could be questions raised about restricting free movement of citizens in case of same-sex marriage. However, there is no explicit case decided today by the ECJ related to such a situation. As shown in this article, it is not clear if Article 9 of the Charter and Article 12 of the ECHR have the same or different substance in question of same-sex marriages.

Different regulations of member states and non-recognition of legal relations contracted abroad cause serious problems in the everyday life of EU citizens in using their right of free movement. Member states know that; hence, it seems a complicated issue as every member state protects marriage in its own way. Also, the Charter does not show in this question any clear solution based on the ECHR and leaves the decisions open.

References

Books and Articles

Bradley D (1996) Family law and political culture. Scandinavian laws in comparative perspective. Sweet & Maxwell, London

Cornides J, Brussels JD (2010) The right to marriage according to the ECHR and the EU fundamental rights charter. http://works.bepress.com/jakob_cornides/32

Ivic S (2009) The four values of the charter of fundamental rights of the European Union. Int J Good Conscience 4(2):278–295, ISSN: 1870-557X

Joamets K (2012) Marriage capacity, social values and law-making process. Int Comp Law Rev 12 (1):97–115

Laffranque J (2006) Legal system of EU and Estonian place in it. AS Juura, Tallinn

Peréz AT (2009) Fundamental rights conflicts in the European Union. Conflicts of rights in the European Union. A theory of supranational adjudication. Oxford University Press, Oxford. http://books.google.ee/books?id=fhEmW4ISqioC&pg=PA5&lpg=PA5&dq=Fundamental+rights+conflicts+in+the+European+union.+Conflicts+and+rights+in+the+European+Union.+A+theory+of+supranational+adjudication&source=bl&ots=wZXQWepJMI&sig=_D7MOUBtVIXS1uXn6UbO8J1HhaI&hl=et&sa=X&ei=sEPuUbbFCero4QT_mIH4Aw&ved=0CGQQ6AEwCA#v=onepage&q=Fundamental%20rights%20conflicts%20in%20the%20European%20union.%20Conflicts%20and%20rights%20in%20the%20European%20Union.%20A%20theory%20of%20supranational%20adjudication&f=false

Pull JA (2006) Questioning the fundamental right to marry. Student Scholarship Papers 26. http://digitalcommons.law.yale.edu/student-papers/26

Official Material

Reding V (2012) Observations on the EU Charter of fundamental rights and the future of the European Union. Speech/12/403. In: XXV congress of FIDE, Tallinn, 31 May 2012

Council Regulation (EC) No 1347/2000 of 29 May 2000 (Brussels II)

Directive 2003/86/EC of 22 September 2003 on the right to family reunification, OJ L 251 of 3.10.2003

Directive 2003/86/EC of 22 September 2003 on the right to family reunification, OJ L 251
Directive 2004/38/EC of the European Parlament and of the Council of 29 April 2004 on the right
   of citizens of the Union and their family members to move and reside freely within the territory
   of the member states amending Regulation (EEC) No 1612/68 and repealing Directives
   64/221/EEC, 68/360/EEC, 72/194/EEC, 73/148/EEC, 75/34/EEC, 75/35/EEC, 90/364/EEC,
   90/365/EEC and 93796/EEC
European Instrument for Democracy and Human Rights (EIDHR) Strategy Paper 2011 – 2013 C
   (2010)2432 21 April 2010 http://ec.europa.eu/external_relations/human_rights/index_en.htm
Report from the Commission to the European Parliament, the Council, the European Economic
   and Social Committee and the Committee of the Regions. 2011. Report on the Application of
   the EU Charter of Fundamental Rights. COM(2012) 169 final.EC 16.4.2012. SWD(2012)
   84final, SWD(2012) 85final
Bringing the Charter to life – opportunities and challenges of putting the EU Charter of Fundamental Rights into practice. Copenhagen Seminar Report. 15–16 March 2012. Danish Presidency of
   the Council of the EU and EU Agency for Fundamental Rights. www.fra.europa.eu/en/publica-
   tion/2012/bringing-charter-life-opportunities-and-challenges-putting-eu-charter-fundamental
Green Paper – Less bureaucracy for citizens: promoting free movement of public documents and
   recognition of the effects of civil status records. European Commission. Green Paper. COM
   (2010)747final
Commentary of the Charter of Fundamental Rights of the European Union
Bringing the Charter to life – opportunities and challenges of putting the EU Charter of Fundamental Rights into practice. Copenhagen Seminar Report. Danish Presidency of the Council of the
   EU and EU Agency for Fundamental Rights. 15–16 March 2012. www.europa.eu/en/publica-
   tion/2012/bringing-charter-life-opportunities-and-challenges-putting-eu-charter-fundamental

Case Law

Case of C-59/85, State of Netherlands v. Ann Florence Reed, [1986] ECR I-1283 (17 April 1986)
Case of C-249/96, Lisa Jacqueline Grant v. South West Trains Ltd., [1998] ECR I-00621
   (17 February 1998)
Case C-148/02 Garcia Avello [2003] ECR I-11613 (2 October 2003)
Case C-406/04 De Cuyper [2006] ECR I-6947 (18 July 2006)
Case of C-122/99 P and C-125/99 P, and the Kingdom of Sweden v Council of the European
   Union, [2001] ECR II-1 (31 May 2001)
Case C-499/06 Nerkowska [2008] ECR I-0000 (22 May 2008)
Case C-353/06 Grunkin and Paul v. Niebüll (14 October 2008)
Case of Rees v. UK ECtHR (Appl. No. 9532781), (17 October 1986)
Case of F.v. Switzerland ECtHR (Appl. No 11329/85), (18 December 1987)
Case of Sheffield and Horsham v. United Kingdom ECtHR (Appl. No 22985/93 and no. 23390/
   94), (30 July 1998), Rep. 1998-V
Case of Cossey v United Kingdom ECtHR (Appl. No 10843/84), (27 September 1990)
Case of I. V. The United Kingdom ECtHR (Appl. No 25680/94), (11 July 2002)
Case of Christine Goodwin v. United Kingdom ECtHR (Appl. No 28957/95) (11 July 2002)
Case of Aresti Charalambous v. Cyprus, ECtHR (Appl. 43151/04), (19 July 2007)
Case of Emonet and others v. Switzerland ECtHR (Appl. No 39051/03), (13 December 2007)
Case of Schalk and Kopf v. Austria ECtHR (Appl. No.3014104), (24 June 2010)
Joint Dissenting Opinion of Judges Rozakis, Spielman and Jebens and of Judge Malinverni
   Concurring Opinion in Case of Schalk and Kopf v. Austria (http://hudoc.echr.coe.int/. . .)
Opinion of advocate general Jacobs, delivered on 22 May 2003. http://curia.europa.eu 11.01.2013
   para. 25
Court Decision of Estonian Administrative Court 18.10.2012 3-12-1446

The Standard of Judicial Review in EU Competition Law Enforcement and Its Compatibility with the Right to a Fair Trial Under the EU Charter of Fundamental Rights

Marco Botta and Alexandr Svetlicinii

1 Introduction

1.1 The Growing Relevance of Fundamental Rights Protection in Competition Law Enforcement

When the EU founding fathers included competition rules in the Treaty of Rome, they were probably not aware of the potential link between the enforcement of competition law and fundamental rights protection. By sanctioning the anticompetitive practices by private undertakings that represented invisible barriers to trade, competition rules aimed at completing the free movement rules were included in the Treaty of Rome.[1] Competition law, therefore, aimed at achieving the establishment of the common market rather than at safeguarding the protection of fundamental rights in Europe. Moreover, the EU founding fathers opted for an

---

[1] A good example of the market integration objectives of EU competition rules is provided in the landmark judgment of the Court of Justice of the European Union (CJEU) in the case *Consten-Grundig*: "...an agreement between a producer and a distributor which tend to restore the national divisions in trade between Member States might be such as to frustrate the most fundamental objections of the Community. The Treaty, whose preamble and content aim at abolishing the barriers between States, and which in several provisions gives evidence of a stern attitude with regard to their reappearance, could not allow undertakings to reconstruct such barriers". Joined Cases 56 and 58–64, *Établissements Consten S.à.R.L. and Grundig-Verkaufs-GmbH v Commission* (1966) ECR 00429, para. 340.

M. Botta (✉)
Institute for European Integration Research, University of Vienna, Vienna, Austria
e-mail: marco.botta@univie.ac.at

A. Svetlicinii
Tallinn Law School, Tallinn University of Technology, Tallinn, Estonia
e-mail: alexandr.svetlicinii@ttu.ee

T. Kerikmäe (ed.), *Protecting Human Rights in the EU*,
DOI 10.1007/978-3-642-38902-3_7, © Springer-Verlag Berlin Heidelberg 2014

administrative rather than a criminal system of competition law enforcement. Under Regulation 17/62,[2] in fact, the European Commission was the sole administrative authority at EU level in charge of enforcing Articles 101 and 102 of the Treaty of Functioning of the European Union (TFEU).[3] For a number of decades, the main function carried out by Directorate General (DG) for Competition of the EU Commission was to review the compatibility of the agreements notified by private undertakings with Article 101 TFEU.[4] On the other hand, the EU Commission devoted limited resources to the investigations on secret cartels, and thus the number of fines imposed on private undertakings due to serious competition law infringements was negligible.[5] Within this context, few commentators argued that the EU Commission was bound to comply with the additional procedural guarantees that characterize criminal proceedings (i.e., right of defense, equality of arms, presumption of innocence).[6]

During the last decade, the system of competition law enforcement has radically changed and the debate concerning the compatibility of its enforcement regime with fundamental rights has gained momentum. In particular, two factors have increased the relevance of the protection of fundamental rights in the context of competition law enforcement: the entry into force of the Lisbon Treaty and the progressive *criminalization* of competition law enforcement. Under Article 6(1) of the Treaty on European Union (TEU),[7] the EU Charter of Fundamental Rights (hereinafter EU Charter) has become binding for the EU institutions and the EU Member States (MS) when they "implement" EU law.[8] Consequently, when the EU Commission conducts competition law investigations, it is bound to comply with the fundamental rights included in the Charter. Furthermore, Article 6(2) TFEU requires the EU to accede to the European Convention of Human Rights (ECHR).[9] Although the provisions included in the EU Charter mirror those ones included in

---

[2] Council Regulation No 17 (EEC): First Regulation implementing Articles 85 and 86 of the Treaty. OJ 013, 21.02.1962.

[3] Consolidated version of the Treaty of the Functioning of the European Union, OJ C-115/99, 9.5.2008. Entered into force on 1.12.2009.

[4] Regulation 17/62, Arts 2–8.

[5] Statistics concerning the number and amount of fines imposed by the European Commission due to competition law infringements is available at http://ec.europa.eu/competition/cartels/statistics/statistics.pdf. Accessed 10 March 2013.

[6] One of the first commentators on the lack of compatibility of the EU competition law enforcement regime with fundament rights was Graupner at the beginning of the 1970s.
   Graupner (1973), p. 291.

[7] Consolidated version of the Treaty on European Union, OJ C-83/15, 30.3.2010.

[8] Charter of Fundamental Rights of the European Union. OJ C-83/391, 30.3.2010. The Charter was adopted in Nice on 7.12.2000 without binding effects. However, since the entry into force of Art. 6 TEU, the Charter has become binding for the EU institutions and the EU MS when they "implement" EU law—Art. 51(1).

[9] Convention for the Protection of Human Rights and Fundamental Freedoms, signed in Rome on 4.11.1950. http://www.echr.coe.int/NR/rdonlyres/D5CC24A7-DC13-4318-B457-5C9014916D7A/0/Convention_ENG.pdf. Accessed 10 March 2013.

the ECHR,[10] the EU accession to the ECHR would have important consequences in the current framework of competition law enforcement. In particular, a private undertaking sanctioned by the EU Commission for a competition law infringement could appeal to the European Court of Human Rights (ECtHR) after having "exhausted the domestic remedies" (i.e., after having appealed the EU Commission decision before the EU General Court and the Court of Justice of the European Union).[11]

The *criminalization* of competition law enforcement is linked to the growing relevance of cartel investigations within the enforcement activities of DG Competition. By introducing a leniency policy[12] and by focusing its investigations on anticompetitive practices that have the *object* of harming the consumers' welfare,[13] DG Competition has progressively increased the number of cartel investigations during the last decade.[14] At the same time, DG Competition has constantly increased the amount of fines imposed on the sanctioned undertakings, claiming that the main objective of higher fines was to ensure *deterrence* against possible future infringements.[15] Nowadays, the fines imposed by DG Competition do not simply aim at *compensating* the damage caused by the anticompetitive practice but also at *punishing* the sanctioned undertaking in order to ensure that the latter will not repeat the same violation in the future. Under the case law of the ECtHR,

---

[10] Under Art. 52(3) of the EU Charter, ". . .this Charter contains rights which correspond to rights guaranteed by the Convention for the Protection of Human Rights and Fundamental Freedoms. . .".

[11] Art. 35(1) ECHR.

In relation to the ongoing negotiations concerning the EU accession to the ECHR and the complex relation between ECtHR and CJEU, see

Harpaz (2009), p. 105.

Lock (2011), p. 1025.

[12] Leniency is a policy that aims at detecting secret cartels by offering to the companies involved in a cartel partial or full immunity from the fine if they actively cooperate with DG Competition by providing evidence to prove the existence of the cartel. The leniency policy was first introduced by the US antitrust authorities at the beginning of the 1990s, and nowadays most of the NCAs in the world have introduced a leniency policy. Commission Notice on Immunity from Fines and Reduction of Fines in Cartel Cases, OJ C-298/17, 8.12.2006.

[13] Art. 101 TFEU sanctions both anticompetitive agreements, which have the *object* as well the *effect* of restricting the degree of competition in the market. An example of object restriction is a cartel, established by the participating companies with the intent to restrict competition. On the other hand, vertical agreements (i.e., licensing or distribution agreements) usually do not aim at restricting competition *per se*, but they have an anticompetitive effect. While object restrictions are *de facto per se* illegal, effect restrictions may be justified under Art. 101(3) TFEU.

[14] See above DG Competition, statistics on fines imposed on cartels.

[15] The *deterrence* effect of cartel fines is emphasized in the EU Commission Notice on the method to calculate fines. The Notice states that "the Commission will pay particular attention to the need to ensure that fines have a sufficiently deterrent effect; to that end, it may increase the fine to be imposed on undertakings which have a particularly large turnover beyond the sales of goods or services to which the infringement relates". European Commission, *Guidelines on the Method of Setting Fines Imposed pursuant to Article 23(2)(a) of Regulation No 1/2003*. OJ C-210/2, 1.9.2006, para. 30.

sanctions that aim at *punishing* the infringer are criminal sanctions, irrespective of their definition under national law.[16] Therefore, although Article 23(5) of the Regulation 1/2003 states that the fines imposed by the EU Commission do not have "a criminal law nature",[17] it is now commonly accepted that the fines imposed by DG Competition should be considered as criminal sanctions under the ECtHR case law.[18] Consequently, the additional procedural guarantees that characterize criminal proceedings would be applicable in the context of the enforcement of EU competition rules.

The relevance of the debate concerning the compatibility of competition law enforcement with basic fundamental rights is not limited to the EU competition rules. Regulation 1/2003, which has replaced Regulation 17/72, has *decentralized* the enforcement of competition law in Europe. Under the old enforcement regime, the national competition authorities (NCAs) and national courts of the EU MS could apply Articles 101(1) and 102 TFEU, while the EU Commission had the exclusive power to exempt notified agreements under Article 101(3) TFEU.[19] Some EU MS decided *autonomously* to establish an NCA (i.e., Germany, France, Italy); Regulation 17/62, in fact, did not bind EU MS to establish an NCA; Regulation 1/2003, on the other hand, has mandated every EU MS to establish an NCA in charge of enforcing both national and EU substantive competition rules (i.e., Articles 101 and 102 TFEU).[20] Regulation 1/2003 did not harmonize the national procedural rules of enforcement of substantive competition rules.[21] However, most of the EU MS that established an NCA after the entry into force of Regulation 1/2003 established an NCA taking DG Competition as an example of an *independent administrative authority*. Countries from Central and Eastern Europe (CEE)[22]

---

[16] In *Engel,* the ECtHR ruled that the categorization of a sanction for the scope of the ECHR is autonomous from its categorization under national law (i.e., classified as administrative or criminal law). According to the ECtHR case law, three criteria have to be analyzed in order to determine whether a sanction has a criminal character: (1) the categorization of the crime under domestic law, (2) the nature of the crime, (3) the nature and gravity of the sanction. The three criteria are alternative, and not cumulative. ECtHR, *Engel and others v. Netherlands.* Judgment issued on 8.6.1976. Application no. 5100/71; 5101/71; 5102/71; 5354/72; 5370/72, para. 82.

[17] Council Regulation (EC) n. 1/2003 of 16 December 2002, on the Implementation of the Rules on Competition Laid down in Articles 81 and 82 of the Treaty. OJ L-1/1, 4.1.2003.

[18] Forrester (2009), p. 817.

[19] In *Delimitis,* the CJEU recognized the direct effect of Articles 101(1) and 102 TFEU, which thus could be enforced by the national authorities of the EU MS. On the other hand, the CJEU ruled that the EU Commission preserved the exclusive right to grant exemptions to notified agreements under Article 101(3) TFEU.

Case C-234/89, *Stergios Delimitis v Henninger Bräu AG* (1991) ECR I-00935.

[20] Art. 35 Regulation 1/2003.

[21] Art. 5 Regulation 1/2003 only lists the NCAs powers in enforcing Art. 101 and 102 TFEU. In particular, the NCAs can adopt decisions requiring an infringement to be brought to the end, order interim measures, accepting commitments and imposing fines. On the other hand, these powers are applied by the NCAs in accordance with the national procedural law.

[22] Fingleton et al. (1997).

and Southeast Europe (SEE)[23] have established their NCAs in the context of the EU enlargement process. On the other hand, "old" EU MS have "spontaneously" reformed the structure of enforcement of their national competition laws in order to progressively align it to the EU best practices.[24] In particular, following the example of DG Competition, the NCAs of the EU MS have increasingly focused their enforcement activities on detecting cartels and imposing fines that have a deterrent effect.[25] Therefore, the *criminalization* of competition law enforcement is not a trend that concerns exclusively EU competition law; it is a common trend in almost every EU MS. Since all the EU MS are Contracting Parties to the ECHR, they should ensure the compliance with fundamental rights in the context of competition law investigations. However, as we will see in the following sections, since the EU MS have structured their NCAs taking DG Competition as a reference point, the tensions between the competition law enforcement and fundamental rights protection that characterize the enforcement of EU competition law become evident at the national level as well. Therefore, the emerging debate on the compatibility of fundamental rights with competition law enforcement does not concern exclusively the EU competition law; such debate also affects the EU MS and candidate countries.

1.2 The Debate Concerning the Compatibility of EU Competition Law Enforcement with the Right to a Fair Trial

One of the tensions between competition law enforcement and the protection of fundamental rights concerns the right to a fair trial included in Article 6 ECHR, as well as in Article 47(2) EU Charter. Article 6(1) ECHR provides that each person involved in criminal or civil proceedings is entitled to fair and public hearings, as well as to a public trial. On the other hand, Article 6(2)(3) ECHR includes additional procedural guarantees in relation to criminal proceedings, such as the principle of presumption of innocence and the right of defense. The determination of whether competition law investigations have an administrative or a criminal nature has thus important repercussions on the application of the *basic* procedural

---

[23] Efremova (2012), p. 23.

[24] Vedder (2004), p. 5.

[25] A good example that shows the tendency of the NCAs to follow the example of DG Competition in focusing their enforcement activities on the cartels detection is the adoption of a Model Leniency Program by the European Competition Network (ECN). The ECN is an informal network of cooperation among the NCAs of the EU MS that is chaired by DG Competition. In 2006, the ECN adopted a model of leniency policy that has been later implemented by most of the NCAs at the domestic level. According to Jaspers and Gauer, the adoption of the leniency model shows that the fight against cartels has become a top priority both for DG Competition and for the NCAs of the EU MS. Gauer and Jaspers (2007), p. 35.

guarantees provided by Article 6(1) ECHR *vis-a-vis* the *additional* guarantees provided by Article 6(2)(3) ECHR.[26]

For a number of years, the compatibility of the EU competition law proceedings with the principle of fair trial has been the subject of an ongoing discussion in academic and professional circles. In particular, two opposite approaches emerged in this discussion. On the one hand, a number of practitioners argued that the enforcement structure of EU competition law does not comply with the principle of "fair trial".[27] In particular, the fact that DG Competition both conducts the investigations and later adopts the decision sanctioning the undertaking subject of the investigations does not comply with Article 6 ECHR (i.e., EU Commission acts both as a *prosecutor* and as a *judge*). Although DG Competition has tried to separate these functions through the introduction of Hearing Officers,[28] the latter do not have real adjudicative powers; the final decision to impose a fine is taken by the College of the Commissioners on the basis of the recommendation put forward by the team investigating the case. In the light of the progressive *criminalization* of competition law enforcement, the administrative system of EU competition law enforcement does not comply with the additional guarantees required by Article 6(2)(3) ECHR. For example, Bronckers and Vallery have argued that the lack of a separate adjudicative body in charge of examining the conclusions of the team in charge of the investigations within DG Competition undermines the principle of presumption of innocence enshrined in Article 6(2) ECHR.[29]

Representatives of the EU Commission, on the other hand, have defended the current system of EU competition law enforcement. In particular, by referring to the ECtHR judgment in *Jussila*,[30] Wils has argued that competition law fines should be considered as *minor* rather than *hard-core* criminal sanctions.[31] According to the ECtHR's ruling in *Jussila*, *minor* criminal sanctions could be imposed by an administrative authority rather than by a judicial body, provided that the

---

[26] An extensive analysis of the ECtHR case law in relation to Art. 6 ECHR is provided by Vitkauskas and others (2009), Article 6. http://www.interights.org/files/107/INTERIGHTS%20Article%206%20Manual.pdf. Accessed 10 March 2013.

[27] See, for instance, Slater et al. (2008), http://www.coleurope.eu/sites/default/files/research-paper/gclc_wp_04-08.pdf. Accessed 10 March 2013.

[28] DG Competition introduced Hearing Officers since the early 1980s. Their function is to chair the meeting between the investigating team of DG Competition and the representatives of the companies following the Statement of Objections to the parties. The Hearing Officers directly respond to the Competition Commissioner, and thus they are not part of the team investigating the case within DG Competition. The main function of the Hearing Officers is to ensure that the investigating team complies with right of access to the file and procedural guarantees throughout the investigations. For an overview of the functions of the Hearing Officers, see http://ec.europa.eu/competition/hearing_officers/index_en.html. Accessed 10 March 2013. Decision 2011/695/EU of the President of the European Commission of 13 October 2011 on the Function and Terms of Reference of the Hearing Officer in certain Competition Proceedings. OJ L-275/29, 20.10.2011.

[29] Bronckers and Vallery (2011), p. 535.

[30] ECtHR, *Jussila v. Finland*, Judgment of 21.5.2003. Application n. 73053/01.

[31] Wils (2011), p. 189.

administrative decision could be subject to *full* judicial review on appeal in front of an independent court.[32] Similarly, Castillo de la Torre has rejected the argument concerning the *criminalization* of competition law enforcement due to the alleged increase of the amount of fines imposed by DG Competition during the last years.[33] According to the author, "the fines imposed in the earliest cartel cases were considered just as heavy as they are today".[34] According to Castillo de la Torre, the argument concerning the recent *criminalization* of competition law enforcement is unfounded: the alleged increase of the fines, in fact concerned the overall number of the fines imposed by DG Competition rather than the proportion of fines in comparison to the annual turnover of the sanctioned undertakings.

Until quite recently, the debate summarized in the previous paragraphs took place at a largely theoretical level.[35] Only in September 2011, the ECtHR recognized in *Menarini* that an NCA could impose a fine due to a competition law violation, despite the lack of separation between prosecution and judicial functions within the NCA.[36] Nevertheless, in order to comply with the principle of fair trial, the administrative decision of the NCA had to be subject to a *full* judicial review on appeal. Following the *Menarini* judgment, the debate concerning the compatibility of the competition law enforcement system has thus shifted from the institutional structure of enforcement of competition law to the standard of judicial review applied by the court that has to review on appeal the decision of the NCA.

This chapter aims at contributing to the ongoing debate concerning the compatibility of EU competition law enforcement with the right to a fair trial by analyzing the scope of judicial review of the EU Commission decisions exercised by the Court of Justice of the European Union (CJEU). In particular, the question discussed in the following pages concerns the compatibility of the standard of judicial review developed by the General Court (GC) and by the CJEU in the field of competition law with the requirement of *full* judicial review introduced by the ECtHR in *Menarini*. In order to answer to this question, the *Menarini* judgment will be analyzed in the following section, followed by an analysis of the standard of review developed by the CJEU in the field of EU competition law.

---

[32] ECtHR, *Jussila v. Finland,* para. 43.

[33] Castillo de la Torre (2009).

[34] Castillo de la Torre (2009), p. 2.

[35] *Jussila* concerned national proceedings relating to a tax matter. Jussila received an administrative pecuniary sanction due to a tax evasion case and challenged the compatibility of such administrative enforcement system with Art. 6 ECHR. Due to the similarities between the tax and the competition law enforcement systems, Wils extended the ECtHR conclusions in *Jussila* to the case of competition law enforcement.

[36] ECtHR, *Menarini Diagnostics S.R.L. v. Italy.* Judgment issued on 27.9.2011. Application n. 43509/08. The authors relied on the translation of the English translation of the Italian language judgment elaborated by Jessica Tristano, available at www.duitbase.it. Accessed 10 March 2013.

2 *Menarini*: Testing the Compatibility of the National Competition Law with the Right to a Fair Trial

2.1 Facts and Ruling

Menarini Diagnostic was an Italian pharmaceutical company fined by the Italian NCA (AGCM)[37] for participation in a cartel of pharmaceutical companies aimed at fixing the sale price of diabetes diagnostic tests. The cartel was prohibited under the national equivalent of Article 101 TFEU.[38] The sanctioned undertaking challenged the administrative decision before the Regional Administrative Tribunal of Lazio (TAR)[39] and later before the Council of State (*Consiglio di Stato*).[40] Both administrative courts rejected appeal, and thus "after having exhausted the domestic remedies" Menarini appealed to the ECtHR.

Menarini argued that the deterrent and punitive nature of the fine imposed by the AGCM represented a clear criminal sanction, and thus the additional procedural guarantees provided by Article 6(2)(3) ECHR were applicable.[41] In addition, TAR and Council of State exercised only a limited judicial control of the AGCM decision[42]: the two administrative courts reviewed the legality of the AGCM decision, but they could not replace the AGCM assessment of facts with their own assessment. In the absence of separation between investigative and adjudicative functions within the AGCM, and due to the fact that both TAR and Council of State exercised only a limited judicial review, the Italian administrative system of competition law enforcement breached the principle of fair trial.

In its ruling, the ECtHR confirmed that a competition law fine had the features of a criminal sanction due to its punitive and deterrent character.[43] However, such fines were *minor* criminal sanctions, which could be imposed by an administrative

---

[37] *Autorita Garante per la Concorrenza ed il Mercato*, http://www.agcm.it/. Accessed 10 March 2013.

[38] Law n. 287 approved on 13.10.1990, "Norme per la Tutela e la Concorrenza del Mercato". Arts 2,3,4 of the Italian Law 287/1990 mirror Arts 101, 102 TFEU. Under Art. 1(1) of the Law 287/1990, the Italian NCA enforce this legislation when Arts 101 and 102 TFEU are not applicable (i.e., when the anticompetitive practice does not affect the intra-Community trade). The text of the Law 287/1990 is available at http://www.agcm.it/normativa/concorrenza/4531-legge-10-ottobre-1990-n-287-norme-per-la-tutela-della-concorrenza-e-del-mercato.html. Accessed 10 March 2013.

[39] *Tribunale Amministrativo Regionale per il Lazio*, http://www.giustizia-amministrativa.it/italia/lazio.htm. Accessed 10 March 2013.

[40] ECtHR *Menarini*, paras 10–21. Under Article 33 of the Law 287/1990, TAR Lazio and the Council of State have exclusive competence to review appeals against the administrative decisions of the Italian NCA.

[41] ECtHR *Menarini*, paras 33–37.

[42] ECtHR *Menarini*, paras 50–56.

[43] ECtHR Menarini, paras 41–42.

authority like the AGCM.[44] Nevertheless, the ECtHR pointed out that the sanction should be subject to a *full* judicial review on appeal by an independent court.[45]

In the present case, the ECtHR recognized that both TAR and the Council of State satisfied the independence criterion.[46] In addition, the two administrative courts carried out a *full* judicial review[47]: they controlled the proportionality and the reliability of the evidence put forward by the AGCM to justify the fine imposed. In view of these considerations, the ECtHR rejected the claim concerning the infringement of Article 6 ECHR.[48]

2.2 The Relevance of **Menarini**

In *Menarini*, the ECtHR upheld the position previously emerged in the literature (i.e., Wils)[49] concerning the compatibility of an administrative system of competition law enforcement with the right to a fair trial due to the *minor* criminal character of the sanctions imposed thereunder. Nevertheless, through its ruling, the ECtHR has opened a new debate concerning the scope of judicial review. On the one hand, the ECtHR introduced in *Menarini* a higher threshold of judicial review to justify an administrative system of competition law enforcement (i.e., *full* judicial review of the NCA decision). On the other hand, the ECtHR upheld the judicial review exercised by TAR and by the Council of State without analyzing in detail the type of review carried out by the two Italian administrative courts.[50] In particular, the Italian courts have always left a certain margin of discretion to the AGCM in carrying out the economic analysis required in competition law investigations, thus limiting their review to the *proportionality* and the *plausibility* of the AGCM's findings.[51]

---

[44] ECtHR *Menarini*, para. 59.

[45] ECtHR *Menarini*, para. 58.

[46] ECtHR *Menarini*, para. 60.

[47] ECtHR *Menarini*, paras 64–66.

[48] ECtHR *Menarini*, para. 67.

[49] Wils (2011).

[50] In the *Menarini* judgment, in fact, the ECtHR dedicated only few paragraphs (i.e., 64–66) to discuss this important issue. Among the commentators, Bronckers and Vallery have expressed dissatisfaction with the manner whereby the ECtHR checked the compliance with the principle of full judicial review by TAR and the Council of State in *Menarini*.
Bronckers and Vallery (2012), p. 44.

[51] This type of standard of review has been reiterated in TAR and Council of State case law. See, for instance, the judgment of the Council of State n. 9575, *Soc. T.I. v. Autorità Garante Concorrenza e Mercato,* issued on 29.12.2010. The judgments of the Council of State are available at http://www.giustizia-amministrativa.it/webcds/frmRicercaSentenza.asp. Accessed 10 March 2013.

This apparent inconsistency between the standard of judicial review developed by the ECtHR and its application in the present case has been strongly criticized by the ECtHR judge Pinto de Albuquerque in its dissenting opinion in *Menarini*.[52] The Portuguese judge noted that in the course of the national proceedings, both TAR and the Council of State had constantly referred to paragraphs of the AGCM decision.[53] According to Pinto de Albuquerque, TAR and Council of State had not carried a careful technical assessment of the AGCM decision; their judicial review was thus *not full*.[54] The diverging views of the ECtHR judges highlighted the difficulties of the application of the principle of full judicial review in individual cases.

The relevance of the *Menarini* judgment goes beyond the compatibility of the Italian system of competition law enforcement with Article 6 ECHR. In fact, as mentioned in the introduction, most of the EU MS share a similar administrative system of competition law enforcement. Moreover, like most of the national courts reviewing NCA decisions, the standard of review developed by TAR and by the Council of State is quite close to the one exercised by the GC and by the CJEU in relation to the decisions of the EU Commission in the field of EU competition law. As we shall demonstrate in the following section, due to the technical nature of competition law analysis, EU and national courts have generally granted a certain margin of discretion to the competition authorities. In the aftermath of the *Menarini* judgment, the question is whether such margin of discretion still complies with the criterion of *full* judicial review introduced by the ECtHR in *Menarini*.

3 CJEU Standard of Review in EU Competition Law and Its Compatibility with the Right to a Fair Trial

3.1 Intensity of Judicial Review

The standard of judicial review is inherently linked to the nature of the process itself. In order to establish the intensity of judicial review, it could be helpful to enumerate various grounds to challenge the EU Commission's decisions. These grounds are reflected in the Article 263 TFEU: lack of competence, infringement of an essential procedural requirement, infringement of the Treaties or of any rule of law relating to their application, or misuse of powers. Article 261 TFEU

---

[52] Dissenting opinion of Judge Pinto de Albuquerque attached to ECtHR judgment, *Menarini Diagnostics S.R.L. v. Italy*. Judgment issued on 27.9.2011. Application n. 43509/08.

[53] Dissenting opinion of Judge Pinto de Albuquerque in *Menarini*, paras 7–8.

[54] Dissenting opinion of Judge Pinto de Albuquerque in *Menarini*, para. 10.

mentions the unlimited jurisdiction of the CJEU with regard to the penalties provided for in the regulations of the European Parliament and the EU Council. Such provision is confirmed in Regulation 1/2003 in relation to the "decisions whereby the Commission has fixed a fine or periodic penalty payment".[55] As reaffirmed by the CJEU in *Danone*, "the [EU] judicature is empowered to exercise its unlimited jurisdiction where the question of the amount of the fine is before it".[56] The CJEU is thereby empowered to cancel, reduce, or increase the fine or periodic penalty payment.

Although the text of the above legal provisions might create an illusion that the CJEU exercises a full and uniform degree of judicial review in relation to the identified issues, the judicial practice demonstrates significant divergence in the intensity of review depending on its subject: correctness of facts, evidential support, legal interpretations, complex economic assessments, etc. There could be instances where the above issues overlap; this would be the case when the application of the substantive legal test might depend on the outcome of the complex economic assessment.

The review over correctness of facts, on which EU Commission bases its findings has traditionally been regarded as intense. AG Tizzano characterized the intensity of the judicial review of facts in the following way:

> With regard to the findings of fact, the review is clearly more intense, in that the issue is to verify objectively and materially the accuracy of certain facts and the correctness of the conclusions drawn in order to establish whether certain known facts make it possible to prove the existence of other facts to be ascertained.[57]

An illustrative example of the CJEU's review of correctness of facts can be found in *Schneider* litigation. In *Schneider/Legrand*, the EU Commission reviewed a merger between two manufacturers of electrical equipment, which were active on the national markets of several EU MS.[58] Due to the differences in the regulatory frameworks in some EU MS, which required the equipment produced by the merging parties to satisfy certain technical standards, the EU Commission concluded that relevant geographical markets are national ones.[59] However, when assessing the dominance of the merging parties, "Commission based its assessment of the impact of the concentration on transnational, global considerations, extrapolated from a single market without demonstrating its relevance at the

---

[55] Council Regulation (EC) n. 1/2003 of 16 December 2002, on the Implementation of the Rules on Competition Laid down in Articles 81 and 82 of the Treaty. OJ L-1/1, 4.1.2003, Art. 31.

[56] Case C-3/06P *Groupe Danone v Commission* [2007] ECR I-1331, para. 62.

[57] Opinion of AG Tizzano in Cases C-12/03 P and C-13/03 P *Commission v Tetra Laval*, para. 86.

[58] Case COMP/M.2283 *Schneider/Legrand* [2001].

[59] *Id.*, paras 193–220.

national level".[60] The GC noted that EU Commission's assessment was "vitiated by errors and omissions which deprive it of probative value".[61]

Similarly, the GC pointed out the EU Commission's omissions in substantiating its claims of collective dominance in *Airtours*. In that case, the EU Commission alleged that UK short-haul package-holiday market was experiencing very moderate growth, which would reinforce the alleged collective dominance of the remaining market players. When examining evidential support that EU Commission presented in substantiation of its claim, the GC found that it was based on a single-page brief prepared at an unknown date.[62] Moreover, the Court observed that it was "apparent from the cursory examination of that document that the Commission's reading of it was inaccurate".[63]

Recalling the unlimited jurisdiction of the CJEU in relation to the fines imposed by the EU Commission, one would observe a thorough review of the factors considered by the EU Commission since the early CJEU judgments. In *Chemiefarma*, for example, the CJEU has reviewed a complex variety of circumstances ranging from the nature of anticompetitive infringement to the size and market shares of the undertakings concerned.[64] In that case, the Court has established an error in the EU Commission's calculation of the duration of infringement, which justified a slight reduction of the initial fine.[65] A similar conclusion in *Dunlop Slazenger* resulted in a 40% reduction of the fine imposed by the EU Commission.[66] In *Pioneer*, the CJEU, referring to its powers of unlimited jurisdiction, slashed the EU Commission's fine by a half for errors of assessment in relation to duration and gravity of the infringement, the intent, the role, and the financial situation of the undertakings concerned.[67]

Although the above instances seem to be relatively straightforward cases where the CJEU revealed inconsistencies and inappropriate usage of evidence, the distinction between the review of facts and review of assessment of facts is not always so obvious. The importance of the distinction between the correctness of evidence and conclusions drawn from it becomes relevant in assessments of complex economic matters, where the EU Commission is granted a certain margin of appreciation.

---

[60] *See* Press Release No 84/02 "The Court of First Instance Annuls the Commission's Decision Prohibiting the Concentration Between Schneider and Legrand and Ordering them to Separate Accordingly", 22 October 2002, available at http://curia.europa.eu/en/actu/communiques/cp02/aff/cp0284en.htm. Accessed 10 March 2013.

[61] Case T-351/03 *Schneider Electric SA v Commission* [2007] ECR II-2237, para. 227.

[62] Case T-342/99 *Airtours v Commission* [2002] ECR II-2585, para. 129.

[63] *Id.*, para. 130.

[64] Case 41/69 Chemiefarma v Commission [1970] ECR 661, paras 180–188.

[65] *Id.*, para. 188.

[66] Case T-43/92 *Dunlop Slazenger International Ltd v Commission* [1994] ECR II-441, paras 178–179.

[67] Case 100/80 *SA Musique Diffusion française and others v Commission* [1983] ECR 1825, paras 123–124.

3.2   Limitations of Judicial Review: Complex Economic Assessments and Manifest Errors

The standard of review related to the errors of assessment in antitrust cases is traditionally found in the *Aalborg Portland* judgment, an Article 101 TFEU case that evolved around the assessment of economic matters. According to the CJEU:

> examination by the Community judicature of the complex economic assessments made by the Commission must necessarily be confined to verifying whether the rules on procedure and on the statement of reasons have been complied with, whether the facts have been accurately stated and whether there has been any manifest error of appraisal or misuse of powers.[68]

Legal treatises explain that under this "manifest error of assessment" standard, "GC will allow the Commission considerable margin of appreciation and will only annul a Commission decision where it finds that the Commission has committed manifest errors of appreciation".[69] At the same time, the CJEU acknowledged the evolution of this standard by distinguishing between *traditional* standard of judicial review and *stricter* standard of review that emerged after the landmark *Tetra Laval* litigation.[70]

The concept of "manifest error of assessment" has been relied on by the CJEU throughout its jurisprudence.[71] It served as a formalistic expression for indicating deficiencies in the EU Commission's assessment. A very typical usage of this terminology can be found in the GC's *Impala* judgment:

> [Commission's finding] is not supported by a statement of reasons of the requisite legal standard and is vitiated by a manifest error of assessment in that the elements on which it is based are incomplete and do not include all the relevant data that ought to have been taken into consideration by the Commission and are not capable of supporting the conclusions which are drawn from them.[72]

The same concept has been used by the GC to justify its abstention from exercising the unlimited jurisdiction over determination of fines in *Wieland-Werke* case. In the latter judgment, the GC held:

> in areas such as determination of the amount of a fine imposed pursuant to Article 15(2) of Regulation No 17, where the Commission has a discretion, for example, as regards the amount of increase for the purposes of deterrence, review of the legality of those assessments is limited to determining the absence of manifest error of assessment.[73]

---

[68] Joined Cases C-204/00 P, C-205/00 P, C-211/00 P, C-213/00 P, C-217/00 P, and C-219/00 P, *Aalborg Portland and Others v Commission*, para. 279.

[69] Faull and Nikpay (2007), p. 588.

[70] *Id.*, p. 590.

[71] *See, for example*, Joined Cases T-346/02 and T-347/02 *Cableuropa SA v Commission* 2003 ECR II-04251, para. 119, and Case T-158/00 *ARD v Commission* 2003 ECR II-03825, para. 194.

[72] Case T-464/04 *Impala v Commission (Impala I)* [2006] ECR II-2289, para. 475.

[73] Case T-116/04 *Wieland-Werke v Commission* [2009] ECR II-1087, para. 32.

At a first glance, it appears that "manifest" implies obvious errors and inconsistencies that can be established by the CJEU without conducting a reassessment of the EU Commission's findings. This understanding of the standard of judicial review was widely shared during the early years of the EU competition law. For example, in the 1990s Brown suggested:

> The CJEU will not attempt to substitute its own view of the effectiveness of competition in relevant markets. Only the Commission has the necessary expertise and fact-finding powers to carry out such a factual analysis. The future role of judicial review by the Community courts is likely to be limited to rulings on important issues of law or procedure and ensuring that the Commission does not make manifest errors in applying the law to the facts.

Similarly, Bebr, summarizing the early CJEU's practice, concluded that "the Court may certainly not be expected to push the extent of its judicial review any further than is absolutely indispensable for ensuring and respecting the principle of rule of law".[74] Advocate General Slynn in an early Article 81 EC case noted: "The question in this case is whether the arguments raised by [the applicant] concerning the Commission's assessment of competition in the relevant market and the inferences it drew from that assessment disclose such manifest error, misdirection or unreasonableness on the Commission's part that the decision must be annulled".[75] In *RJB Mining*, the GC also confirmed similar understanding of the word *manifest*: "the failure [by the EU Commission] to observe legal provisions is so serious that it appears to arise from an obvious error of evaluation".[76] Thus, initially the scope of judicial review was regarded as limited to the errors in application of law and *manifest* errors in application of the law to the facts, an approach that clearly demonstrated significant deference to the EU Commission's assessment. Irrespective of the reasons behind intensifying judicial review of the EU Commission's decisions, the lack of clarity concerning the standard of judicial review led to the following situation: the CJEU on several occasions substituted the EU Commission's assessment by its own. The Court ruled that the evidence put forward by the EU Commission was unconvincing and thus concluded that there had therefore been a manifest error of assessment on the side of the EU Commission. This *de novo* assessment of the evidence already evaluated by the EU Commission would appear closer to the concept of *full* review rather than to the limited review of the *manifest* errors of assessment.

---

[74] Bebr (1981), p. 139. The author adds that "it is idle to emphasize in this connection that an appropriate reasoning of a judgment supporting an evaluation of economic facts may be a proper guarantee for a judicial review, exercised properly and within the necessary limits".

[75] Case 43/85 *ANCIDES v Commission* [1987] ECR 3131.

[76] Case T-156/98, *RJB Mining plc v Commission* [2001] ECR II-337, para. 87.

3.3 Full Judicial Review and Margin of Appreciation

The attribution of the margin of assessment recognizes the complexity of the assessment and existence of alternative interpretations of the given facts. It acknowledges that a specialized agency like the EU Commission is better placed to carry out these complex assessments than courts. Legal framework restricts the scope of judicial review in the area where the agency exercises its margin of assessment since the legislator intended to give the ultimate say in these matters to the administrative agency. The term "margin of discretion", although being often used in the EU jurisprudence,[77] in our view appears somewhat misleading. In the absence of a detailed analysis, it creates an impression that the EU Commission has the discretionary powers (i.e., unlimited within its margins) to make decisions on matters of economic assessment. In order to avoid this confusion and add clarity to this term, we prefer to use the expressions "margin of appreciation", "margin of assessment", or "certain freedom of evaluation",[78] expressions that were likewise used in the EU jurisprudence.[79]

The margin of appreciation should be viewed as an exception from the full judicial review exercised by the courts over the decisions of administrative agencies. According to judge Legal, the limited judicial control should take place in three types of cases: (1) when the contested decision incorporates the use of discretionary powers that the institution holds, when the dispute at hand is more political than legal, or when no available source of law dictates a particular answer to the problem posed; (2) when the decision implies an assessment of a highly technical nature that the judge is not better prepared or, even in some cases, less well prepared than the agency to provide an objective answer to the questions posed; (3) when the assessment on which the decision rests has already been conducted by an independent and an impartial authority, like a jury or a quasi-jurisdiction, which if the court were to fully review for the second time would lead to a duplication.[80]

---

[77] Case C-12/03P *Commission v Tetra Laval* [2005] ECR I-0987, paras 37–40: "CFI...required [Commission] to satisfy a standard of proof and to provide a quality of evidence in support of its line of argument which are incompatible with the *wide discretion* [emphasis added] which it enjoys in assessing economic maters".

[78] As suggested by Christoforou in Reeves et al (2006), p. 172.

[79] Case 210/01 *General Electric v Commission* [2005] ECR II-5575, para. 63.

[80] Legal (2006), p. 109. According to Judge Legal, the discretion with regard to economic matters "must be in the choice of the approach best suited to the analysis of a given situation or phenomenon. It can be a choice of economic methodology, no theory being inadmissible as long as it provides useful tools to come to a convincing result". Legal (2006), p. 115.

The discretion in economic assessments has been confirmed in a number of CJEU's judgments.[81] According to some commentators, the significance of the EU Commission's discretion lies in the fact that once it has undertaken a comprehensive investigation and supported its conclusion with a solid evidence, the CJEU would not annul the EU Commission's decision even in a case where the CJEU's own assessment would differ from that of the EU Commission. In relation to fines imposed for the infringements of EU competition law where the CJEU is expected to exercise the unlimited review, a certain margin of discretion has been allowed to the EU Commission within its Fining Guidelines.[82] In particular, the EU Commission can assess the appropriate amount of the fine taking into consideration the duration of the infringement, the deterrent effect of the sanction,[83] as well as attenuating circumstances (i.e., degree of cooperation showed by the sanctioned undertaking during the investigations).[84] In *Heineken*, the GC confirmed that "the Commission enjoys a broad discretion as regards the method for calculating fines" so that "in areas such as determining the amount of a fine…where the Commission has such a discretion, review of the legality of its assessments is limited to determining the absence of manifest error of assessment".[85] Likewise, in *Carbon Tokai*, the GC stated that in relation to the quality and usefulness of cooperation by the cartelists, the Commission has "a wide discretion" and only the "manifest abuse of that discretion" should be penalized by the Court.[86] Similarly, in *FMC Foret*, the GC acknowledged that "the Commission has a discretion as regards the application of attenuating circumstances".[87]

In turn, the CJEU has refused to substitute its assessment for that of the GC exercising "its unlimited jurisdiction as to the amount of the fines imposed on undertakings",[88] thus leaving certain issues in the "wide discretion" of the EU Commission. Hence, the overview of the CJEU's practice in exercising its "unlimited jurisdiction" led some commentators to conclude that "over the last 30 years,

---

[81] Case T-102/96 *Gencor v Commission* [1997] ECR II-0879, paras 164–165; Joined Cases C-68/94 and C-30/95 *France v Commission* [1998] ECR I-1375, paras 223–224; Case T-342/99 *Airtours v Commission* [2002] ECR II-02585, para. 64; Case T-342/00 *Petrolessence v Commission* [2003] ECR II-01161, para. 101.

[82] Guidelines on the method of setting fines imposed pursuant to Article 23(2)(a) of Regulation No 1/2003. Official Journal C 210, 1.09.2006, pp. 2–5.

[83] See Svetlicinii (2010), p. 318.

[84] Forrester (2011), p. 194.

[85] Case T-240/07 *Heineken v Commission*, paras 308–309.

[86] Joined Cases T-236/01, T-239/01, T-244/01, T-246/01, T-251/01 and T-252/01 *Tokai Carbon v Commission* [2004] ECR II-1181, para. 371.

[87] Case T-191/06 *FMC Foret v Commission*, para. 333.

[88] See Joined Cases C-125/07 P, C-133/07 P, C-135/07 P and C-137/07 P *Erste Group Bank et al v Commission* [2009] ECR I-8681, para. 187. See also Case C-291/98 P *Sarrió v Commission* [2000] ECR I-9991, paras 96 and 97, and Joined Cases C-238/99 P, C-244/99 P, C-245/99 P, C-247/99 P, C-250/99 P to C-252/99 P and C-254/99 P *Limburgse Vinyl Maatschappij and Others v Commission* [2002] ECR I-8375, para. 617.

one of the main characteristics of the EU Courts' unlimited jurisdiction has been the discrepancy between the judge's ample powers and the very limited—and at times insufficient—use made of such powers".[89]

3.4 Full Judicial Review in Antitrust Cases in the Aftermath of KME Case Law: Myth or Reality?

The debate about the standard of judicial review in EU competition law cases and its compatibility with the fair trial principle under Article 6 ECHR as applied by the ECtHR in *Menarini* has been recently reinvigorated in the aftermath of the *Chalkor*[90] and *KME*[91] judgments issued by the CJEU at the end of 2011.

In the *KME* case, the EU Commission imposed a EUR 39 million fine on the undertakings forming part of the KME group for participation in a set of anticompetitive agreements on the copper plumbing tubes market.[92] On appeal before the CJEU, the appellant argued that the GC[93] had violated its fundamental right to full and effective judicial review by failing to conduct a thorough review of the EU Commission's decision. According to KME, the GC has "deferred to an excessive and unreasonable extent to the Commission's discretion".[94] Advocate General Sharpston, in her opinion, has addressed the issue whether the GC exercised the full jurisdiction within the meaning of Article 6 ECHR and the relevant case law of the ECtHR.

Unlike the Advocate General, the CJEU in its assessment of the KME's pleas chose to refer solely to Article 47 of the EU Charter rather than to Article 6 ECHR. In explaining the relationship between the GC's judicial review and the EU Commission's margin of assessment, the CJEU simply reiterated its statement in *Tetra Laval*[95]:

whilst the Court recognizes that the Commission has a margin of discretion with regard to economic matters, that does not mean that the Community Courts must refrain from reviewing the Commission's interpretation of information of an economic nature. Not

---

[89] Barbier de La Serre and Winckler (2012), p. 369.

[90] Case C-386/10P *Chalkor v Commission*, judgment of 8 December 2011.

[91] Case C-272/09P *KME Germany and others v Commission*, judgment of 8 December 2011.

[92] Commission Decision C(2004)2826 of 3 September 2004, Case COMP/E-1/38.069—*Copper plumbing tubes*.

[93] Case T-127/04 *KME Germany and others v Commission* [2009] ECR II-01167.

[94] Opinion of AG Sharpston in Case C-272/09P *KME Germany and others v Commission*, paras 40–41.

[95] Case C-12/03P *Commission v Tetra Laval* [2005] ECR I-0987.

only must the Community Courts, inter alia, establish whether the evidence relied on is factually accurate, reliable and consistent but also whether that evidence contains all the information which must be taken into account in order to assess a complex situation and whether it is capable of substantiating the conclusions drawn from it.[96]

Therefore, "the Courts cannot use the Commission's margin of discretion. . .as a basis for dispensing with the conduct of an in-depth review of the law and of the facts".[97] Finally, the CJEU reached the conclusion that „the review of legality provided for under Article 263 TFEU, supplemented by the unlimited jurisdiction in respect of the amount of the fine, provided for under Article 31 of Regulation No 1/2003, is not therefore contrary to the requirements of the principle of effective judicial protection enshrined in Article 47 of the EU Charter".[98]

The significance of the *KME* precedent lies primarily in the fact that the CJEU for the first time has expressly affirmed the compatibility of the EU competition law system with the right to a fair trial (although only under the EU Charter, not under ECHR). While there have been various suggestions as to why the CJEU decided to avoid the reference to ECHR,[99] the Court has affirmed that Articles 261 and 263 TFEU provide the Courts with sufficient legal powers to conduct an adequate control of the EU Commission's decisions, which would guarantee the right to a fair trial under Article 47 of the EU Charter. According to the *KME* ruling, the EU Commission's discretion, which in some instances remains "substantial" or „wide", does not prevent the GC "from carrying out the full and unrestricted review, in law and in fact, required of it".[100] This statement appears to be in line with the requirements laid down by the ECtHR in *Menarini*: "judicial body with full jurisdiction with the power to quash in all respects, in facts or in law, decision rendered by the lower body".[101] This led some authors to assume that the CJEU is gradually intensifying its standard of review and narrowing down the EU Commission's margin of discretion.[102] Other authors have argued that the *KME* precedent "falls short of a coherent framework for appraising whether the EU system of review complies with the requirement of a fair trial".[103] While awaiting the emerging case law, where the ECtHR would have an opportunity to further substantiate the compliance of its judicial review with the fundamental rights guaranteed in the EU Charter and ECHR, we submit that the mere reiteration of *Tetra Laval* formula of judicial review outside the merger control context does not

---

[96] Case C-272/09P *KME Germany and others v Commission*, judgment of 8 December 2011, para. 94.

[97] *Id.*, para. 102.

[98] *Id.*, para. 106.

[99] See Sibony (2012), pp. 1989–1995.

[100] *KME* judgment, para. 109.

[101] *Menarini* judgment, para. 59.

[102] Nikolic (2012), p. 587.

[103] Sibony (2012), p. 2000.

resolve the problem of compliance of various limitations on the allegedly *full* jurisdiction of the CJEU that have been discussed above.

4   Concluding Remarks

The progressive *criminalization* of competition law enforcement has produced a vibrant debate concerning the compliance of the EU competition enforcement regime with the right to a fair trial. *Menarini* eliminated the concerns previously expressed by a number of authors concerning the compatibility of the administrative system of competition law enforcement with Article 6 ECHR. In that ruling, the ECtHR defined competition law fines as "minor" criminal sanctions, which could thus be imposed by an administrative authority like an NCA or EU Commission. Nevertheless, the ambiguous requirement of *full* judicial review introduced by the ECtHR has opened a new debate in relation to the standard of judicial review exercised by the CJEU/GC in reviewing the decisions of the EU Commission. During the last two decades, the EU Courts in Luxembourg have progressively broadened the scope of their judicial review. Nevertheless, it is unclear at the moment whether the *Tetra Laval* standard of judicial review complies with the *Menarini* requirement of a full judicial review.

In *KME*, the CJEU positively *self-assessed* the compatibility of its standard of judicial review with Article 47 of the EU Charter. However, it is unclear whether the ECtHR would achieve the same conclusion in relation to Article 6 ECHR. The *Menarini* judgment referred to the compatibility of the enforcement regime of the national competition law with Article 6 ECHR. Only when the EU accedes to the ECHR will the ECtHR be able *to verify* the correctness of the *self-assessment* made by the CJEU in *KME*. In fact, when the EU joins the ECHR, a company fined by EU Commission will be able to appeal to the ECHR "after having exhausted the domestic remedies" (i.e., after having appealed the EU Commission decision to the GC and CJEU). Taking into consideration that 3 years after the entry into force of the Lisbon Treaty the EU is still not a Contracting Party of the ECHR, we do not expect any time soon an ECtHR judgment assessing the compatibility of the EU competition law enforcement system with Article 6 ECHR.

Even if we assumed that the ECtHR would consider CJEU standard of review in line with its *Menarini* case law, the issue would still remain open at the national level. As previously noted by the authors, at the level of EU MS and candidate countries national courts do not always perform full judicial review of the NCA decisions.[104] In particular, in the new EU MS and candidate countries, national courts often limit their review to the procedural aspects of the NCA decisions. Therefore, following the example of Menarini Pharmaceutical, a company sanctioned by the NCA of one ECHR, Contracting Parties could appeal to the ECtHR,

---

[104] Svetlicinii and Botta (2012), p. 489.

arguing that in the context of national proceedings the national courts did not conduct a *full review* of the NCA decision. In such cases, the ECtHR could achieve a different assessment in comparison to the conclusions reached in *Menarini* in relation to the standard of judicial review applied by the Italian courts.

In conclusion, while the *potential* diverging views between the courts in Luxembourg and Strasbourg will be clarified only when the EU accedes to the ECHR, in the coming years the ECtHR is expected to rule on new cases concerning the compatibility of the national standard of judicial review in competition cases with the requirement of *full* judicial review. As a consequence, the compatibility of the standard of judicial review and the right to a fair trial is likely to remain one of the more debated issues in the field of competition law.

References

Barbier de La Serre E, Winckler C (2012) A landmark year for the law on fines imposed in EU competition proceedings. J Eur Compet Law Pract 3(4):351–370

Bebr G (1981) Development of Judicial Control of the European Communities. Martinus Nijhoff, The Hague

Bronckers M, Vallery A (2012) Business as usual after Menarini? MLex Magazine 44–47 (January-March 2012)

Bronckers M, Vallery A (2011) No longer presumed guilty? The impact of fundamental rights on certain dogmas of EU competition law. World Compet 34(4):535–570

Castillo de la Torre F (2009) Evidence, proof and judicial review in cartel cases. In: Proceedings of the 2009 EU Competition Law and Policy workshop organized by the European University Institute. http://www.eui.eu/Documents/RSCAS/Research/Competition/2009/2009-COMPETITION-Castillo.pdf. Accessed 10 Mar 2013

Efremova V (2012) Evolution of competition law in South-Eastern European countries on the way towards EU membership. Mediterr Compet Bull 6:23–43

Gauer C, Jaspers M (2007) ECN Model Leniency Programme — a first step towards a harmonised leniency policy in the EU. Compet Policy Newsl 1:35–38

Graupner F (1973) Commission decision-making on competition questions. Comm Mark Law Rev 10:291

Faull F, Nickpay A (2007) The EC Law of Competition, Oxford University Press

Fingleton J, Fritsch M et a l(eds) (1997) Rules of competition and east–west integration. Kluwer Law International, The Hague

Forrester I (2009) Due process in EC competition cases; a distinguished institution with flawed procedures. Eur Law Rev 34(6):817–843

Forrester I (2011) A challenge for Europe's judges: the review of fines in competition cases. Eur Law Rev 36(2):185–207

Harpaz G (2009) The European Court of Justice and its relations with the European Court of Human Rights: the quest for enhanced reliance, coherence and legitimacy. Comm Mark Law Rev 46:105–141

Legal H (2006) Standards of proof and standards of judicial review in EU competition law. In: Hawk BE (ed) Proceedings of the 2005 Fordham Competition Law Institute

Lock T (2011) Walking on a tightrope: the draft ECHR accession agreement and the autonomy of the EU legal order. Comm Mark Law Rev 48:1025–1054

Nikolic I (2012) Full judicial review of antitrust cases after KME: a new formula of review? Eur Compet Law Rev 33(12):583–588

Reeves T, Legal H, Christoforou Th, Steuer R (2006) Standards of proof and standards of judicial review in EC competition law roundtable. In: Hawk BE (ed) Proceedings of the 2005 Fordham Competitive Law Institute

Sibony A-L (2012) Case C-272/09P, KME Germany and others v commission, judgment of the Court of Justice (second chamber) of 8 December 2011, nyr. Comm Mark Law Rev 49:1977–2002

Slater D, Thomas S, Waelbroeck D (2008) Competition law proceedings before the European Commission and the right to a fair trial: no need for reform?. GCLC working Paper 04/08. http://www.coleurope.eu/sites/default/files/research-paper/gclc_wp_04-08.pdf. Accessed 10 Mar 2013

Svetlicinii A (2010) Epilogue of the plasterboard litigation: how much legal certainty in the commission's treatment of repeated infringements? Eur Law Rep 10:318–322

Svetlicinii A, Botta M (2012) Article 102 TFEU as a tool for market regulation: "excessive enforcement" against "excessive prices" in the new EU member states and candidate countries. Eur Compet J 8(3):473–496

Vedder H (2004) Spontaneous harmonization of national competition laws in the wake of the modernization of the EC competition law. Compet Law Rev 1(1):5–21

Vitkauskas D and others (2009) Right to a fair trial under the European Convention on human rights (Article 6). Interights, London. http://www.interights.org/files/107/INTERIGHTS%20Article%206%20Manual.pdf. Accessed 10 Mar 2013

Wils W (2011) EU antitrust enforcement powers and procedural guarantees: the interplay between EU law, national law, the charter of fundamental rights of the EU and the European Convention on Human Rights. World Compet 34(2):189–213

European Court of Asylum—Does It Exist?

Lehte Roots

1 Introduction

The inclusion of asylum and refugee issues in the competence of the European Union after the Treaty of Amsterdam is a significant development in the international refugee law. Every year, thousands of persons apply for asylum in European Union countries. In 2011, there were more than 870,000 asylum applications submitted in the world.[1]

This chapter assesses the role of the CJEU (Court of Justice of European Union) and the ECrtHR (European Court of Human Rights) in the asylum law development in Europe. Right of asylum is also recognized by some EU member states as one of the fundamental rights that have been stated in the constitution of the countries.[2] EU law, European Convention of Human Rights, and constitutional rights are very much interrelated and connected. We can find some rights in all these three levels, and at the same time it is diverse how countries apply those rights. In German and Italian constitutions we can find the right for asylum, but in Estonian or Latvian constitution there is no clearly stated right to asylum available.

In the analysis, special attention is paid on the Bosphorus ruling[3] made by the ECrtHR as the basis of the protection of fundamental rights and the balance between the two important courts in Europe.

The relationships between the directives and international refugee and human rights treaties is governed by art. 351of the TFEU. This provision regulates the

---

[1] http://www.unhcr.org/cgi-bin/texis/vtx/home/opendocPDFViewer.html?docid=4fd6f87f9& query=statistics 2011, Accessed 15.01.2013.

[2] For example Italy, Germany.

[3] Bosphorus Hava Yollari Turizm v. Ireland, App. No. 45036/98, EctHR, 30 June 2005.

L. Roots (✉)
Tallinn Law School, Tallinn University of Technology, Akadeemia tee 3, 12618 Tallinn, Estonia
e-mail: lehte.roots@ttu.ee

T. Kerikmäe (ed.), *Protecting Human Rights in the EU*,
DOI 10.1007/978-3-642-38902-3_8, © Springer-Verlag Berlin Heidelberg 2014

relationship between EC law and international treaties concluded by Member States prior to the entry into force of the TEC or, for acceding states, before the date of their accession. Paragraph 1 of Art. 351 establishes that the rights and obligations arising from those treaties shall not be affected by the provisions of the TFEU.

Nevertheless, even when the EU Treaty and TFEU confer powers on the EU to conclude international agreements, international refugee and human rights treaties do not bind the EU as such, as they have not joined the treaties. In the Opinion 2/94, it was stated that there was no legal basis for the EU to accede to the human rights treaties.[4]

Article 78 of the TFEU establishes an obligation for EU secondary legislation on asylum to comply with the Refugee Convention and its Protocol[5] and with other human rights treaties, which would include the European Convention on Human Rights[6] and the Convention against Torture.[7] Derived from this, it can be argued that art. 78 of TFEU is *lex specialis* in comparison to art. 351.

2   Who Has the Jurisdiction?

International asylum law is regulated by the 1951 Geneva Convention and its protocol from 1967. The 1951 Geneva Convention itself does not give any specific court jurisdiction to review the asylum cases. While the 1951 Geneva Convention was under preparation, no one seemed to think about creating an international court or a body that would be composed of experts in charge of overseeing its implementation by State Parties, on the model of the monitoring systems included later on in the UN human rights conventions adopted from the mid-1960s.[8] As the parties to the Convention are the states, it applies only in case the states between themselves have some disputes or misunderstandings on the application of this Convention.

When the UNHCR was created, the Statute of the organization gives the UNHCR the "*task of supervision international conventions providing for the protection of refugees*".[9] The states are obliged to cooperate with the UNHCR.[10] It is noteworthy

---

[4] Opinion 2/94, Accession by the Communities to the European Convention for the Protection of Human Rights and Fundamental Freedoms [1996] ECRI-1759.

[5] Protocol relation to the status of Refugees, adopted 31 Jan 1967, entered into force 4 Oct 1967, 606 UNTS 267. See more also in Lambert (2006).

[6] European Convention on Human Rights and Fundamental Freedoms, adopted 1950, entered into force 3 September 1953, 213 UNTS 221.

[7] Convention against Torture and Other Cruel, Inhuman or Degrading Treatment or Punishment, adopted 10 December 1984, entered into force 26 June 1987, 1464 UNTS 85.

[8] Article 38 of the Convention: "*Any dispute between parties to this Convention relating to its interpretation or applications, which cannot be settled by other means, shall be referred to the International Court of Justice at the request of any one of the parties to the dispute*".

[9] Preamble, §6.

[10] Ibid.

that the word "convention" is used in plural form. It is an important statement because the Convention has been later modified and the modification done with the protocol in 1967 has made the convention, in our time, a regulatory document to be applied. For a long time, domestic and administrative and judicial institutions were left on their own in the interpretation of the Convention in the local level.

Gil-Bazo states that *"When conflicts of obligation arise between those derived from the EC law and those derived from pre-existing international human right treaties, Member States must give priority to those pre-existing human rights treaties"*.[11]

She has based her argumentation on the previous case law. In the Burgoa case, the ECJ stated that paragraph 1 of art. 307 *"is of general scope and it applies to any international agreement, irrespective of the subject matter"*. It also clarified that the provision does not alter the nature of such agreements' and, therefore, does not "adversely affect the rights which individuals may derive from them".[12]

When we take into account the *lex posteriori* principle, we should give priority to EU law as the latest available regulation after the human rights treaties. Furthermore, despite of the preexisting treaties, paragraph 2 of art. 351 imposes an obligation on Member States to take all appropriate steps to eliminate the incompatibilities between them and EU law.

3 European Court of Human Rights

The ECrtHR initially has been silent about the rights of foreigners and also did not mention asylum. First initial provisions relating to aliens allow to restrict the rights of foreigners.[13] The content of the additional protocols of ECHR Protocol no 4 (art. 4)[14] and Protocol 7 (art.1)[15] is relevant for foreigners. There is no right for asylum stated in the ECHR. Nevertheless, the Strasbourg Court plays an important indirect role in cases relating to asylum seekers through its case law on several

---

[11] See Gil-Bazo (2007).

[12] C 812/79 Attorney General v Burgoa [1980] ECR 2787, §6 and §10.

[13] Art 5.1 of ECHR on arrest and detention of a person to prevent his unauthorized entry into the country or against whom deportation or extradition is contemplated and art. 16 on restrictions on the political activities of aliens.

[14] Article 4 of Protocol no 4 of ECHR prohibits the collective expulsion of aliens.

[15] Article 1 of Protocol no 7 of ECHR gives procedural safeguards relating to expulsion of aliens: (1) An alien lawfully resident in the territory of a State shall not be expelled therefrom except in pursuance of a decision reached in accordance with law and shall be allowed: (a) to submit reasons against his expulsion, (b) to have his case reviewed, and (c) to be represented for these purposes before the competent authority or a person or persons designated by that authority. (2) An alien may be expelled before the exercise of his rights under paragraph 1.a, b and c of this Article, when such expulsion is necessary in the interests of public order or is grounded on reasons of national security.

provisions of the Convention such as article 3,[16] which regulates prohibition of torture; article 8,[17] respect of family and private life; and article 13,[18] the right to an effective remedy.

Comprehensively, the court has used art. 39 of its rules of procedure on interim measures.[19] As asylum control was not for a long time the competence of the EU, asylum seekers turned to the ECrtHR as the last instance court to find the answers to their questions. It is also more convenient for the individual to use the opportunity to ask the opinion of the ECrtHR, as the individuals do not have a chance to turn to the CJEU directly. It is up to the domestic judge to decide whether or not to ask a preliminary ruling from the CJEU in the asylum case in order to guarantee the right application of EU law.[20]

4   Court of Justice of the European Union

After the Lisbon Treaty, the Court of Justice of the European Union has gained full competence to give consistent interpretation of the EU asylum law; however, it still does not have the competence to interpret the ECHR. The attention that needs to be paid to the application of the ECHR in the EU is highly relevant in the view of three important developments of the European Union law.

Before the Lisbon Treaty amendments, there were several concerns about the application of the EU asylum law by the domestic courts, as there was a limitation under art. 68 of the EC Treaty to the access of the preliminary ruling procedure. Also, Advocate General highlighted the problem that these limitations raise serious questions about the compatibility of the current status with the Charter of Fundamental Rights and the ECHR.[21] After the Lisbon Treaty, the Charter has become an integral part of the EU primary legislation. There is clearly stated in the primary legislation of the EU, in TEU art. 6.3, that *"fundamental rights, as guaranteed by the European Convention on Human Rights and Fundamental Freedoms and as*

---

[16] Chahal v UK on expulsion of aliens; Cruz Varas and Others v Sweden, Vilvarajah and Others v UK, Salah Sheek v The Netherlands. On the implementation of Dublin II Regulation, see AA v Greece, MMS v Belgium and Greece.

[17] Fawsie v Greece, Saidoun v Greece, Rahimi v Greece. In 2010, the Court held that Greece was in breach of art 8 combined with art 14 for refusing to give family allowances to refugees on the ground that they were not Greek nationals, nationals of another EU Member State, or of Greek origin.

[18] Jabari v Turkey, Conka v Belgium, Gebremedhin v France.

[19] See more in Errera (2007) and Lambert (2006). Also, case Mamatkulov and Askarov v Turkey, the State parties are under an obligation to comply with them. The Court has repeatedly used it in cases relating to Sri Lanka.

[20] Article 267 TFEU. Read more about the preliminary ruling from Barents (2009).

[21] See Jacobs (2003) p. 343.

they result from the constitutional traditions common to the Member States, shall constitute general principles of the Union's case law".

It is noteworthy that the Charter of Fundamental Rights is also stating right for asylum as one of the fundamental rights of human beings.[22] And according to art. 6.2 of the TEU, the EU should find a way to join the European Convention of Human Rights, which makes the EU a subject under the international law where the ECrtHR has its jurisdiction. This step leads us to the mixed and joint jurisdiction of the asylum law.

The EU has its limited competence in international relations, and it is given by the treaties to it. The Union can conclude international agreements. Once concluded, these agreements "are binding upon the institutions of the Union and on its Member States" (Article 216 TFEU).

When the Treaty of Rome in 1957 was signed, there was no slight idea that asylum can become the competence of the European Community. Now we can find asylum regulated in art. 3.2 of the TEU and Articles 67 and 78 of the TFEU. The effect is that refugee and asylum law in EU Member States is primarily composed of the 1951 Geneva Convention and of a series of EU instruments issued by directives, regulations, and decisions. Another consequence of the delegation of the powers in asylum law gave the ECJ the role of a "supra national court". This influence comes mainly via the preliminary ruling procedure when domestic courts ask for the interpretation of the EU law under art. 267 TFEU. It helps the creation of the EU own asylum principles from part of the rest of the world who are also parties to the 1961 Geneva Convention.

Preliminary ruling is a court-to-court procedure, unique instrument of cooperation between national courts and the CJEU. Finally, it is up to the domestic court to decide whether it is necessary to request the CJEU interpretation of certain provisions of EU law or not.[23] The CJEU has delivered rulings on refugee and asylum issues. One was the action brought by the European Parliament against the decision of the Council on their respective powers on the procedure of adoption of the common list of safe countries of origin.[24]Others were the preliminary ruling references from the domestic courts.

The Court has issued its opinion on the Qualification Directive[25]: on the interpretation of article 15(c) on subsidiary protection[26]; on articles 2(c), 7(1), 11-1 (e),

---

[22] Article 18 of the Charter of Fundamental Rights of EU.

[23] Art 234 TFEU says that the Member State court may refer to European Court, but the court itself in several rulings have concluded that there is an obligation to refer C-393/98 Ministerion Publico and António Gomes Valente [2001] ECR I-1327.

[24] C-133/06, European Parliament v Council of the European Union, 2008 ECR I-3189.

[25] Council Directive 2004/83/EC of 29 April 2004 on minimum standards for the qualification and status of third country nationals or stateless persons as refugees or as persons who otherwise need international protection and the content of the protection granted *OJL 304, 30/09/2004 P. 0012–0023.*

[26] Case C.465/05, Meki Elgafaji and Noor Elgafaji v Staatsecretaris van Justitie, Grand Chamber, 2009, ECR I-921. See also Errera (2011b) pp. 93–112.

and 15 relating to cessation[27]; on article 12 (1) (a) on exclusion[28]; and one on article 12 (2) (b) and (c) on exclusion and art. 3[29] on religious persecution.[30] Other cases were related to the procedural aspects of the Dublin II regulation[31] and procedures directive.[32]

5 The Charter of Fundamental Rights

The Charter of Fundamental Rights of the European Union is a most relevant instrument, as it recognizes the right as they result, in particular, from the constitutional traditions and international obligation common to the Member States.[33]

From art. 6.1 of TEU, we can find that "The Union recognizes the rights, freedoms and principles set put in the Charter of Fundamental Rights of the European union of 7 December 200, as adopted at Strasbourg on 12 December 2009, which shall have the same legal values as Treaties".

Article 18 of the Charter gives us the clue that asylum is recognized as one of the fundamental rights of the EU: "*The right to asylum shall be guaranteed with due respect for the rules of the Geneva Convention of 28 July 1951 and the Protocol of 31st July 1967 relating to the status of refugees and in accordance with the Treaty on European Union and the Treaty on the Functioning of the European Union*".[34] Article 19, §2, states the prohibition of *refoulment*, which is also an important provision for foreigners and previous asylum seekers.

For example, the qualification directive issued in 2004 takes the Charter as its reference in its preamble.[35] The link between the Charter of Fundamental Rights and the ECHR is explained in its article 52(3). It explains us that the meaning and scope of the rights shall be the same as those laid down by the Convention of the

---

[27] Joined Cases C-175/0, C176/08, C178/08 and C-179/98, Aydin Salahadin Abdulla, Kamil Hasan, Ahmed Adem, Hamrin Mosa Rashi and Dler Jamal v Bundesrepublik Deutschland, 2 March 2010. See also Errera (2011a) pp. 521–537.

[28] C- 31/09 Nawras Bobol v Bevandorlasi es Allampolgarsagi Hivatal.

[29] Joined Cases C-57/09 and C-101/09, Bundesrepublik Deutschland v B and D.

[30] C-71/11 Y and C-99/11 on religious persecution.

[31] C-19/08, Migrationsverket v Petrosian, C-411/10 NS, C-493/10 ME and others, C-620/10, Kastrati, C-4/11 Puid, C-164/11 CIMAD et GISTI.

[32] C-69/10 Samba Diouf, C-175/11 HID.

[33] Preamble of the Charter.

[34] Article 18 of the Charter on Fundamental Rights.

[35] Recital 10 of the directive.

Protection of Human Rights and Fundamental Freedoms, which application is controlled by the European Court of Human Rights in Strasbourg.

It is worth mentioning that the Charter has been used as a reference[36] by the court even before it became a binding document. A number of pending references mention provisions of the Charter among other instruments.[37]

6 Refugee Status and Subsidiary Protection Under the Qualification Directive

Even when one would presuppose that the EU is not bound by international refugee and human rights treaties as such, EU secondary legislation must correspond to human rights as general principles of EU law. Article 6(2) of the TEU establishes that "The Union shall accede to the European Convention for the Protection of Human Rights and Fundamental Freedoms. Such accession shall not affect the Union's competences as defined in the Treaties". There is no word about acceding the UN 1951 Convention and its protocols.

On 29th of April 2004, the Council of the European Union adopted Directive 2004/83/EC on minimum standards for the qualification and status of third country national or stateless person as refugees or as persons who otherwise need international protection and the content of the protection granted.[38]

The directive contributes to the clarification of some of the elements of the refugee definition in the UN Convention on the Status of Refugees. It helps to create the EU common asylum system derived from the notion of UN 1951 Refugee Convention.

Member States have interpreted the directive differently, for example, persecution that can arise from the non-state actors (art. 6),[39] as well as recognition of gender- and child-specific forms of persecution [art. 9(2)]. So there is a need for a court interpretation on this field. From the previous EU case law, the fundamental rights, as they result from the constitutional traditions and international obligations common to the Member States, are binding as general principles of Community law.[40]

---

[36] See Bolbon, §38; Abdulla, §53-54; and B and D, §78.

[37] In Case C-411/10, art 18 was referred; in Case C-69/10 Samba Diouf, delivered on March 1, 2011, art 47 of the Charter was quoted.

[38] [2004] OJ L 304/12.

[39] See more in Phuong (2003).

[40] C 29/69 Staudr [1969] ECR 419, §7.

7   Bosphorus Case[41] and the Court Jurisdiction

The judgment of the European Court of Human Rights in Bosphorus[42] states that the Member States may be held accountable on the implementation of EC law. The court recalled that Member States can subject themselves to the rule of an international organization compatible with the ECHR as long as that organization has equivalent standards to the ECHR, in terms of substantive protection and the procedural system for enforcement. When states are "considered to retain Convention liability in respect of treaty commitments subsequent to the entry into force of the Convention",[43] the Court established that if such equivalent protection is considered to be provided by the organization, the presumption will be that a state has not departed from the requirements of the Convention when it does no more than implement legal obligations flowing from its membership of the organization. The presumption can be rebutted only if it is considered that the protection of Convention rights was manifestly deficient.[44]

The accession of the EU to the ECHR has been discussed for some time. In its Opinion 2/94, the ECJ held that EC lacked the competence to accede.[45] When the Lisbon Treaty amendments came, according to said amendments and to Protocol 14 to the ECHR, these obstacles to accession have been removed.

Article 6(2) TEU not only gives the European Union the competence to conclude an accession treaty but also puts it under an obligation to effectuate it, as it states that the Union shall accede to the ECHR. In the Bosphorus case, the ECtHR reemphasized the responsibility of the Member State for the application of secondary EU law.

In this case, Ireland impounded an aircraft by implementing EC regulation, which transposed a UN Security Resolution, providing sanctions against the Federal Republic of Yugoslavia. The applicant company alleged an infringement of its right to property contained in art. 1 Protocol 1 ECHR. The ECtHR held that the European Union's legal system protected fundamental rights in a manner "equivalent to the Convention".

The Bosphorus presumption postulates that where the Member State had no discretion in implementing EU secondary law, it is presumed that a State has acted

---

[41] See more in Costello (2006) p. 87.

[42] Bosphorus Hava Yollari Turizm v. Ireland, App. No. 45036/98, EctHR, 30 June 2005.

[43] App No 45036/98 Bosphorus Hava Yollari Turizm Ve Ticaret Anonim Sirketi (Bosphorus Airways) v Ireland [GC], judgment of 30 June 2005, Reports 2005-V, (2006) 42 EHRR 1, 155–156.

[44] Ibid.

[45] Accession of the Community to the European Human Rights Convention, (Opinion 2/94), ECR 1996, I-1759.

in compliance with the Convention.[46] When the case is manifestly deficient, this presumption is rebuttable.[47]

Nevertheless, the responsibility of the Member State for EU action can only be found when the Member State authorities have acted in a certain manner. Otherwise, the EU's action is not within their jurisdiction, as required by art. 1 ECHR.

The argument of the autonomy of the EU legal order has to be also taken into account. There are several cases that have reminded this principle over the years.[48] In Costa v Enel, the ECJ made it clear that EEC Treaty constituted an independent source of law. In that case, the ECJ substantiated a concept of autonomy as the reason domestic legal provisions cannot override provisions of the Treaty and thereby established primacy of EU law over domestic law. In the light of that decision, it is evident why the Member State applying the EU law cannot apply it reversely. It would be infringement of the EU law supremacy principle.

One can also have a quick look at article 19(1) TEU and Article 344 TFEU, which confer exclusive jurisdictions on the ECJ to interpret the Treaties. Bearing this in mind, one can conclude that there can be no ECtHR jurisdiction over the legislation of the EU.

Certain problems will arise to interpret these article after the EU accession to the ECHR if it becomes part of the EU law, but it will not become part of the Treaties as art. 19(1) TEU and Article 344 TFEU allow the ECJ to interpret the Treaties.

In such cases as Bosphorus, which concern the conduct by a Member State required by EU legislation, the ECtHR will normally be asked to find that the piece of legislation was incompatible with the Convention. Therefore, the Member States will be held responsible as a proxy for the Union.

Article 36(1) of the ECHR gives a right to take part in the proceedings for the third party. It says that "a High Contracting Party one of whose nationals is an applicant shall have a right to submit written comments and to take part in hearings". And art. 36 (2) ECHR allows the President of the Court to invite any High Contracting Party that is not a party to the proceedings or any person concerned who is not the applicant to submit written comments or take part in hearings.

In case the EU accedes to the ECHR, one can conclude that every time the foreigner has a case in the ECtHR the EU as a party to the Convention has a right to take part in the proceedings. There are also drawbacks because the third party does not have an obligation to intervene. After accession to the ECHR, it would make sense that the Union intervenes whenever the case is brought against one of its Member States, and in that sense Bosphorus case is a good example as only EU has a power to declare the Regulation void.

---

[46] Bosphorus (2006) 42 E.H.R.R. 1 at 155 and 156.

[47] Bosphorus (2006) 42 E.H.R.R. 1 at 156.

[48] C-402/05 & 415/05 Kadi v Council of the European Union, C-6/64 Costa v Enel, C-459/03 Commission v Ireland.

Argumentation supporting the idea that EU accession to the ECHR does not increase the overall scope of rights protection is based partly on the Connolly judgement, where it was confirmed that art. 52(3) of the Charter imposes the duty to comply with the minimum standard of the ECHR.[49] Art. 52(3) of the Charter says: "In so far as this Charter contains rights which correspond to rights guaranteed by the Convention for the Protection of Human Rights and Fundamental Freedoms, the meaning and scope of those rights shall be the same as those laid down by the said Convention. This provision shall not prevent Union law providing more extensive protection".

It is important to note that the EU law can provide more extensive protection than the ECHR itself.

One problem that can arise when the EU is not part of the ECHR is art. 52(2), which says that rights are guaranteed within the limits of the TFEU.

Furthermore, as the Charter also recognizes fundamental rights that result from the constitutions of the Member States,[50] it can easily be concluded that when EU joins the ECHR it does not really help to increase the protection of the rights that are actually already protected. Besides that, all EU member states are parties to the ECHR and have to apply these principles derived from the ECHR in their current legislation and practice.

It can be easily argued that this kind of double or triple protection might increase the sensation of the protection, but in fact the laws are just copying the same principles. The problem is not in having few legislation but in applying the legislation in practice, when the fundamental principles of ECHR are not followed.

An additional problem to the EU's accession to the ECHR is related to the jurisdiction of different courts. Does the ECtHR become superior over the ECJ?

The ECHR gives only minimum rights that must be protected, and the EU law can be always more generous, as is stated in art. 52 (3) of the Charter.

Also the problem of EU responsibility arises. Which institution can be held responsible under the ECHR if the EU law violates the Convention?

In the Bosphorus case, the ECtHR decided that action of the Member States that is no more than implementing their obligations under EU law is presumed to be in accordance with the ECHR as long as the ECJ provides comparable protection to that provided by the ECHR. In case the protection derived from ECHR is deficient in a particular case, this presumption can be disproved. It develops from the principle laid down in art. 52(3), which encourages the Union to provide more extensive protection.

It is art. 52(2) of the Charter of Fundamental Rights that also confirms that any rights recognized by the Charter for which there is a provision in the Treaties shall be exercised under the conditions and within the limits defined by the Treaties.

The "double standard" of review of MS action, depending on whether it is determined autonomously or on the basis of EU law might not be justified and

---

[49] Case C-274/99 P, [2001] ECR I-1611.

[50] Article 52(4).

acceptable to all Member States. The supremacy of EU law is accepted by many countries, including Estonia. Member States in bona fide apply the EU law, as the infringement of the application of the EU law is also penalized; therefore, the MS should not be penalized for the application of the EU law.

Nevertheless, as the EU country is also part of the ECHR it should have common sense to control its action also related to its international obligations and not obligations towards EU law. There is no other party to the Convention whose constitutional provisions are not reviewable by Strasbourg. The need to review EU primary law and its conformity with the ECHR might arise from the lack of competence of the EU to amend its primary law. It is up to the member states to make changes to the treaties. By passing the review rights to Strasbourg, EU will stay in conflict within itself. It can create joint liability or conflict of several liabilities to the Member State. It seems that it depends on the applicant against whom (Member State or EU) the case will be brought. At the same time, it is unfair towards the applicant in cases where the responsibility is not clearly defined.

Normally, the ECtHR will be asked to review which piece of legislation was incompatible with the ECHR. The Member State would be therefore held responsible as a proxy for the Union and the other MS, and we may conclude that there is no need to hold the EU responsible. A Member State as a separate legal identity must also follow its international obligations, not only its EU obligations, and full responsibility for the conduct of the MS can be put on the MS. Therefore, double review is not necessary as MS is often the implementing part of the EU law and, while implementing EU rules, it has to respect human rights.

In order for an individual application to the ECtHR to be admissible, art. 35(1) ECHR tells that the applicant must exhaust all domestic remedies within 6 months of the final decision. It shows that the ECtHR review has a subsidiary character. An applicant should first bring the action against the EU or a Member State.

The difference can be made between cases involving EU law that are directed against the EU and those directed against a Member State involving application of the EU law, as domestic remedies are contained in the respondent party's legal system.

Review of the legality of an act in the EU can be done under art. 263(4) TFEU. Individuals can only access the European Union's courts under the individual complaints procedure found in art. 263 (4) TFEU:

> Any natural or legal person may /.../ institute proceedings against an act addressed to that person or which is of direct and individual concern to them, and against a regulatory act which is of direct concern to them and does not entail implementing measures.

Being part of the ECHR, the procedure before the ECJ would no longer be considered as international case and ECJ would be regarded as a domestic court.

Problem will arise from art of 35(2) of the ECHR because it will not render a complaint inadmissible because it has already been submitted to "another procedure of international investigation or settlement". Therefore, the procedure before the ECJ has to be finished and remedy should be sought before the EU court in order to satisfy the requirements of Art. 35(1) ECHR.

The Luxemburg court (ECJ) is the only court that can interpret the Treaties. The agreement must not affect powers of the EU institutions, and the ECtHR must not be given jurisdiction to interpret the Treaties in a binding fashion. These principles are founded by the ECJ in its rulings of Kadi and Germany v Council of the European Union.

In Kadi, the ECJ highlighted that not only does the autonomy of EU law prevent an agreement from affecting the allocation of powers within the EU, but an agreement must also not have the effect of prejudicing the constitutional principles of the Treaty, which include respect for fundamental rights.[51]

The principle nevertheless has to be linked to another ECJ decision where the hierarchy of EU laws have to be respected and the primary law takes priority over Union agreements and secondary law.[52]

Based on the above-mentioned analysis, the Bosphorus ruling does not change the current situation. The ECtHR does not have jurisdiction to place remedies on the EU, as it has no right to interpret the treaties. It is up to ECJ to control EU legislation development and its compliance with the ECHR, as after the accession it is part of the EU law. The confusion of the hierarchy of norms is nevertheless still in place, and it depends much from the prospective where it is seen from.

8   Conclusion

As Steve Peers has noted, " The effective application in practice of any set of legal rules depend to a large degree on the judicial system established to rule on the interpretation, validity, legal effect and enforcement of those rules".[53] As the current analysis has shown, asylum rules can be shaped by the ECJ, ECtHR, and Member States. The EU system has been created to ensure uniform interpretation, effective enforcement, and sufficient judicial review measures.

Taking into account the previous analysis at the moment for the EU Member State that is bound by the EU law and its secondary legislation, it is relevant to follow the secondary legislation issued in the framework of asylum. It ensures the application of *lex posteriori* and *lex specials* within the Member States. If EU asylum law required Member States to violate their obligations under international refugee law and international human rights law, the relevant EC law would be invalid, without further obligation on Member States to denounce the treaties. It can be assumed that the Union, by joining the ECHR, would accept the jurisdiction of the ECtHR and the latter would be, in principle, open to individuals' actions against the Union.

---

[51] Kadi C-402/05, E.C.R. I-6351.

[52] Germany v Council of the European Union C-122/95, E.C.R. I-973.

[53] Peers (2007).

As Hinajeros states, *"The ECtHR could then deal with such an action in two different ways: on the one hand, it could treat the Union just like any other signatory to the Convention, meaning that it would simply examine the substance of each complaint, if admissible. On the other hand, the Court could establish a presumption in favour of the Union, applying the 'equivalent protection' doctrine that it has developed in relation to the EC"*.[54]

After the accession of the EU to the European Convention of Human Rights and the development of the case law, there might emerge a need for the review of the situation.

References

Books and Articles

Barents R (2009) Directory of European Union case law on the preliminary ruling procedure. Kluwer Law International, Alphen aan den Rijn

Costello C (2006) The Bosphorus Ruling of the European Court of Human Rights: fundamental rights and blurred boundaries in Europe. Hum Rights Law Rev 6:87

Errera R (2007) The European Court of Human Rights and interim measures: scope of powers and issues for domestic courts. In: Mole N (ed) Asylum and the European Convention on Human Rights. Council of Europe Publishing, Strasbourg

Errera R (2011a) Cessation and assessment of new circumstances: a comment on Abdulla, ECJ, 2 March 2010. Int J Refug Law 23:521–537

Errera R (2011b) The CJEU and subsidiary protection: reflections on Elgafaji - and after. Int J Refug Law 23:93–112

Gil-Bazo M-T (2007) Refugee status and subsidiary protection under EC law: the qualification directive and the right to be granted asylum. In: Baldaccini A et al(ed) Whose freedom security and justice? EU immigration and asylum law and policy. Hart Publishing, Oxford

Hinarejos A (2009) Judicial control in the European Union. Reforming jurisdiction in the intergovernmental pillars. OUP, Oxford, p 179

Jacobs F (2003) Effective judicial protection of individuals in the European Union, now and in the future. In: Andens M, Usher J (eds) The Treaty of Nice enlargement and constitutional reform. Hart Publishing, Oxford

Lambert H (2006) The EU asylum qualification directive—its impact on the jurisprudence of the United Kingdom and international law. Int Comp Law Q 55:184

Peers S (2007) The jurisdiction of the Court of Justice over EC immigration and asylum law: time for a change? In: Baldaccini A et al(ed) Whose freedom security and justice? EU immigration and asylum law and policy. Hart Publishing, Oxford

Phuong C (2003) Persecution by non-state agents: comparative judicial interpretation of the 1951 refugee convention. Eur J Migr Law 4:521–532

---

[54] Hinarejos (2009).

Case Law

App. No(s) 13163/87, 13164/87, 13165/87, 13447/87, 13448/87, Vilvarajah and Others v UK, A 215

App. No15576/89 Cruz Varas and Others v Sweden, A201

App No 22414/93 Chahal v UK, Reports 1996-V

App No 45036/98 Bosphorus Hava Yollari Turizm Ve Ticaret Anonim Sirketi (Bosphorus Airways) v Ireland [GC], judgement of 30 June 2005, Reports 2005-V, (2006) 42 EHRR

App No 40035/98 Jabari v Turkey

App No 51564/99 Conka v Belgium

App No 1948/04 Salah Sheek v The Netherlands

App No 25389/05 Gebremedhin v France

App No 40080/07 Fawsie v Greece

App No 40083/07 Saidoun v Greece

App No 12186/08 AA v Greece

App No 8687/08 Rahimi v Greece

App No. 30696/09 MMS v Belgium and Greece

App No. 46827/99 and 46951/99 Mamatkulov and Askarov v Turkey

C-6/64 Costa v Enel

C 29/69 Staudr [1969] ECR 419

C 812/79 Attorney General v Burgoa [1980] ECR 2787

C 812/79 Attorney General v Burgoa [1980] ECR 2787

C-122/95Germany v Council of the European Union, E.C.R. I-973

C-393/98 Ministerion Publico and António Gomes Valente [2001] ECR I-1327

C-274/99 P, [2001] ECR I-1611

C-459/03 Commission v Ireland

C-402/05 & 415/05 Kadi v Council of the European Union, E.C.R. I-6351

C.465/05, Meki Elgafaji and Noor Elgafaji v Staatsecretaris van Justitie, Grand Chamber, 2009, ECR I-921.

C-133/06, European Parliament v Council of the European Union, 2008 ECR I-3189

C-19/08, Migrationsverket v Petrosian,

C- 31/09 Nawras Bobol v Bevandorlasi es Allampolgarsagi Hivatal

C-620/10 Kastrati

C-493/10 ME and others

C-69/10 Samba Diouf

C-4/11 Puid

C-164/11 CIMAD et GISTI

C-175/11 HID

C-71/11 Y and C-99/11 on religious persecution

Joined cases C-175/08, C176/08, C178/08 and C-179/98, Aydin Salahadin Abdulla, Kamil Hasan, Ahmed Adem, Hamrin Mosa Rashi and Dler Jamal v Bundesrepublik Deutschland, 2 March 2010.

Joined Cases C-57/09 and C-101/09, Bundesrepublik Deutschland v B and D,

Joined Cases C-411/10 N.S v Secretary of State for the Home Department and (C-493/10) M. E., A. S. M., M. T., K. P., E. H. v Refugee Applications Commissioner, Minister for Justice, Equality and Law Reform

Official Materials

Accession of the Community to the European Human Rights Convention, (opinion 2/94), ECR 1996, I-1759

Council Directive 2004/83/EC of 29 April 2004 on minimum standards for the qualification and status of third country nationals or stateless persons as refugees or as persons who otherwise need international protection and the content of the protection granted OJL 30, 30/09/2004 P. 0012 - 0023

Convention against Torture and Other Cruel, Inhuman or Degrading Treatment or Punishment, adopted 10 December 1984, entered into force 26 June 1987, 1464 UNTS 85.

European Convention on Human Rights and Fundamental Freedoms, adopted 1950, entered into force 3 September 1953, 213 UNTS 221 http://www.unhcr.org/cgi-bin/texis/vtx/home/opendocPDFViewer.html?docid=4fd6f87f9&query=statistics 2011, 15.01.2013

Opinion 2/94, Accession by the Communities to the European Convention for the Protection of Human Rights and Fundamental Freedoms [1996] ECRI-1759

Protocol relation to the status of Refugees, adopted 31 Jan 1967, entered into force 4 Oct 1967, 606 UNTS 267

Free Movement of Students in the EU

Kari Käsper

1 Introduction

An interesting testing ground for the effectiveness of EU law for solving issues related to human rights might be the topic of free movement of people, more specifically the free movement of people. It is an intersection of fundamental rights as guaranteed by the Charter of Fundamental Rights, as well as economic rights embedded in the treaties since the creation of the European communities in the 1950s. In this context, it is possible to examine the free movement rights in general and their development. After that, it can be analysed what, if any, impact has the mainstreaming of human rights in EU law had on this topic. The article is limited to this specific aspect of free movement of students who are EU citizens.

The aim of the article is to show how free movement rights have been developed and elaborated in the European Union. Different rights for the status of persons are then elaborated upon, after which the focus shifts to students as a specific subgroup of persons exercising their free movement rights. The article does not focus on non-EU students because they face a different set of circumstances and status. *One of the important aspects is also to analyse the role of education in the EU and the powers of the EU in that sector to see whether rights guaranteed by the EU can be utilised. Education is also the area that Member States have wanted to exclude from harmonisation.*

The article seeks to analyse whether fundamental rights (especially those specified in the Charter of Fundamental Rights) can be used to protect against

This article is based on Master Thesis by the author defended in 2012 at Tallinn University of Technology.

K. Käsper (✉)
Tallinn Law School, Akadeemia tee 3, 12618 Tallinn, Estonia
e-mail: kari.kasper@ttu.ee

obstacles created by the Member States. Also, one specific barrier relating to language-based discrimination of students is analysed in detail, as some Member States (including Estonia) are providing higher education without tuition fees in the official state language and charging fees for studies in another language.

This article is mainly limited to discussion and analysis of the free movement of students from human rights point of view. The Bologna quality enhancement process and other areas will not be covered in detail. This is due to the fact that the analysis on higher education is an indicator on the overall legal issues prevalent in the economic and social policy coordination in the EU.

2 Free Movement Rights in the European Union

The free movement rights in the European Union originate from the economic common market, which was established with the 1958 Treaty of Establishing the European Economic Community or the so-called Treaty of Rome. The treaty established the common market where goods, services, capital, and workers would be able to move freely. This stems from an economic logic of benefits achieved with deeper economic integration, so that in addition to the abolition of custom duties and quantitative restrictions between Member States and the establishment of common customs rules vis-a-vis third countries, the free movement of production resources (i.e., services, workers, and capital) would be achieved.[1] The prevalent aim of this was to create the common market, which is the aim that the CJEU initially used in the interpretation of these rules. There were, however, significant obstacles for moving for people, so that only very few actually used these rights.

Barnard identifies different sets of obstacles that were present in the early days of the EEC. These were social (not wanting to move without their families), economic (fear of losing pensions in their home state), cultural (familiarity and comfort with life in their own Member States), and linguistic (lack of language skills).[2] There were a number of secondary law instruments that were designed to overcome these problems, which Barnard claims was the start of an erosion of the link between economic activity and free movement rights.[3] This assessment can be agreed with; it was yet another example of Jean Monnet's well-known spill-over effect.

In 1987, the Single European Act introduced the concept of the single market and the idea that by the end of 1992, an internal market should be created, with the abolishment of further legal and technical barriers in the Community. In Maastricht, a step further was taken with the introduction of the Treaty of European Union, which became effective from 1993. The Treaty of Maastricht introduced the

---

[1] Barnard (2010), pp. 3–30.

[2] Ibid., p. 224.

[3] Ibid., p. 224.

concept of European Union citizenship, which included an inherent right of free movement in the EU. Although a major step towards deeper integration, the free movement rights were still subject to limitations and restrictions, so that the concept of EU citizenship did not mean a lot in practical terms. The area of freedom, security, and justice was subsequently introduced, matters related to residence were transferred from third pillar to Community pillar with the Treaty of Amsterdam, and the concept of citizenship-related free movement rights was strengthened.

The adoption of EU citizens free movement directive in 2004,[4] which replaced a number of previous directives and codified some of the CJEU case law in the area of free movement, was not a major innovation. It, however, remains an important piece of legislation in the area. The Directive follows the logic that those EU citizens and their family members who are economically active and migrate have strong legal basis to access and obtain residence rights in another EU member state.

With the Treaty of Lisbon, no major innovations were undertaken in the area of citizenship. The Charter of Fundamental Rights includes the same free movement provisions as TFEU itself. With the Charter, however, not extending any powers or competences of the Union, it is questionable whether there is any further progress at all in this regard in terms of the Treaty of Lisbon. Therefore, the current state of integration supports the grouping of individuals in terms of rights of residence in other MS based on their status as a worker, family member of a worker, jobseeker, self-employed person, student, or other EU citizen.

The CJEU case law on free movement rights has evolved to support at least limited rights for people who are not economically active coming from their EU citizenship. This has been criticised, as this expansion does not have sufficient connection with the aims of the treaty and makes the issue of reverse discrimination more pronounced.[5] Davies points out that with the strict application of Article 18 TFEU, the CJEU has made national citizenship rather irrelevant.[6] Jacobs distinguishes different stages of CJEU techniques: first, citizenship was used to broaden the scope of the non-discrimination principle; second, it was used to further broaden the scope of the non-discrimination principle in the context of market freedoms; and finally, it started to use citizenship as an independent source of rights.[7]

The main differentiating factor is whether the persons are economically active or not. According to Directive 2004/38/EC, all EU citizens have the right to remain in a Member State for three months, but for residence longer than 3 months, they will

---

[4] Directive 2004/38/EC of the European Parliament and of the Council of 29 April 2004 on the right of citizens of the Union and their family members to move and reside freely within the territory of the Member States amending Regulation (EEC) No 1612/68 and repealing Directives 64/221/EEC, 68/360/EEC, 72/194/EEC, 73/148/EEC, 75/34/EEC, 75/35/EEC, 90/364/EEC, 90/365/EEC and 93/96/EEC, Official Journal L 158, 30.4.2004, pp. 77–123.

[5] Tryfonidou (2009), pp. 1616–1617.

[6] Davies (2005), pp. 43–56.

[7] Jacobs (2007), p. 593.

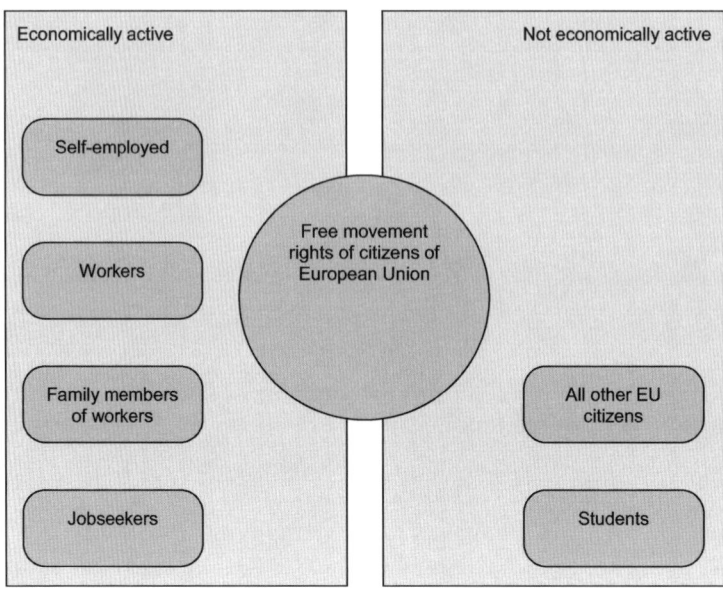

Fig. 1 Classification of EU citizens based on their economic status

be treated differently according to their status in that country. That status is connected with the state of economic activity and, as more recently developed by the CJEU, level of integration in the host member state (Fig. 1). The differences are even more pronounced when considering the issues of equal treatment in social matters. The worker as the most protected economically active EU migrant has full rights not to be directly or indirectly discriminated against in social matters based on Regulation 492/2011,[8] which recently replaced Regulation 1612/68.[9] This has moved beyond simple non-discrimination matters, but workers sometimes have to be guaranteed even more favourable treatment as host state citizens.[10] Any justifications for obstacles for free movement of workers have to fulfil a strict proportionality test. Other categories enjoy significantly lower protections, as demonstrated in Table 1.

This system is remarkably different from the US, where there is a federal citizenship and everyone has the right to freely move to start anew in a new State even if he/she lacks the resources to support himself/herself initially.[11] The

---

[8] Regulation (EU) No 492/2011 of the European Parliament and of the Council of 5 April 2011 on freedom of movement for workers within the Union, Official Journal L 141-1, 27.05.2011, pp. 1–12.

[9] Regulation (EEC) No 1612/68 of the Council of 15 October 1968 on freedom of movement for workers within the Community, Official Journal L 257, 19.10.1968, pp. 2–12.

[10] Known as the concept of reverse discrimination. See Barnard (2010), pp. 230–232.

[11] Strumia (2005–2006), pp. 727–736.

Table 1 Residence and equality rights in matters of social benefits of migrants who are EU citizens

Category	Right of access to the MS (residence and fees)	Right to receive social benefits on equal terms with nationals
Workers	Full rights, based on Article 45 TFEU and secondary legislation, mostly Directive 2004/38	Full rights, based on Article 45 TFEU and secondary legislation, specifically Regulation 492/2011
Family members of workers	Rights initially dependent on workers and secondary legislation, mostly Directive 2004/38	Rights initially dependent on workers and secondary legislation, specifically Regulation 492/2011
Self-employed	Full rights, based on Article 49 TFEU and secondary legislation, mostly Directive 2004/38	Some rights, based on Article 49 TFEU
Jobseekers	Limited rights, based on Article 45 TFEU and secondary legislation, mostly Directive 2004/38	Rights dependent on the level of integration and on the fact that the person has previously worked in the MS
Students	Rights dependent on declaration of sufficient resources not to burden the social system and having been accepted to an accredited educational establishment, based on Article 21(1) TFEU and secondary legislation, such as Directive 2004/38	Initially no rights, dependent on level of integration in the society demonstrated by length of stay, additional rights as recipients of services; health care rights divergent from MS to MS
All other citizens	Rights dependent on ability to demonstrate sufficient resources not to burden the social system, based on Article 21(1) TFEU and secondary legislation, Directive 2004/38	Initially no rights, dependent on level of integration in the society demonstrated by length of stay, additional rights as recipients of services

American judicial concept of the right to travel is based on a deep-rooted ideology of "a new beginning" that is missing from the EU framework, which rewards with free movement rights only those who are either able immediately or within a short period of time to economically contribute to the new host member state with their labour or those who have sufficient resources to support themselves so much as not to become a burden to the social system of host member state. This divergence in approaches can, of course, be explained by the different concepts of citizenship in a US federal or Union level. When there is little EU-wide social security scheme and social benefits and taxes are left upon Member States, it makes no sense for individual Member States to provide social benefits in an equal amount to both their own nationals and any migrants from other EU member states. It can be questioned if and for how long the lack of rights remains sustainable, especially with the increased benefits mobility of not economically active people bring, as well as whether this supports development of European unity. It is also unfortunate that there is a classification of EU citizens based on the economic status.

Students represent a most interesting category within this classification. Although they are mostly not economically active yet, they have the potential of becoming economically active and contributing to the economy of the host or home Member State. This makes it conceptually more difficult to restrict the students' rights of access to residence or social benefits, especially regarding the importance that is put on student mobility, which should support the quality of higher education in Europe.

It is also clear from the statistical data that many of the students work while studying.[12] This means their status as students might at times be overlapped by their status as a worker, which further complicates matters, especially when the work is not continuous. In terms of the free movement of workers, students might have difficulties proving that the work they did in addition to being full time student is effective and genuine work and not purely marginal and ancillary.[13] Indeed, initially the main focus of early academic literature on the subject included the possibility that students should be treated akin to workers.[14]

2.1 Higher Education and EU Law: Soft Measures Without EU Harmonisation

Education has not always held an important place in the EU context. Cooperation at the EU level started on an economic level; matters relating to education were originally firmly outside of EU competence, along with topics such as culture; and coordination of anything in this sphere was a purely intergovernmental exercise. It is difficult to tell why education was so unconnected from the area of economic integration, but it could be attributed to the development of the economy as a whole at the time of the drafting of the Treaties (mostly low-skilled and not so much related to services), as well as the low level of European integration, which meant that it was relatively uncommon to study in another country. One could also speculate that this was because education not only is a provider of skills and knowledge for economic purposes but also serves other societal needs such as developing patriotic, religious, cultural, and other values. Supranational regulation in the sphere of education would have meant that the Member States lose, at least partially, tools in creating and preserving their national identity. This argumentation might be valid for the area of primary or secondary education, but it is questionable whether this also applies for a quality tertiary education today.

It is important to distinguish between different aspects of EU law in higher education. In 1976, there was a Ministers of Education meeting within the Council and the Council adopted a Resolution to undertake an action programme in the field

---

[12] Orr et al.

[13] Case 53/81, *D.M. Levin v Staatssecretaris van Justitie*, [1982] ECR 1035.

[14] See, for example, De Witte (1989), p. 77.

of education.[15] The fact that Council was involved, in addition to the ministers, was remarkable because it shows that there had been an understanding that education is something where there is a role to be played by the Community as well.[16] However, this understanding did not translate into any substantive legislation using the Community legal framework,[17] nor was there substantive coordination in educational policies within the EEC member states. Gori believes that this was most probably due to the fact that Member States realised that there was a risk to their education systems from Community action even in limited areas and wanted to prevent this from happening.[18]

In the negotiations leading to the Treaty on European Union, there emerged a divide between Member States and the Commission regarding Community role in education.[19] The Commission saw education and vocational training through an economic prism, as an indispensable tool to achieve competitiveness of European economy by providing high-quality, mobile, and skilled workforce. For this, it needed clear and enforceable laws to overcome the protectionism of national educational systems.

On the other hand, Member States entered the negotiations with the clear aim of limiting the expansive interpretation of the competences of EU law in the area of education by the CJEU (to be discussed below). They contested the definition of higher education as vocational training and wanted to clearly delimit where EU competence ends, even by overruling existing case law of the CJEU by way of Treaty amendment.[20] This fact speaks volumes about how central education, including higher education, was for the sovereignty of Member States and how they did not envisage a great role for supranational regulation in this area.

Therefore, it was clear that Commission and Member States wanted to see education in the treaties, but for opposing reasons: the Commission wanted to get a strong legal basis to propose harmonisation legislation, and the Member States wanted to see clear limits in what they perceived as a sort of "competence creep" by the EU dealing with educational matters that they had not delegated to it. The wording of Article 165 (ex article 149 ECT) is the one that also remains applicable today: although it foresees a role for the EU in higher education, bringing it into the

---

[15] Resolution of the Council and of the Ministers for education meeting within the Council of 9/2/76 comprising an action programme in the field of education, OJ C 38 of 19 February 1976.

[16] Gori (2001), p. 20.

[17] With the single exception of Directive 77/486 on the education of children of migrant workers.

[18] Gori (2001), p. 21.

[19] Ibid., pp. 55–71.

[20] Ibid., p. 63.

scope of the Treaties, it clearly prohibits harmonisation of legislation in the area.[21] The following article on vocational training is almost identical and also excludes any possibility of harmonisation of laws of Member States.

Having achieved their goal of stopping any EU-led harmonisation in higher education for the foreseeable future, European states suddenly in the end of the 1990s embarked on their own massive reform and harmonisation of European higher education through what is now known as the Bologna Process. Totally intergovernmental and outside of the EU in its nature, it has had a huge impact in European higher education (including all Member States of the EU).

Therefore, it can be concluded that although the Commission has repeatedly tried with the support of the CJEU to expand EU political and legislative competence in the field of education, this has not been very successful and, in terms of policymaking and legislation, Member States are firmly in the driver's seat. However, the CJEU has been reluctant to "let go" of the area of education and has used

---

[21] The current wording of Article 165 TFEU is as follows: "1. The Union shall contribute to the development of quality education by encouraging cooperation between Member States and, if necessary, by supporting and supplementing their action, while fully respecting the responsibility of the Member States for the content of teaching and the organisation of education systems and their cultural and linguistic diversity.

The Union shall contribute to the promotion of European sporting issues, while taking account of the specific nature of sport, its structures based on voluntary activity and its social and educational function.

2. Union action shall be aimed at:

— developing the European dimension in education, particularly through the teaching and dissemination of the languages of the Member States,

— encouraging mobility of students and teachers, by encouraging inter alia, the academic recognition of diplomas and periods of study,

— promoting cooperation between educational establishments,

— developing exchanges of information and experience on issues common to the education systems of the Member States,

— encouraging the development of youth exchanges and of exchanges of socio-educational instructors, and encouraging the participation of young people in democratic life in Europe,

— encouraging the development of distance education,

— developing the European dimension in sport, by promoting fairness and openness in sporting competitions and cooperation between bodies responsible for sports, and by protecting the physical and moral integrity of sportsmen and sportswomen, especially the youngest sportsmen and sportswomen.

3. The Union and the Member States shall foster cooperation with third countries and the competent international organisations in the field of education and sport, in particular the Council of Europe.

4. In order to contribute to the achievement of the objectives referred to in this Article:

— the European Parliament and the Council, acting in accordance with the ordinary legislative procedure, after consulting the Economic and Social Committee and the Committee of the Regions, shall adopt incentive measures, excluding any harmonisation of the laws and regulations of the Member States,

— the Council, on a proposal from the Commission, shall adopt recommendations."

existing EU competences to define new rights for individuals in the area based on the cases it has been asked to adjudicate.[22]

3 Right to Education as a Human Right

As social rights gain more prominence, it is increasingly important to look at the right to education as a social human right. Although the human rights framework does not include a right to access to education in another country, issues related to human rights are still important to consider when discussing issues related to access to education and social benefits.

The European Convention of Human Rights protects the right to education. Article 2 of Protocol 1 to the Convention states:

> No person shall be denied the right to education. In the exercise of any functions which it assumes in relation to education and to teaching, the State shall respect the right of parents to ensure such education and teaching in conformity with their own religious and philosophical convictions.[23]

This, combined with Article 14 on non-discrimination, provides a tool to consider discrimination in the provision of education. However, the ECtHR has refused to interpret the Convention and its protocols in a way that would protect the rights of migrant students to reside in another country.[24] It clarified that the right of access is guaranteed by the Convention only after the right of education is already provided to foreigners by national rules. States are also entitled to regulate and limit access as they see fit even when the matter falls within the jurisdiction of the Convention.[25] Therefore, practices such as *numerus clausus* systems or admission examinations are perfectly compatible with Article 2 of Protocol 1. Gori claims that even though limited in nature, the Convention as an international law instrument has had the strongest impact in the area of education.[26] However, that impact has limited relevance in the framework of the issues considered in this thesis due to fact that the rights of migrant students are not well protected. As the thesis is not

---

[22] For a complete overview, see Käsper and Kerikmäe (2012), pp. 399–413.

[23] Article 2 of Protocol to the Convention for the Protection of Human Rights and Fundamental Freedoms of 20 March 1952, available on the Internet at http://www.echr.coe.int/NR/rdonlyres/D5CC24A7-DC13-4318-B457-5C9014916D7A/0/CONVENTION_ENG_WEB.pdf, last accessed 12 May 2012.

[24] Application no 7671/76 and 14 other applications, Decision of the Commission of the Convention on the Admissibility of the Applications, 15 Foreign Students vs The United Kingdom, 19 May 1977, available on the Internet at http://cmiskp.echr.coe.int/tkp197/view.asp?action=open&documentId=804246&portal=hbkm&source=externalbydocnumber&table=F69A27FD8FB86142BF01C1166DEA398649, last accessed 12 May 2012.

[25] Gori (2001), p. 371.

[26] Ibid., p. 376.

focusing on access to higher education in general, it is not necessary to consider the case law of the ECHR in this context further.

The Charter of Fundamental Rights has a certain political and legal significance because the issues related to access to education for EU migrant students concern the application of EU law in the area. The Charter includes several rights that touch upon the area of mobile students. Article 14 of the Charter proclaims that "[e] veryone has the right to education and to have access to vocational and continuing training".[27] The latest implementation report of the Charter[28] does not unfortunately include any cases or activities related to the right to education, so there seems to be little impact in the area of education. The political impact of having the right to education mentioned in the Charter is important in itself because not all the social rights found their way into the Charter. The Charter also restates the existing prohibition of discrimination, which does not necessarily need to be strengthened.[29] Relevant articles also include Article 34, which proclaims that "Everyone residing and moving legally within the European Union is entitled to social security benefits and social advantages in accordance with Union law and national laws and practices"[30] and Article 45, which guarantees the right to move and reside freely within the territory of the Member States. When discussing the Charter and its impact, regard is to be had, however, on the limitation provided for in Article 51, which states that "The Charter does not extend the field of application of Union law beyond the powers of the Union or establish any new power or task for the Union, or modify powers and tasks as defined in the Treaties".[31]

3.1 Fighting Discrimination with Discrimination: Language-Based Differentiation as a Solution to Access to Education and Social Benefit Issues

One of the solutions that could be proposed is to take advantage of the already-existing natural barrier of language differences and allow Member States to limit benefits and privileged access to studies in the language of the Member States, with specific exceptions to those Member States that use the same language. When a

---

[27] Charter of Fundamental Rights of the European Union, Official Journal C 83, 30.3.2010, pp. 398–403.

[28] Commission Staff Working Document on the Application of the EU Charter of Fundamental Rights in 2011—Accompanying document to the Report from the Commission to the European Parliament, the Council, the European Economic and Social Committee and the Committee of the Regions—2011 Report on the Application of the EU Charter of Fundamental Rights, SWD(2012) 84 final, available on the Internet at http://eur-lex.europa.eu/LexUriServ/LexUriServ.do? uri=SWD:2012:0084:FIN:EN:PDF, last accessed 12 May 2012.

[29] Article 21 of the Charter of Fundamental Rights.

[30] Charter of Fundamental Rights.

[31] Ibid.

student is able to learn the language of the Member State, that should be sufficient to provide the student with equal access and benefits with nationals, as it would also show "certain degree of integration" or at least a great motivation at that. The language-based distinction would also support the notion of cultural diversity of the Europe and would allay fears of Member States that they would lose the use of their language in higher education.[32] It is also the most important "natural" barrier that will probably impact the choices of students for a long time.[33]

One should consider, however, whether such language-based barrier would not in itself amount to illegal discrimination according to EU law. EU law in the area of discrimination based on language is not a fully developed one. There have been several important decisions by the CJEU, but many gaps still remain in understanding where exactly to draw the line between the perceived need to preserve Europe's linguistic diversity and to essentially allow Member States to be protectionist of their languages and the wider goal of further economic and social integration in Europe while protecting the rights of EU economic migrants.

In order to consider whether language-based barriers for student mobility could be legal or illegal, one should look at other areas of EU law. There is very little case law on language requirements as barriers to free movement. The landmark case regarding EU law requirements regarding language is the controversial *Groener* case,[34] which concerned the issue of whether Ireland could require a citizen of another Member State to possess knowledge of the Irish language in order to teach at an English-speaking institution. Anita Groener, who had been teaching in a temporary capacity at an art college in Dublin, applied for a permanent position, in which it was required to have knowledge of the Irish language, although in her work she did not need to use it. The CJEU, surprisingly, allowed the requirement to stand without even considering it in the context of the free movement of workers. It was based on an expansive interpretation of Article 3 of Regulation 1612/68, which is in conflict with other interpretations of the Treaties, where the Court has been restrictive in allowing Member States to justify behaviour that disrupts the rights of migrant workers. Indeed, the CJEU in *Groener* refused to follow the grammatical interpretation of the Regulation, which had stated that the "provision shall not apply to conditions relating to linguistic knowledge required by reason of the nature of the post to be filled". In this case, knowledge of Irish was not required by the nature of the post, but the CJEU still found a way to consider the important role of the preservation of the Irish language and its connection to national identity. The Court said that "The EEC Treaty does not prohibit the adoption of a policy for the protection and promotion of a language of a Member State which is both the

---

[32] See Huisman and van der Wende (2004), p. 355 for a brief discussion on the issues related to impact of the greater acceptance of English as the *lingua franca* of higher education and its impact to different countries.

[33] Van der Mei (2005), p. 239.

[34] Case C-379/87, *Anita Groener v Minister for Education and the City of Dublin Vocational Educational Committee*, [1989] ECR 3967.

national language and the first official language".[35] However, Member States do not have an unlimited discretion in the manner. The CJEU warned:

> However, the implementation of such a policy must not encroach upon a fundamental freedom such as that of the free movement of workers. Therefore, the requirements deriving from measures intended to implement such a policy must not in any circumstances be disproportionate in relation to the aim pursued and the manner in which they are applied must not bring about discrimination against nationals of other Member States.[36]

The Court, however, went on to approve of the Irish measure:

> The importance of education for the implementation of such a policy must be recognized. Teachers have an essential role to play, not only through the teaching which they provide but also by their participation in the daily life of the school and the privileged relationship which they have with their pupils. In those circumstances, it is not unreasonable to require them to have some knowledge of the first national language.[37]

Creech claims that much of the opinion of the Court is open for serious questioning.[38] He also questions why the Court did not simply call it to fall under free movement of persons but then find it justified based on public policy, which would have been easier to do there, rather than using Regulation 1612/68, which did not include any public policy exception *per se*. Garben calls the decision "somewhat surprising".[39] It is indeed difficult to recognise that this was the same court that had shown little to no sensitivity regarding educational autonomy. Therefore, at least based on the *Groener* case, it could be said that language issues are considered to be by the court somewhat more sensitive than those relating to education. However, one should emphasise that the Court still felt that language issues fall within EU law and that any infringement of EU law that is justified by language policies must meet the Court's proportionality test. The application of such a test seems to be rather problematic because some people have questioned the Court's judgment regarding the fact that the proportionality test is met in the eyes of the Court in *Groener*, when looking at the factual situation in Ireland. Or as Creech puts it, "the theoretical, and remote, possibility that one day an Irish-speaking aspiring artist would wish to speak to Mrs. Groener in Irish does not seem sufficient to justify the infringement of Mrs. Groener's present and concrete Treaty-based right to work in the Emerald Isle". [40] He also wonders why a Dutch art teacher should be required to speak Irish in a place where it would likely never be used, when the President of Ireland who symbolically represents the entire country cannot effectively use it himself. The decision also contrasts with the approach taken by the

---

[35] Ibid., para. 19.

[36] Ibid., para. 19.

[37] Ibid., para. 20.

[38] Creech (2005), p. 103.

[39] Garben (2011), pp. 101–102.

[40] See Creech (2005), p. 104 ff.

Court against the promotion of domestic goods in the *Buy Irish* case,[41] which was decided earlier in 1982.

It is an open question whether the specific circumstances of the *Groener* case were limited to Ireland and the special status the Irish language has in that country or whether the judgment has real impact in other countries where there are different issues at work. The Court mentions the "special linguistic situation of Ireland" and refers to an officially bilingual situation, so Creech comments that the case might not apply at all in countries where there is only one official language.[42]

The *Groener* case differs also from the treatment France has received from the Commission in respect of its language laws relating to labelling of goods, where the Commission has been vigilant in trying to protect consumer interests rather than the French language.[43]

When considering the possible impact of ECHR case law to language-based discrimination, then the court has clarified this not to mean that there is right to be educated in any language of their choice.[44] Therefore, one could assume that a restriction based on language might not be considered a form of indirect discrimination based on nationality, or, alternatively, if it is considered to be discriminatory, it could be justified on the basis of the need to preserve national identity and cultural heritage.

The counter-arguments to such an approach are also strong. It would not support the idea of European unity, as it would reinforce any existing and problematic language barriers. The issue of how to compensate influx of students to countries that use languages that are widely spoken, such as the UK, Germany, or France, will arise. The risks are bound to be high with such an approach, as well as the possibility that this approach could be adopted in other areas of the EU, which might not be desirable for further integration purposes.

4 Conclusion

The article looked at only a very narrow set of issues related to free movement of students and their rights from a human rights perspective. First, different categories of EU citizens were described and compared vis-à-vis their rights as migrants in another EU Member State. Second, students as a special category was distinguished and issues of both access to education and access to social benefits were covered. The paper also looked at possibilities to create human-rights-based arguments for

---

[41] Case 249/81, *Commission of the European Communities v Ireland*, [1982] ECR 4005.

[42] Creech (2005), p. 107.

[43] See the discussion in Creech (2005), pp. 107–109. See also the detailed analysis of the French Toubon law in Feld (1998), pp. 153–202.

[44] Gori (2001), p. 369.

migrants to receive rights in another Member State, but it was concluded that existing rights are rather weak in this regard. Also, a special circumstance of linguistic discrimination was analysed as a potential barrier for free movement of students, concluding that the picture is not so clear.

It can be concluded that the area of free movement rights for students and, more generally, the area of education and related rights are still under intense debate in the EU. As can be seen from the above analysis, not much is certain and the Charter of Fundamental Rights has not (yet?) provided tools to clarify the situation. At the same time, issues related to education are becoming more and more important for the EU to tackle as a whole. It would be interesting to see more activity on behalf of the Luxembourg court in this area, including shift from economic arguments to more fundamental-rights-based ones.

Further, research is needed in the area of education regulation in the European Union level, both in terms of social benefits issues and issues relating to tuition fees and access. The area of higher education is fundamental for the success or failure of the European integration project. Thus, more clarity and detail are necessary in rules that govern free movement of students. Provided that the CJEU is willing to follow this route, fundamental-rights-based challenges to barriers could form a new path forward in this matter.

References

Books and Articles

Barnard C (2010) The substantive law of the EU: the four freedoms, 3rd edn. Oxford University Press, Oxford, pp 3–30

Creech RL (2005) Law and language in the European Union: the paradox of a Babel "United in Diversity". Europa Law Publishing, Groningen

Davies G (2005) 'Any Place I Hang My Hat?' or: residence is the new nationality. Eur Law J 11 (1):43–56

De Witte B (1989) Educational equality for community workers and their families. In: De Witte B (ed) The European Community Law of Education. Nomos, Baden Baden

Feld SA (1998) Language and the globalization of the economic market: the regulation of language as a Barrier to Free Trade. Vanderbilt J Transnatl Law 31:150–202

Garben S (2011) EU Higher Education Law: the bologna process and harmonization by stealth, European Monographs Series Set, Kluwer Law International, Alphen aan den Rijn/ Frederick

Gori G (2001) Towards an EU right to education. Kluwer Law International, The Hague

Huisman J, van der Wende M (eds) (2004) On cooperation and competition. National and European Policies for the Internationalisation of Higher Education. ACA Papers on International Cooperation in Education. Lemmens, Bonn

Jacobs FG (2007) Citizenship of the European Union – a legal analysis. Eur Law J 13(5):591–610

Käsper K, Kerikmäe T (2012) Access to higher education in the EU: evolving case law of the CJEU. Eur J Law Reform 14(4):399–413

Strumia F (2005–2006) Citizenship and free movement: European and American features of a judicial formula for increased comity. Columbia J Eur Law 1:727–736

Tryfonidou A (2009) In search of the aim of the EC free movement of persons provisions: has the Court of Justice missed the point? Common Market Law Rev 46:1616–1617

Van der Mei AP (2005) EU Law and education: promotion of student mobility versus protection of education systems. In: Dougan M, Spaventa E (eds) Social welfare and EU Law, Essays in European Law. Hart Publishing, Oxford

Official Material

Charter of Fundamental Rights of the European Union

Directive 2004/38/EC of the European Parliament and of the Council on the right of citizens of the Union and their family members to move and reside freely within the territory of the Member States amending Regulation (EEC) No 1612/68 and repealing Directives 64/221/EEC, 68/360/EEC, 72/194/EEC, 73/148/EEC, 75/34/EEC, 75/35/EEC, 90/364/EEC, 90/365/EEC and 93/96/EEC

Regulation (EU) No 492/2011 of the European Parliament and of the Council on freedom of movement for workers within the Union

Regulation (EEC) No 1612/68 of the Council on freedom of movement for workers within the Community

Resolution of the Council and of the Ministers for education meeting within the Council of 9/2/76 comprising an action programme in the field of education (19 February 1976)

Article 2 of Protocol to the Convention for the Protection of Human Rights and Fundamental Freedoms (20 March 1952)

Application no 7671/76 and 14 other applications, Decision of the Commission of the Convention on the Admissibility of the Applications, 15 Foreign Students v. The United Kingdom (19 May 1977)

Commission Staff Working Document on the Application of the EU Charter of Fundamental Rights in 2011 - Accompanying document to the Report from the Commission to the European Parliament, the Council, the European Economic and Social Committee and the Committee of the Regions – 2011 Report on the Application of the EU Charter of Fundamental Rights, SWD (2012) 84 final

Case Law

European Court of Justice

Case 53/81 *D.M. Levin v Staatssecretaris van Justitie* (23 March 1982)

Case 249/81, *Commission of the European Communities v Ireland* (24 November 1982)

Case C-379/87*Anita Groener v Minister for Education and the City of Dublin Vocational Educational Committee* (28 November 1989)

Fundamental Rights of Athletes in the EU Post-Lisbon

Katarina Pijetlovic

1 Introduction

Whereas sport is not the first thing that springs to mind in the context of fundamental rights, the interaction between the two fields is a dynamic one. Sporting federations are monopolistic self-governing bodies possessing a degree and scope of regulatory latitude unmatched by any private entity in other industries. The boundaries of legal control of these entities have always presented a policy problem for both Member States and the EU institutions. On the one hand, the right of sport to self-govern is widely acknowledged in the EU policy documents; on the other, the exercise of such high degree of autonomy has global impact and often results in breaches of law, including fundamental rights of sportspersons. In such events, athletes may turn to the internal dispute-settling bodies established by the federations in charge of their sporting discipline. In case of negative outcome, they may appeal to the Court of Arbitration for Sport, whose decisions are reviewable only on very limited basis by the Swiss Federal Tribunal. It is therefore of utmost importance that the principles of fair trial, now enshrined in Article 47 of the Charter of Fundamental Rights of the EU ("the Charter") in the system of distribution of sporting justice are observed. As shall be illustrated, this is often not the case. For example, there is a serious failure to comply with the fair trial guarantees before some of the sports dispute-settlement bodies in the prosecution of corruption offences, as well as with Article 49(3) of the Charter, which provides for the proportionality of criminal penalties. The recourse to the ordinary courts is excluded by the standard consent agreements that athletes sign in the beginning of each season, and the signing of which is a precondition for participation in the competitions. As the European social dialogue process in sports is still in its infancy, the athletes in many sporting disciplines neither have the opportunity

K. Pijetlovic (✉)
Tallinn Law School, Tallinn University of Technology, Akadeemia tee 3, 12618 Tallinn, Estonia
e-mail: Katarina.Pijetlovic@ttu.ee

T. Kerikmäe (ed.), *Protecting Human Rights in the EU*,
DOI 10.1007/978-3-642-38902-3_10, © Springer-Verlag Berlin Heidelberg 2014

and proper representation to negotiate the terms of such agreements, nor can they otherwise affect their content. Moreover, the provisions and the implementation of the World Anti-Doping Code (WADC) adopted by the World Anti-Doping Agency (WADA), which is applicable virtually across all sporting disciplines, entail a number of concerns regarding athletes' rights to privacy and the right to rest, i.e., Articles 7 and 31 of the Charter, respectively.

This chapter addresses the outlined issues and argues for the application of the Charter to the rules and practices of the sport-governing bodies due to their monopolistic state-like competences, as well as the scope of their regulatory authority. The sports-related jurisprudence in the EU thus far revolved around the economic rights of athletes under the internal market and competition provisions. *The key point made by this contribution is that the Charter can be used in the familiar analytical framework devised for the regulatory rules in sport under those provisions to support and supplement athletes' economic arguments and counter-balance the reliance on Article 165 TFEU concept of "specificity of sport" by the governing bodies seeking to justify their restrictive measures.* In order to illustrate the real-life issues, we will refer to the regulation of tennis, the most popular individual sport in the world.

2 EU Sports Competences and Institutional Structures

Since 1997, Directorate-General for Education and Culture of the European Commission has included the Sport Unit,[1] which is responsible for cooperation within the Commission and with other EU institutions on sport-related issues, cooperation and meetings with national and international sports institutions, organisations, and federations. Following the entry into force of the Lisbon Treaty, the Ministers responsible for sport of the 27 EU Member States can now meet in the formal setting of the Council.[2] In its role as interpreter of the EU law, the Court of Justice of the European Union (the Court) played a central role in the interpretation of the existing economic provisions in the sporting context.[3]

---

[1] http://ec.europa.eu/sport/index_en.htm.

[2] For example, there was a meeting of EU Sports Directors in Genval on 16–17 September 2010. See http://ec.europa.eu/sport/consultation-cooperation/co-operation-with-the-member-states_en.htm.

[3] See, e.g., cases such as Case 36/74 *Walrave and Koch v. Union Cycliste Internationale and others* [1974] ECR 1405; Case 13/76 *Gaetano Donà v. Mario Mantero* [1976] ECR 1333; Case C-415/93 *Union Royale Belge Sociétés de Football Association and others v. Bosman and others* [1995] ECR I-4921; Joined Cases C-51/96 and C-191/97 *Christelle Deliège v. Ligue francophone de judo et disciplines associées ASBL, Ligue belge de judo ASBL, Union européenne de judo and François Pacquée* [2000] ECR I-2549; Case C-176/96 *Jyri Lehtonen and Castors Canada Dry Namur-Braine ASBL v. Fédération royale belge des sociétés de basket-ball ASBL (FRBSB)* [2000] ECR I-2681; Case C-325/08 *Olympique Lyonnais SASP v. Olivier Bernard and Newcastle United FC*

Until the entry into force of the Lisbon Treaty on 1 December 2009, the EU did not have direct legislative competence to regulate sport. The traditional instruments were (and still are) therefore essential to protect the core objectives of the Union when the rules and activities of sporting bodies obstruct the functioning of internal market and distort competition. These include the TFEU rules on competition (Articles 101 and 102 TFEU), rules on freedom of movement for workers (Articles 45–48 TFEU), self-employed (Articles 49–55 TFEU), and freedom to provide services (Articles 56–62 TFEU).

Article 165(1) TFEU, included under Title XII on Education, Vocational Training, Youth and Sport, states that "[t]he Union shall contribute to the promotion of European sporting issues, while taking account of the *specific nature of sport*, its structures based on voluntary activity and its *social and educational function*" [emphasis added]. According to Article 165(2), "Union action shall be aimed at: [. . .] developing the European dimension in sport, by promoting fairness and openness in sporting competitions and cooperation between bodies responsible for sports, and by *protecting the physical and moral integrity of sportsmen and sportswomen, especially the youngest sportsmen and sportswomen*". Unlike the primary law provisions on, for example, fundamental rights and environmental protection, Article 165 TFEU does not contain a horizontal clause.

Article 2(5) TFEU in combination with Article 6 TFEU gives the Union a competence to carry out actions that support, coordinate, or supplement the actions of the Member States in the area of sport and that do not entail harmonisation of the Member States' laws or regulations. However, the examination of the equivalent past prohibitions of harmonisation and their treatment by the Court[4] suggests that harmonising measures can be taken as long as they are nominally based on another Treaty competence and convergence can be achieved in practice by using other legal basis to pass the harmonising legislation.[5] This indicates the possibility for the fundamental rights of athletes to be protected via, for instance, legislation facilitating their free movement in their capacity as service providers or employed persons.

3 Sport and Fundamental Rights

Access to sport on a non-discriminatory basis is considered by some academics as an emerging human right.[6] It has been recognised as such under Fundamental Principles of International Olympic Committee's Olympic Charter,[7] which states

---

judgment of grand Chamber of the Court delivered on 16 March 2010; and Case C-519/04 *David Meca-Medina and Igor Majcen v. Commission* [2006] ECR I-6991.

[4] Such as in the fields of social policy, education, vocational training, culture, and public health.

[5] See the European Parliament, Directorate-General for Internal Policies, Study on the Lisbon Treaty and EU Sports Policy (2010), p. 13.

[6] See, e.g., Brems and Lavrysen (2012), p. 228.

[7] http://www.olympic.org/Documents/olympic_charter_en.pdf.

that *"[t]he practice of sport is a human right. Every individual must have the possibility of practising sport, without discrimination of any kind [...]"*. Article 13 of the UN Convention on the Elimination of Discrimination against Women,[8] which has been signed by all EU Member States, lists the right to participate in sport on a non-discriminatory basis as one of the social rights. Article 1 of the UNESCO International Charter of Physical Education and Sport (1978)[9] provides that *"[e]very human being has a fundamental right of access to physical education and sport*, which are essential for the full development of his personality. The freedom to develop physical, intellectual and moral powers through physical education and sport must be guaranteed both within the educational system and in other aspects of social life." Article 30(5) of the UN Convention on the Rights of Persons with Disabilities,[10] of which both the EU and its Member States are signatories, includes the obligation to take appropriate measures to ensure the rights of persons with disabilities to participate on an equal basis with others in sporting activities. Whether or not sport can be considered as a fundamental right still remains a controversial topic. However, an issue that is free of any controversy is that sport has given rise to numerous human rights concerns. Some of the most notorious examples involve human trafficking, in particular, of young football players from Africa to Europe[11]; negative impact of sporting mega-events (such as Olympic Games and FIFA World Cup) on housing of disadvantaged groups in the society and their displacement in order to build the necessary infrastructure[12]; and various discriminatory practices such as prohibition on women to compete in certain sporting disciplines[13] and different treatment of trans-genders and homosexuals.[14] The list goes on.

There has never been the case before the Court and the Commission dealing with fundamental rights of athletes. Similarly, the topic is not very conspicuous among EU sports law academics, and there are no academic texts available on the Charter in the sporting context. There is no available study in the EU in the field of human rights and sport to date. The Commission's Strategy for Equality between Women

---

[8] http://www.un.org/womenwatch/daw/cedaw/text/econvention.htm.

[9] http://unesdoc.unesco.org/images/0021/002164/216489E.pdf.

[10] http://www.un.org/disabilities/convention/conventionfull.shtml.

[11] See, e.g., Backe Madsen and Johansson (2008).

[12] See, e.g., Morel (2012), pp. 229–259.

[13] See, e.g., the speech by Annette Hofmann at Play the Game conference in Cologne "Women Challenge the IOC in Court: The Case of Ski Jumping" 5 October 2011, and BBC News "Women Fight Olympic Ski Jump Ban" 21 April 2009.

[14] See the speeches at Parallel Session on Transgender Challenges at Play the Game conference in Cologne, 5 October 2011, and P. Griffin "Inclusion of Transgender Athletes on Sport Teams" available at http://www.transgenderlaw.org/resources/Griffinarticle.pdf.

and Men 2010–2015 is set out, *inter alia*, to encourage the mainstreaming of gender issues into sport-related activities.[15] The statistics suggest that the number of women in leadership positions in sport is alarmingly low. In its research on racism, discrimination, and exclusion in sport, the EU Agency for Fundamental Rights found that that despite significant progress made in the past years, incidences of racism and ethnic discrimination affect sport at professional as well as amateur levels.[16]

Despite the inadequate efforts at the EU policy level, it must be emphasised that the main responsibility for organisation and promotion of sport, as well as for any sporting rule and practice giving rise to violation of fundamental rights, remains exclusively with the sport-governing bodies. They possess a high degree of discretion in the performance of their central roles and enjoy monopolistic position regarding regulation and organisation of their respective disciplines, as shall be explained next.

4 Sport-Governing Bodies as Addressees Under the Charter

According to Article 51 of the Charter, the circle of addressees includes the institutions, offices, and agencies of the Union, with due regard to the principle of subsidiarity, and Member States when they are implementing EU law. The provisions of the Charter do not extend the field of application of Union law, and therefore a party cannot successfully invoke its provisions where the measure or action being challenged falls outside the scope of Union law. In addition, the Charter does not have *direct* horizontal effect and is formally addressed to the actions of public authorities.[17]

In contrast to the rules and practices that can be attributed to public authorities, sporting rules and practices emanate from actions of private entities. International sports associations are normally registered in the commercial register in accordance with the law of the country of incorporation. However, regardless of such formal status, there is perhaps no other economic sector in which private bodies have the same scope of regulatory latitude as in sports sector[18] and within which they

---

[15] Communication from the Commission to the European Parliament, the Council, the European Economic and Social Committee and the Committee of the Regions of 21 September 2010—Strategy for equality between women and men 2010–2015 [COM(2010) 491, final].

[16] European Union Agency for Fundamental Rights "Racism, ethnic discrimination and exclusion of migrants and minorities in sport: a comparative overview of the situation in the European Union", October 2010. Available at http://fra.europa.eu/sites/default/files/fra_uploads/1207-Report-racism-sport_EN.pdf.

[17] For indirect horizontal effect of the Charter see De Mol (2012), pp. 280–303; Safjan and Miklaszewicz (2008), pp. 475–486; and Papadopoulous (2011), pp. 437–447.

[18] Para. 3.7 of the J.L. Arnaut, *Independent European Sport Review* (2006).

constructed what legal anthropologists would refer to as a semi-autonomous social filed.[19] Sporting authorities rely on commercial sponsorship and sales of broadcasting rights to sporting events rather than state funding and thus have a high degree of financial autonomy. In terms of political autonomy, many Member States have expressly delegated public authority to their national sport bodies.[20]

In addition, some sporting bodies are powerful participants in the global affairs, and their influence should not be underestimated: for example, Fédération Internationale de Football Association (FIFA) has direct contacts with many heads of State from its Swiss headquarters, while the International Olympic Committee (IOC) has been granted the observer status at the United Nations. Nevertheless, the autonomy of these bodies is not unlimited, and the sporting industry has relatively recently in the history undergone the process of juridification.[21] In its 2007 White Paper on Sport, the European Commission emphasised that "most challenges can be addressed through self-regulation respectful of good governance principles, *provided that EU law is respected*".[22] Also in various other EU sports policy documents, the right to self-govern is conditional upon respect for EU law.[23] Although the autonomy was initially self-proclaimed, subsequently it became a matter of express or implicit delegation of competence by public to private bodies to regulate themselves within the confines of the law. In terms of their substantive powers, the true legal status of sport-governing bodies can be found on the equilibrium between private and public authorities.

Furthermore, a classic European sport model is based on a pyramid structure where only one federation per country and per discipline can be a member of the European and global governing body that are at the apex of the pyramid.[24] The "one-federation-per-sport" structure reveals the apparent monopolistic position of the governing bodies. They pass the rules and regulations specifying the procedures for prosecuting various sporting offences and imposing disciplinary sanctions that in turn affect the athlete's livelihood and sometimes permanently terminate their careers, they determine the athlete selection criteria for certain competitions, and they rule every other aspect of their discipline, claiming unfettered competences

---

[19] See, e.g., Greenfield and Osborn (2004), p. 171.

[20] Germany is the extreme example as national sports organisations enjoy a very high degree of autonomy, the federal and Länder governments having delegated policymaking in the field of sport to them.

[21] A term used to describe the process by which sport leaves the safe zone of internal self-regulation and becomes a subject to ordinary laws. Under this process, "what were intrinsically social relationships between humans within a 'social field' become imbued with legal values and are understood as constituting legal relationships – thus social norms become legal norms". See Gardiner et al. (2005), pp. 84–88.

[22] European Commission White Paper on Sport, COM(2007) 391 final, para. 4 [emphasis added].

[23] Notably in Communication from the Commission to the European Parliament, the Council, the European Economic and Social Committee, and the Committee of the Regions "Developing the European Dimension in Sport" COM(2011) 12 final, 18. 1. 2011.

[24] European Model of Sport, Consultation Document of DG X, European Commission.

relating to doping, corruption, exception from normal labour laws, etc. The impact that these regulations have on the sportspersons is no different than the impact of formal laws passed by the states. In addition, they are far reaching in their scope as, when passed by the international federations, they apply globally to all the athletes and regulate in a collective manner every aspect of their professional lives and often some aspects of their private lives. Because international sporting federations possess state-like competences whose regulatory effect is equivalent to those of state action, the question of the accountability for violations of law and the fundamental rights, in particular, is a pressing one.[25]

It is submitted that sports-governing bodies, due to their specific nature, global influence, and vast regulatory competence, ought to be considered as addressees under the Charter. This proposition is assisted by two distinct facts: first, the Court normally applies functional rather than formalistic approach in its teleological interpretation of the provisions of EU law, and second, the public/private divide has not been very pronounced (if at all) when it comes to treating sporting organisations under the EU law.

Article 6 TEU accords the value of primary EU law to the Charter, which puts it on equal footing with the Treaties. It is exactly in the sporting cases that involved questions on the application of internal market provisions of the TFEU, *expressis verbis* addressed to the Member States, that the Court extended the protection on fundamental economic rights of internal market to private bodies such as sporting federations. Namely, in the 1974 *Walrave* judgment, the Court specified that the prohibition of discrimination enshrined in those provisions does not apply only to action of public authorities but also to "rules of any other nature aimed at regulating in a collective manner gainful employment and the provision of services".[26] As the justification for this approach, it considered that the fundamental objectives of the Union (related to freedom of movement *in casu*) would be frustrated by obstacles resulting from the exercise, by associations or organisations not governed by pubic law, of their legal autonomy.[27] The approach of giving direct horizontal effect to free movement of persons has been confirmed in the subsequent sports case law, such as *Bosman*, *Deliège*, and *Lehtonen*,[28] and it became clear that sporting federations are addressees under the internal market provisions that are otherwise expressly directed at actions of the Member States. Furthermore, the non-sporting *Viking* judgment implies that provisions of the TFEU are capable of *horizontal* effect in cases where collective action of individuals *produces regulatory effects*

---

[25] Brems and Lavrysen (2012), p. 227.

[26] Paragraph 17. In Case 36/74*Walrave* [2012], one of the questions related to the horizontal direct effect of the TFEU Articles 18, 45, and 56, as the respondent in the case, *Union Cycliste International*, was not a body governed by public law but a private sporting organisation.

[27] *Ibid.* para 18.

[28] Case C-415/93*Bosman* [1995], Joined Cases C-51/96 and C-191/97 *Deliège* [2000], Case C-176/96 *Lehtonen* [2000].

similar to those resulting from State action.[29] The same judgment specified that "the fact that certain provisions of the Treaty are formally addressed to the Member States does not prevent rights from being conferred at the same time on any individual who has an interest in compliance with the obligations thus laid down".[30] Along these lines of logic and due to the equivalent legal status of the Charter with the primary Union law, the exercise of legal autonomy of organisations that do not formally fall under the scope of public law and whose actions therefore cannot be attributed to Member State could diminish the protection of human rights (as further detailed in the Charter) the Union is founded on.[31] Combined with the specific nature and status of sport-governing bodies and the scope of their regulatory influence, that fact should provide a sufficient trigger for the application of the Charter in such (quasi-)vertical situations and support arguments in favour of holding sporting bodies accountable for the breaches of the EU's bill of rights.[32] This approach was implied by the EU Expert Group on Anti-Doping set up by the Council of the EU that considered certain aspects of the World Anti-Doping Code in contravention with the Charter.[33]

5 The Concept of "Specificity of Sport" as a Restriction on the Fundamental Rights of Athletes

It is generally accepted that there should be no difference in protection of fundamental rights of athletes and any other economically active person in the EU. This in turn also means that the rights of athletes are not unconditional. In addition to the rights sometimes being restricted due to the conflict with other rights and freedoms, in the sporting context the rights of athletes are further conditioned by the concept of "specificity of sport". The concept has been established, recognised, and taken into account in the jurisprudence of the Court[34] and the Commission practice. Following Lisbon Treaty amendments, it was included in Article 165(1) TFEU, imposing a positive constitutional obligation on the Union to "contribute to the

---

[29] Case C-438/05 *Viking Line* judgment of 11 December 2007, para 79; Case C-341/05 *Laval* judgment of 18 December 2007.

[30] *Ibid.*, para 58.

[31] See Art. 2 TEU.

[32] Alternatively, nothing in the Charter indicates that *indirect* horizontal effect of its provisions is precluded. This is supported by the Court's jurisprudence in cases like C-144/04 *Mangold v Helm* [2005] E.C.R. I-09981 and Case C-555/07 *Kücükdeveci* [2010], judgment of 19 January 2010. However, even in the context of indirect horizontal effect, it should not be forgotten that we are not talking about classic private operators to which many policy questions, such as whether the obligation to comply with the fundamental freedoms would be excessively burdensome, apply.

[33] For details, see the discussion below in the subparagraph on anti-doping control.

[34] See, e.g., Case C-325/08 *Bernard* judgment of grand Chamber of the Court delivered on 16 March 2010.

promotion of European sporting issues, while taking account of the *specific nature of sport* [...]". It is utilised to justify practices in breach of EU economic freedoms that would not be allowed in any other industry.

European Commission explained that in order to assess the compatibility of sporting rules with any provisions of EU law, it considers the *legitimacy of the objectives pursued* by the rules, whether any restrictive effects of those rules are *inherent* in the pursuit of the objectives and whether they are *proportionate* to them.[35] Objectives *specific to the sporting community* accepted by the Court as legitimate so far were, for example, ensuring regularity of competitions (players can effectively be transferred to another club only during short window in-between seasons, which limits their ability to find work for most of the year),[36] maintaining the balance between clubs by preserving a certain degree of equality and uncertainty as to results, encouraging the recruitment and training of young players (on the first professional transfer of a football player, the club that trained him must get financial compensation, thus limiting player's attractiveness for the clubs that want to sign him),[37] and combating doping in order for competitive sport to be conducted fairly, including the need to safeguard equal chances for athletes, athletes' health, the integrity and objectivity of competitive sport, and ethical values in sport.[38] White Paper on Sport addressed some of the general aspects and divided the approach to the concept into *the specificity of the sport structure* (including, notably, the autonomy and diversity of sport organisations, a pyramid structure of competitions from grassroots to elite level and organised solidarity mechanisms between the different levels and operators, the organisation of sport on a national basis, and the principle of a single federation per sport) and *the specificity of sporting activities and of sporting rules* (such as separate competitions for men and women, limitations on the number of participants in competitions, or the need to ensure uncertainty concerning outcomes and to preserve a competitive balance between clubs taking part in the same competitions).[39] Commission Staff Working Document on Sport and Free Movement of January 2011 states that "the specificity of sport cannot be used as an excuse for making a general exception to the application of free movement rules to sports activities. Exceptions from the EU's fundamental principles must be limited and based on specific circumstances".[40] This places emphasis on a case-by-case approach.

The concept of specificity of sport can be expected to continue playing the same restrictive role on the scope of the rights guaranteed under the Charter as it did in

---

[35] Commission Communication on Developing European Dimension in Sport (2011), para. 4.2.

[36] Case C-176/96 *Lehtonen* [2000].

[37] Case C-415/93 *Bosman* and Case C-325/08 *Bernard*.

[38] Case 519/04 *Meca-Medina*.

[39] White Paper on Sport, para. 4.1.

[40] Commission Staff Working Document "Sport and free Movement" Brussels SEC(2011) 66/2— Accompanying document to the Commission Communication on Developing European Dimension in Sport (2011), p. 7.

relation to economic freedoms and provide a unique set of justifications that shield the rules and practices of the sport-governing bodies from falling foul of the applicable EU law. Whereas there exists no constitutional requirement to take into consideration Article 165 TFEU in the Union's legislative action, the Court's treatment of that provision in *Bernard* supports the view that "the new sports competence may have given further weight to sports-related arguments" and that the concept of specificity of sport gained additional significance.[41]

However, as will be explained next, both the specificity of sport and Charter arguments can take place only within the scope of the EU economic provisions. As such, the Charter may be utilised as to support the legal arguments of athletes in the framework of their economic rights and thus provide a counterbalance to the concept of specificity of sport.

6 Charter as a Supplementary Avenue of Legal Argument and Counterbalance Against Specificity of Sport

The requirement to respect fundamental rights defined in the context of the Union is only binding within the scope of Union law,[42] and the Charter may not have the effect of extending the field of application of Union law beyond the powers of the Union as established in the Treaties.[43]

Thus far in the EU law, the difference between economic and non-economic sporting activities was crucial to establish the EU competence in the matter. In *Walrave*, the Court famously held that "*the practice of sport is subject to Community law only in so far as it constitutes economic activity*".[44] This jurisdictional threshold will therefore act as a trigger for bringing the sporting case under the scope of the Union law and, consequently, for the application of the Charter. Furthermore, it is an established case law that self-employed professional sportspersons constitute service providers within the meaning of Articles 56/57 and "undertakings" for the purposes of Articles 101 and 102 TFEU, that players employed by the sports clubs are "workers" within the meaning of Article 45 TFEU, and that their activities can constitute economic activities that fall within the scope of those provisions. Purely amateur pursuit will not benefit from the economic provisions of the Treaty and will fall outwith the Union competence. These provisions conferring substantive rights onto their respective subjects of

---

[41] See the European Parliament, Directorate-General for Internal Policies, Study on the Lisbon Treaty and EU Sports Policy (2010), and Pijetlovic (2010), pp. 858–869.

[42] Case 5/88 *Wachauf* [1989] ECR 2609, Case C-260/89 *ERT* [1991] ECR I-2925, Case C-309/96 *Annibaldi* [1997] ECR I-7493.

[43] See the Explanations relating to the Charter of Fundamental Rights (2007/C 303/02), available at http://eur-lex.europa.eu/LexUriServ/LexUriServ.do?uri=OJ:C:2007:303:0017:0035:en:PDF.

[44] Case 36/74 *Walrave and Koch* [1974] ECR 1405, para. 4.

protection are directly effective and as such can be relied on before the national courts.

Furthermore, the Court held in *Meca-Medina* that "[i]f the sporting activity in question falls within the scope of the Treaty, the conditions for engaging in it are then subject to all the obligations which result from the various provisions of the Treaty".[45] The conditions for engaging in the remunerated sport are set by the sport-governing bodies. It was therefore confirmed in *Meca-Medina* that rules and practices of such bodies that govern economic activity of professional sportsperson must satisfy the requirements of TFEU provisions, in particular, those provisions that seek to ensure free movement and unrestricted competition. The Court then set out a test for regulatory rules in sport holding that not every restriction on the freedom of action necessarily falls within the prohibition laid down in Article 101:

> For the purposes of application of that provision to a particular case, account must first of all be taken of the overall context in which the decision of the association of undertakings was taken or produces its effects and, more specifically, of its *objectives*. It has then to be considered whether the consequential effects restrictive of competition are *inherent* in the pursuit of those objectives [...] and are *proportionate* to them.[46]

The same test for compatibility of the restrictive measures as spelled out by *Kraus* and *Gebhard*[47] can be found in internal market area.[48] It is in the framework of *Meca-Medina* test and equivalent test under objective justification framework for the rules in breach of internal market provisions that fundamental rights under the Charter can be used to support athletes' arguments. Simply put, in the legal disputes involving application of EU law, the Charter is for athletes what specificity of sport is for the governing bodies and acts as a counterbalance to that concept.

> Hypothetical example: using Charter to support athletes' economic rights
> A French football player is disqualified by UEFA (the governing body for European football) from the Champions League (a pan-European football club competition) because he has a neck tattoo that says: "Allah is great". He may challenge the rules of UEFA under Article 45 TFEU that provide for freedom of movement of employed persons. He may claim that prohibition of participation in Champions League is a severe restriction on his

---

[45] Case 519/04 *Meca-Medina*, para. 28.

[46] *Ibid.*, para. 42. [emphasis added] This test applies to Article 102, as well by virtue of the Court's decision in C-250/92 *DLG* case, a precursor to C-309/99 *Wouters* and C-519/04 *Meca-Medina* in which this test was applied to both Articles 101 and 102.

[47] Case C-19/92 *Kraus* [1993] ECR I-1663, para. 32, and Case C-55/94 *Gebhard* [1995] ECR I-4165, para. 37.

[48] It is of importance to mention that in sports cases, the Union's competition and free movement rules converge to a high extent and that, contrary to established case law, both indirectly discriminatory and non-discriminatory measures *and directly discriminatory measures* benefit from *open list* of public policy justifications. At the same time, public policy objectives can be relied on in the framework of Article 101 and 102 TFEU under *Meca-Medina* framework [although in competition law normally only economic justification under Article 101(3) TFEU can be used]. While the EU competition rules are clearly addressed to private undertakings, internal market rules are addressed to Member States. Sports federations are a subject to both set of norms.

professional opportunities and that no club would employ him if he cannot participate in that competition. UEFA may try to objectively justify its measure on the basis that displaying any religious symbols and slogans in sport would run counter to its robust implementation of policy of equality and fight against racism. The policy in itself is, no doubt, pursuing an objective worthy of protection under EU law. However, the suitability and proportionality of the rules would be hard for UEFA to prove: why it was not possible to have the same objective achieved with less restrictive means and why the disqualification of a player on that basis was even suitable and necessary for the achievement of the objective. UEFA might invoke specificity of sport in terms of football's enormous influence on masses and its social and educational function mentioned in Article 165(1) TFEU and claim that the successful implementation of their policy demands measures showing zero tolerance towards any religious slogans that can be interpreted by the masses as a sign of intolerance towards other religions.

In demonstrating the unsuitability and disproportionality of the rules the football player will assert that disqualification is not capable of achieving the objective as the policy itself manifests religious intolerance and is in either case exceeding what is necessary to attain its aim. To support his arguments, he may claim violation of his rights under Article 10 of the Charter that provides for freedom of religion including freedom, either in public or in private, to manifest religion or belief. It would be more difficult for the Court to provide a sound reasoning for accepting as proportionate a rule that violates fundamental rights than it would be otherwise. The violation of fundamental rights will therefore play an opposing role in the balancing act to the specificity of sport and its different demands to those of other industries due to its immense social impact and educational role. It is in this manner that the Charter may be used in the interpretation of the Union's economic provisions in the sporting sector.

Were our hypothetical athlete self-employed, which is the case in individual sports, he could have brought an action against governing body under Article 56, 101 and 102 TFEU. The same test and the same arguments would apply.

With this analytical background in mind, what follows is the examination of some of the more prominent human rights issues in sport. First, however, we will look at the contractual arrangements that supply to the sporting bodies *pacta sunt servanda* argument as a rationale for the application to athletes of all the rules they adopt (along with the fundamental rights concerns they raise). This argument quickly reaches its limits under the conditions described in the following subsection.

7   Contracts of Adhesion and Athlete Representation: Implications for Article 12 of the Charter

The freedom of association was relied on by the UEFA in the *Bosman* case to take the challenged UEFA rule out of the scope of Union law because, as the German government argued, the intervention by public authorities in the autonomy enjoyed by a sporting federation must be confined to what is strictly necessary.[49] The Court responded that the right guaranteed by Article 11 of the ECHR and constitutional

---

[49] Case C-415/93 *Bosman* [1995] ECR I-4921, para. 72.

traditions of the Member States is one of the fundamental rights protected by the Community legal order.[50] It then qualified this statement stipulating that the UEFA rules in question, which acted as an obstacle to economic freedom under Article 45 TFEU, could not be seen as necessary to ensure enjoyment of that freedom by the sporting associations, by the clubs, or by their players, nor could they be seen as inevitable result thereof.[51] This was a confirmation by the Court that neither fundamental rights nor the autonomy of the sporting federations is unlimited and will have to be assessed against requirements of Union's economic freedoms guaranteed to individuals. The decision left open the possibility that fundamental rights may be relied on by the governing bodies themselves to justify the breach of Union's free movement rules when they can be seen as necessary and inevitable for the enjoyment of fundamental right relied on by the associations themselves or by the clubs or players associated to them.

According to the Secretary General of EU Athletes, another important step in balancing athletes' fundamental rights against the specificity of sport is developing effective social dialogue.[52] Moreover, Commission Communication on Developing European Dimension in Sport states that "good governance in sport is a condition for the autonomy and self-regulation of sport organisations".[53] One of the important aspects of good governance is the representation of all stakeholders in the transparent and democratic decision-making process. In Europe, unlike in the US,[54] the social dialogue and collective bargaining agreements in sports are still in their infancy. Since 2001, the Commission has been supporting projects for the consolidation of social dialogue in the sport sector globally and specifically in the football sector.[55] Studies were conducted to identify the social partners[56] and the labour-related themes and issues suitable to be dealt by means of social dialogue in professional football[57] and also in some other professional sports.[58] Nevertheless,

---

[50] *Ibid.*, para. 79.

[51] *Ibid.*, para. 80.

[52] Palmer (2011).

[53] Communication "Developing the European Dimension in Sport", para. 4.1

[54] For the US, see Halgreen (2004).

[55] See list of projects in fn. 6, section 5.3 in Commission Staff Working Document, The EU and Sport: Background and Context, Accompanying Document to the White Paper on Sport, COM (2007) 391 final.

[56] See *Promoting Social Dialogue in European Professional Football (Candidate EU Member States)*, Report for the European Commission, November 2004, and *Study on the Representativeness of the Social Partner Organisations in the Professional Football Player Sector*, Report for the European Commission, Project No VC/2004/0547 (2006).

[57] See *Study into the Identification of Themes and Issues which can be Dealt with in a Social Dialogue in the European Professional Football Sector*, Report for the European Commission, May 2008. See also the press release in *The International Sports Law Review* 1–2 (2008), p. 109.

[58] Such as cycling. See *Study into the Identification of Themes and Issues to be Dealt with in a Social Dialogue in the European Professional Cycling Sector*, report for the European Commission (2009).

the representation and bargaining strength of athletes in most of the sports in Europe can be described as very weak, as creating conditions for social dialogue process that can produce collective bargaining agreements has not been the priority for most of the sport-governing bodies. As the Grand Chamber of ECtHR held in *Demir and Baykara* on the basis of Article 11 ECHR, the right to conclude collective agreements is "one of the principal means – even the foremost of such means – for trade unionist to protect their interests".[59] Article 12 of the Charter provides for the equivalent freedoms of assembly and of association, which encompass the right of everyone to form and to join trade unions for the protection of his or her interests. With this background in mind, it is important to consider whether sport-governing bodies have a *positive* obligation to create conditions in which the interests of athletes affiliated to them, as the potential social partners, are properly represented.[60]

The mandate of the sport-governing bodies is multifaceted and includes both rights and responsibilities towards all levels and all aspects of their discipline. Democratic, representative, and transparent process of decision making is among those responsibilities that are the part of principles of good governance and, in turn, a condition for their rights related to the exercise of regulatory autonomy. This conditionality has so far been only a slogan in policy and theory, while reality portrays quite a different picture.

An example from the tennis governance will serve to illustrate the problems associated with the lack of proper athlete representation in practice. Namely, men's professional is governed by the ATP,[61] an association that was initially established to represent the interests of professional players. Today, ATP is run by the Board of Directors consisting of three tournament organiser representatives, three player representatives, and a chairman, who is the Executive Chairman and President of the ATP. "Player representatives" include a former tournament director, former executive and agent at IMG (a major sports sponsor, management and media company that owns many of the leading tennis tournaments), and one former tennis player who currently works as a tennis commentator.[62] The ATP Player Council representing players has ten current professional players as their members, while no person in the Player Council advises players on the legal issues. They can deliver advisory opinions to the Board of Directors, which has the power to accept or reject the Player Council's suggestions. Much like it transpires from its modest role, this body is generally regarded as having no power to influence any of the ATP decisions.

Further to this apparent flaw in the governance, a tennis player must sign the standard Consent and Agreement with ATP at the beginning of each season in order

---

[59] *Demir and Baykara v. Turkey* [2008] ECHR 1345.

[60] There are also implications for the rights set out in Articles 27 and 28 of the Charter on right of collective bargaining and action.

[61] Association of Tennis Professionals.

[62] See ATP official website http://www.atpworldtour.com/Corporate/Management.aspx.

to participate in competitions. By the terms of the Agreement, the player, *inter alia*, consents to abide by the ATP Official Rulebook and the Uniform Tennis Anti-Corruption Programme that are not a part of the Agreement, so the provisions on, for example, what constitutes violation of the rules or the standard of proof and sanctions in case of offence does not show up on the face of the Agreement but only in the subsections of the detailed regulations to which it refers. The Agreement is partly an arbitration agreement granting exclusive jurisdiction to Court of Arbitration for Sport (CAS) to review the disputes between a player and the ATP.[63] It states that "no claim, arbitration, lawsuit or litigation shall be brought in any other court or tribunal". By the terms of the Agreement, decisions of CAS are final and non-reviewable. A manager of the Rules and Competition at the ATP reported that while players do receive the Agreement prior to the start of each season, the overwhelming majority does not sign it until they arrive to their first season tournament and are prompted by the ATP staff before their first match to sign it or be disqualified from the competition (i.e., be denied access to provision of their services).[64] Hence, such contract of adhesion creates a "take-it-or-leave-it" situation as players had no opportunity to affect its terms at any stage.[65]

In *Cañas v ATP Tour* the Swiss Federal Tribunal (the only body with jurisdiction to review CAS judgments, albeit on a limited basis) ruled on this matter and held that such waiver of appeal is void because the athletes' purported consent to such exclusion agreements does "obviously not rest on a free will" and is therefore "tainted *ab ovo*":

> [E]xperience has shown that, by and large, athletes will often not have the bargaining power required and would therefore have to submit to the federation's requirements, whether they like it or not. Accordingly, any athlete wishing to participate in organised competition under the control of a sports federation whose rules provide for recourse to arbitration will not have any choice but to accept the arbitral clause, in particular by subscribing to the articles of association of the sports federation in question in which the arbitration clause was inserted[. . .].[66]

By analogy to this judgment, and subject to the notion of severability, *nothing* that players "agree" to via the agreement is valid and enforceable.

The extent and the type of rights that can be contractually waived is itself debatable. The ECtHR noted in *Osmo Suovaniemi v. Finland* that "waiver may be permissible with regard to certain rights but not with regard to certain others. A

---

[63] In addition, Section I (1) of the Uniform Tennis Anti-Corruption Programme provides that any decision related to corruption offence may be appealed exclusively to CAS.

[64] In her report, only 2–5 players out of ca. 3,000 return the signed forms before the season begins.

[65] Montmollin and Pentsov argue that "the athlete who wants to participate competition does not have a choice and must accept the arbitration clause, in particular by adhering to the by-laws of the sports federation containing the arbitration clause, all the more when the athlete is a professional. Otherwise, he would be confronted by the following dilemma: agree to arbitration or practice his sport as an amateur". See De Montmollin and Pentsov (2011), p. 207.

[66] *Cañas v ATP Tour and others* 4P.172/2006 (2007) (Switz.), ATF 133 III 235, translated in 1 SWISS INT'L ARB. L. REP. 65, 84–85.

distinction may have to be made even between different rights guaranteed by Article 6".[67] In general, for the waiver to be valid, it has to be agreed knowingly and voluntarily and no element of duress can be present.[68] Add to this equation the manner of entry into agreement and the *Cañas v ATP Tour* judgment of the Swiss Federal Tribunal and more likely than not the athletes will be able to successfully argue that they are not bound by the rules that constitute waiver of *any* of their fundamental rights and other mandatory rules for the protection of the weaker party. Only a *voluntary* fundamental rights waiver *negotiated in good faith* between the two sides of the industry *and in the full knowledge of the legal ramifications* would necessitate different treatment and, depending on the nature of the rights in question, would stand a chance to survive a legal challenge.

The state of affairs just described carries, *inter alia*, implications for the rights guaranteed under Article 12 of the Charter. If the mandate of a monopolistic self-governing regulator includes ensuring the proper representation in their decision making, and if such representation does not exist, this certainly leads to assumption that they are effectively denying the right of athletes to protect their interests as envisaged by the Charter. Representation of all the stakeholders is also a pre-condition for their autonomy conditional upon the respect for law. This is not favourable state of affairs for the sporting bodies either as the collective agreements present a method that can keep legal disputes to a minimum or, in line with the Court's jurisprudence in the *Albany*, *Brentjens*, and *Drijvende Bokken*, agreements concluded in the context of collective bargaining between employee and employer trade unions that improve working and employment conditions fall outside the scope of Article 101(1) TFEU[69] and would likely not be challenged on any other basis.

It is to be remembered, however, that the violation of the Charter rights by sporting bodies will be dependent on violation of athletes' economic rights and may be used to supplement their legal arguments under TFEU economic provisions. From the internal market and competition law perspective, the entry into compulsory agreements is the precondition for entry into the market for provision of professional tennis player services and access to the ATP's essential organising services that can be seen as constituting an analogous necessity for the operation on the market to the "essential facilities". Much like the access to essential facilities, the access to the monopolised organising services should be provided on reasonable terms. It must be acknowledged that if the clauses in the standard agreements were favourable for the athletes and not in breach of their economic freedoms, there would be no basis in the EU law for the legal challenge to the manner of putting

---

[67] *Osmo Suovaniemi and others v. Finland*, 23 February 2009, No. 31737/96.

[68] Landrove (2006), p. 81.

[69] Case C-67/96 *Albany International BV v. Stichting Bedrijfspensioenfonds Textielindustrie* [1999] ECR I-5751; Cases C-115, 116, & 117/97 *Brentjens' Handelsonderneming BV v Stichting Bedrijfspensioenfonds voor de Handel in Bouwmaterialen* [1999] ECR I-6025; and Case C-219/97 *Drijvende Bokken* [1999] ECR I-6121.

forth and the manner of acceptance of such clauses. The autonomy conditional upon respect for principles of good governance remains a policy slogan that has no discrete basis for challenge in EU law. The conditions stipulated in the unilaterally imposed standard clauses may, however, present an abuse of dominant position by the governing bodies under Article 102 TFEU, an illegal agreement under Article 101(1) TFEU, or a restriction on the free movement of athletes, in which case the avenue to challenge the unrepresentative and compulsory system that leads to the acceptance of the agreement is wide open. Within the *Meca-Medina* framework or equivalent internal market objective justification test, the arguments on violation of Article 12 of the Charter can be added to help illustrate the lack of inherency and/or disproportionality of the unrepresentative structures and the scheme that was at the inception of, and responsible for, the breach of athletes' economic rights.

8 Fair Trial Guarantees in the System of Sporting Justice

Sport-governing bodies have their regulatory and organisational rules spelled out in their statutes, charters, regulations, codes, and other rulebooks and constitutions, as the case may be. As already clear, they take decisions that can have profound economic effects on many different actors in the world of sport, such as athletes and clubs. For the administration of the whole body of rules, regulations, and decisions issued by sports organisations, referred to as the *lex sportiva*, the Olympic Movement established the Court of Arbitration for Sport (CAS) in 1984 as its highest arbitration body for resolving sport-related disputes. CAS has a sole jurisdiction to rule on the commercial issues in the disputes related to sport, and it acts as an appellate body of the last instance in disciplinary cases, most of which concern breach of anti-doping rules and corruption offences by athletes. The CAS Panel decides the disputes according to the rules of law chosen by the parties or, in the absence of such a choice, according to *lex fori* (Swiss law).[70] Hence, CAS jurisprudence itself has become one of the main sources of *lex sportiva*. The impact of their arbitral awards is similar to that of judicial bodies' decisions.

CAS arbitral awards are appealable only to Swiss Federal Tribunal and can be reviewed only on the grounds of procedural public policy guarantees under Article 190(2) of Swiss Federal Code on Private International Law, such as fair trial.[71] In *Lazutina* case, Swiss Federal Tribunal implied that fair trial guarantees must be

---

[70] CAS Statutes, 2012 edition, Article R45. For more information on the Court of Arbitration for Sport, see, for e.g., Blackshaw (2009), pp. 45–99.

[71] Article 190 (2) of Swiss Federal Code on Private International Law sets out procedural public policy guarantees and specifies that an arbitral award can be challenged only "if a sole arbitrator was designated irregularly or the arbitration tribunal was constituted irregularly; if the arbitration tribunal erroneously held that it had or did not have jurisdiction; if the arbitration tribunal ruled on matters beyond the claims submitted to it or if it failed to rule on one of the claims; if the equality of the parties or their right to be heard in an adversarial proceeding was not respected; and if the

respected before the CAS in its arbitration proceedings.[72] Does it suffice that the Swiss Federal Tribunal has *ex post facto* power to consider whether the CAS respected procedural public policy guarantees, including fair trial guarantees, provided that one of the parties challenged the arbitral award on the basis of Article 190(2) of Switzerland's Federal Code on Private International Law? This and a number of other pertinent questions related to minimum fair trial guarantees before CAS were examined by Černič, who convincingly argued that Article 6 ECHR as developed by the ECtHR should also apply to CAS proceedings.[73] He noted that judicial review of respect for fundamental fair trial guarantees by the Swiss Federal Tribunal does not suffice to ensure the respect for fair trial guarantees before the CAS, and it only takes place if the arbitral award is challenged before the Swiss Federal Tribunal.[74] Therefore, the CAS should be responsible for safeguarding respect for fair trial guarantees in its proceedings.

Černič identified the following problems related to the right to fair trial before the CAS: the appointment of qualified arbitrators and their later selection in individual cases is not very transparent, the time it takes to resolve procedures is several times longer than envisaged and thereby violates athlete's rights,[75] the publication of proceedings has not yet gained a foothold as a fundamental principle in sports arbitration procedures, and the standard of proof employed is too low.

With the purpose of illustrating the standard of proof issues in sport, we will continue with our tennis example in which the clauses in the compulsory standard agreements described *supra* in this chapter lead to the application and enforcement of Uniform Tennis Anti-Corruption Code (UTACP), which contains a number of articles not in conformity with the right to fair trial.[76]

According to Article G(3)(a) of the UTACP, "the standard of proof shall be whether the PTIO has established the commission of the alleged Corruption Offense by a *preponderance of the evidence*. [. . .]". However, match fixing is a criminal offense, and standard of proof more appropriate to criminal offences should be used to prove the charges of match fixing. It is well established by the case law of the ECtHR that the notion of a "criminal charge" is an autonomous concept that is a matter of ECHR law.[77] The principle laid down by the ECtHR for

---

award is incompatible with Swiss public policy". Fair trial guarantees in the Swiss legal order also form part of public policy.

[72] *A. and B. v. IOC and FIS (Lazutina)*, 4P.267–270/2002 (1st Civ. Ct., 27 May 2003).

[73] Černič (2012), pp. 259–283.

[74] *Ibid.* 279.

[75] The *Contador* case took one and a half years to resolve, which is three times longer than the time envisaged for appeal procedures.

[76] The UTACP is mainly geared towards the fight against match-fixing offences in which a person (often a tennis player, sometimes organised syndicates) attempts to affect the outcome of his/her own or other players' match by fixing the score in advance. This gives opportunity to earn hefty profits against the odds on the sports-betting market. It is available at http://www.tennisintegrityunit.com/UTACP-2012.pdf.

[77] *Engel and Others v. Netherlands* (1979–80) 1 E.H.R.R. 647.

identifying a criminal charge is known as the "*Engel* criteria". They are the classification of the offence under national law, the nature of the offence, and the nature and severity of the potential penalty.[78]

The UTACP itself deals with the match-fixing offences under the designation of "corruption offences". In the EU sports policy, match fixing is a criminal offence. The study on match fixing in sport by the Commission emphasised the need to fight this form of sports corruption through criminal legislation:

> Resorting to *criminal justice in the fight against match-fixing* shows that sporting manipulation can be not only a "simple" breach of sporting rules but also an offence against the public in a broader sense.[79]

In its Communication on Sport, the Commission similarly states that

> [m]atch-fixing violates the ethics and integrity of sport. Whether related to influencing betting or to sporting objectives, it is a form of corruption and as such *sanctioned by national criminal law*.[80]

Under the national laws of all the EU Member States, match fixing constitutes a criminal offence and is dealt with under their criminal legislation.[81] Member States apply criminal standard of proof to establish whether any such offence took place. The treatment of match fixing under Member States' laws and Commission policy is illustrative of the disproportionality of the standard of proof under the UTACP. Sanctions for the breach of the UTACP under that code may carry a lifetime ban from participating in professional tennis in any capacity even for the first *attempt* to fix a match, while fines are not just compensatory but *punitive* in nature, exceeding the offenders' ability to pay[82] (this in itself should be examined under Article 49 (3) of the Charter requiring that severity of penalties must not be disproportionate to the criminal offence). In Member States' laws, more serious cases of match fixing may lead to imprisonment. The criminal standard of proof should therefore be the applicable standard for proving that corruption offence took place.

The rules that provide for lower standard of proof violate the athletes' right to fair trial under Article 6 of the ECHR and Article 47 of the Charter. Rules and

---

[78] *Ibid.*

[79] "Match-fixing in sport: a mapping of the criminal law provisions in EU 27" (March 2012), pp. 15–16. Available at http://ec.europa.eu/sport/news/documents/study-sports-fraud-final-version_en.pdf.

[80] Commission Communication "Developing the European Dimension in Sport" January 18, Brussels, COM(2011) 12 final, para. 4.5.

[81] "Match-fixing in sport: a mapping of the criminal law provisions in EU 27" (March 2012), pp. 15–16.

[82] Decisions in *Köllerer* and *Savic* cases before the Anti-Corruption Hearing Officer are kept secret and not published, but both players received a lifetime ban and a fine of 100,000 and 85,000 USD, respectively. Redacted CAS awards confirming the ban but lifting the fines are available at http://www.tas-cas.org/recent-decision.

practices adopted for the purpose of fighting match fixing in sports should be designed so as to not deprive athletes of fundamental rights. If they go that far, it will be more difficult to prove their proportionality under the test framework developed in paragraph 42 of *Meca-Medina* and under the internal market objective justification framework. As regards the severity of the sanctions, it will be virtually impossible to prove their proportionality in the context of the economic argument if they are disproportionate under Article 49(3) of the Charter.

In the first instance, disciplinary cases are usually dealt with at the level of the competent authorities of the sport in question by their internal quasi-judicial dispute-settlement mechanisms. The conflation of prosecuting, investigative, and adjudicating functions in one body in the enforcement of the rules, which is often the case in sporting justice, appears problematic from the point of view of Article 47 of the Charter.

The first sentence of Article 6(1) ECHR providing for a hearing before *an independent and impartial tribunal* applies to civil as well as to criminal proceedings. In order to establish under Article 6 of the ECHR whether a body can be considered "independent", regard must be had, inter alia, to the manner of appointment of its members and their term of office, to the existence of guarantees against outside pressures, and to the question whether the body presents an appearance of independence.[83] The rule against bias (*nemo judex in sua causa*) is a principle of natural justice and forms an indivisible part of the right to fair trial. In the legal systems of EU Member States, the rule against bias requires the adjudicator to be free from any interest in the case—in the jurisprudence of the UK courts, this can be financial that automatically disqualifies the adjudicator[84] or where there is the *likelihood of the appearance of bias*[85] (so there is no need for *actual* bias).

Tennis has its Anti-Corruption Hearing Officer (AHO) that acts as an adjudicator for the offences of the UTACP. He is financed by the Tennis Integrity Unit (investigators) that is financed by the Governing Bodies of tennis, including ATP (prosecutors). Tennis Integrity Board, which appoints the AHO, was excluded from the list of respondents before CAS proceedings because it was argued by the tennis Governing Bodies that it is "*simply a representative body of the other four respondents [i.e. the representative of the Governing Bodies]*".[86] Due to the structural links with the tennis Governing Bodies, appointment by Tennis Integrity Body, physical location in the same office, and financial dependence on the tennis Governing Bodies, AHO does not appear as an independent and impartial

---

[83] See, inter alia, the ECHR judgment of 28 June 1984 *Campbell and Fell v. United Kingdom* Series A no. 80, pp. 39–40, para. 78.

[84] *Dimes v Grand Junction Canal Co* (1852) 3 HLC 759.

[85] *Locabail (UK) Ltd v Bayfield Properties* [2000] 1 All ER 65.

[86] Footnote omitted.

body. Yet its decisions have an effect of permanently excluding a tennis player not only from the market for provision of tennis player services but also from coaching, managing, and any other economic activity that can give access to the tournaments and imposing fines that by far exceed the player's ability to pay.[87] This arrangement is yet another point for reform under the fair trial requirements, as it can constitute an abuse of dominant position by the tennis Governing Bodies and a system of enforcement incompatible with economic provisions under TFEU due to the failure to meet the principle of proportionality.

In as far as the dispute concerns a restriction on the EU economic freedoms via the enforcement of the UTACP provision, an athlete that loses a case before the AHO and CAS may turn to the Commission to examine the sporting rule in question (not review the CAS decision *per se*) and thereafter appeal to the Court. In fact, any rule that involves alleged breach of the EU law by a sporting federation may be brought to the attention of the Commission, which will act only if it considers that there is "EU interest" in the case,[88] which could prove a high burden to bear for the individual athletes. Conversely, national courts protect individual interests, but they are very reluctant to examine the rules that affect the entire sporting discipline on a global level, and any case brought before national courts that has an EU element will likely be referred to the Court on a preliminary reference procedure.

Finally, it remains to be mentioned that in its Communication on Sport

> the Commission underscores the need for anti-doping rules and practices to comply with EU law in respecting fundamental rights and principles such as [...]the right to a fair trial and the presumption of innocence. Any limitation on the exercise of these rights and freedoms must be provided for by law and respect the essence of those rights and the principle of proportionality.[89]

There is no reason the same considerations of fundamental rights and fair trial should not apply also to all other sporting rules and practices that restrict the athletes' economic freedoms.

---

[87] See *David Savic* and *Daniel Köllerer* cases before the AHO [the decisions are secret, but decisions (on appeal) by CAS provide a lot of insight]. Appeal to CAS costs tens of thousands of Euros, including lawyer and tribunal fees, and this is an amount that not many tennis players can afford, especially not after they have been imposed severe fines that only the richest of them can pay.

[88] The General Court's judgment in T-24/90 *Automec Srl v Commission*, para 86, provides a test for the existence of the European Union interest in the case. Accordingly, in assessing such interest, the Commission in particular looks at (1) the scope of the investigation required, (2) the probability of establishing the existence of the infringement, and (3) the significance of the infringement from the point of view of the internal market.

[89] Para. 2.1 [emphasis added].

9 Anti-Doping Control: Right to Privacy and the Right to Rest

World Anti-Doping Agency (WADA) was set up in 1999 at the initiative of the International Olympic Committee (IOC). It is a private and non-governmental agency financed by the IOC and the governments of the world. The agency is responsible for the conduct of scientific research, updating of the annual list of prohibited substances, anti-doping education, development of anti-doping capacities, and monitoring of its World Anti-Doping Code (WADC).[90] This code harmonises the rules and regulations governing anti-doping virtually across all sports and all countries. It has been incorporated in the 2005 UNESCO International Convention against Doping in Sport—so far, 145 governments ratified this convention and aligned their national policies on anti-doping.[91]

Testing of athletes can be done in competition and out of competition. It is the out-of-competition testing and "whereabouts" rule that has been a subject of most of the human rights controversy. *Any* professional athlete at any time (from 6:00 to 23:00) is a subject to potential visit from the agents who will gather his/her urine or blood sample (a procedure that is in itself so intrusive that it raises privacy concerns). However, a selected pool of elite players (for example, 50 first players in tennis) will additionally be a subject to "whereabouts" reporting requirement, which means that they have to, on a quarterly basis, *a priori* designate 1-h slot each day between 6:00 and 23:00 at a specific location where they will be available to the anti-doping agents for testing. The testing visits are conducted without prior notice. It is simply expected from the athletes to be there where they said they would at the time they designated for every day of the year. The so-called ADAMS system may be used to change the information if the athlete's whereabouts change. If an athlete misses three tests in an 18-month period, he/she will be banned for at least a year.[92]

Article 31(2) of the Charter provides for the "right to limitation of maximum working hours, to daily and weekly rest periods and to an annual period of paid leave". Working Time Directive[93] protects the right to rest in more details. According to its Article 3, Member States must ensure that workers have a minimum of 11 h of *uninterrupted* rest in a 24-h period, and on the top of this, Article 5 provides for at least 24 h of *uninterrupted* rest in a 7-day period, but derogations can be justified for technical, organisational, or work reasons or according to Article 17 "on account of the specific characteristics of the activities concerned". Article 7 requires 4 weeks of

---

[90] http://www.wada-ama.org/en/World-Anti-Doping-Program/Sports-and-Anti-Doping-Organizations/The-Code/.

[91] For more on WADA see http://www.wada-ama.org.

[92] For more information on the anti-doping programme, see World Anti-Doping Code available at http://www.wada-ama.org/Documents/World_Anti-Doping_Program/WADP-The-Code/WADA_Anti-Doping_CODE_2009_EN.pdf.

[93] Directive 2003/88/EC of the European Parliament and of the Council of 4 November 2003 concerning certain aspects of the organisation of working time, *OJ L 299 18.11.2003 p. 9–19.*

paid annual leave. It is clear that WADA's "whereabouts" rule goes against the requirements of Articles 3, 5, and 7 of the Working Time Directive, as well as Article 31(2) of the Charter. What will not be clear without a legal challenge is whether it may be a good candidate for the derogation and whether it is not possible to organise effective control while allowing athletes one day a week to be free from being included in the reporting obligations.

A panel of 27 EU Member State experts considered that many aspects of WADA "whereabouts" rule contravene EU law, in particular, its privacy laws. Another aspect of anti-doping control relates to ensuring the adequate level of personal data protection in accordance with the Directive on Data Protection[94] and as nowadays also required by Article 8 of the Charter. In the light of proportionality principle, the expert group of 27 invited WADA and anti-doping organisations to reassess the collection of whereabouts as conceived today and, more in general, the current retention period of processed data. WADA responded that these statements went beyond the mandate of expert group, saying they contain "some regrettable factual errors and could potentially undermine the fight against doping".[95] Furthermore, Soek noted that the countries that ratified the UNESCO convention allowed private anti-doping organisations to invade the lives of their subjects anytime, anywhere, and without notice, when in fact according to Article 8(2) ECHR violating the privacy of persons is only *reserved to* "*a public authority*" and on a limited basis.[96] This is yet another reason the Charter should be applicable to the sporting organisations.

As noted by Černič, there are two conflicting values in a contemporary [doping control]: "whether the prevention of doping may undermine the protection of athletes' fundamental human rights, and whether the protection of fundamental human rights may impede the suppression of doping".[97] In the context of the EU objective justification framework, there is no doubt that objectives of anti-doping policy are legitimate. What will be at stake in the examination of the rules under the EU law is their proportionality. In fact, the most extreme example of the review of the proportionality of the sporting rules is the examination by the Commission and the EU Courts of the IOC anti-doping rules in *Meca-Medina*.[98] The case involved two professional swimmers who were found to have breached the sport's anti-doping rules adopted by the IOC. They tested positive for nandrolone and were suspended for the period of 4 years by the Doping Panel of International Swimming

---

[94] Directive 95/46/EC of the European Parliament and of the Council of 24 October 1995 on the protection of individuals with regard to the processing of personal data and on the free movement of such data, *OJ L 281, 23.11.1995 p. 31–50.*

[95] The Guardian: "EU puts WADA whereabouts rule in doubt" 21 April 2009.

[96] Soek (2008), p. 100.

[97] Černič (2012), p. 261.

[98] Case C-519/04 *Meca-Medina* [2006] ECR I-6991.

Federation, which implemented the rules for their discipline.[99] Contesting the anti-doping rules, the applicants asserted that they were in breach of Articles 101 and 102 and Article 56 on freedom to provide services:

> [...] First of all, the fixing of the limit at 2 ng/ml is a concerted practice between the IOC and the 27 laboratories accredited by it. That limit is scientifically unfounded and can lead to the exclusion of innocent or merely negligent athletes. In the applicants' case, the excesses could have been the result of the consumption of a meal containing boar meat. Also, the IOC's adoption of a mechanism of strict liability and the establishment of tribunals responsible for the settlement of sports disputes by arbitration (the CAS and the ICAS) which are insufficiently independent of the IOC strengthens the anti-competitive nature of that limit. [...].[100]

The swimmers raised their claim under both freedom to provide services and competition provisions of the Treaty. In addition to the test in paragraph 42 of that case cited above in this chapter, the Court also acknowledged in paragraph 48:

> the penal nature of the anti-doping rules [...] and the magnitude of the penalties applicable if they are breached are capable of producing adverse effects on competition because they could, if penalties were ultimately to prove unjustified, result in an athlete's unwarranted exclusion from sporting events, and thus in impairment of the conditions under which the activity at issue is engaged in. It follows that, in order not to be covered by the prohibition laid down in Article [101 TFEU], *the restrictions thus imposed by those rules must be limited to what is necessary* to ensure the proper conduct of competitive sport[...].Rules of that kind could indeed prove excessive by virtue of, first, the conditions laid down for establishing the dividing line between circumstances which amount to doping in respect of which penalties may be imposed and those which do not, and second, the severity of those penalties.

Judgment in *Meca-Medina*, paragraphs 42 and 48, in particular, are generally applicable to all regulatory rules in sport, and any aspect of anti-doping policy may be tested against these legal parameters. In that judgments, the objectives of anti-doping control accepted by the Court as legitimate were the need to safeguard equal chances for athletes, athletes' health, the integrity and objectivity of competitive sport and ethical values in sport. After the Treaty of Lisbon amendments, the sporting organisations may more readily rely on the concept of specificity of sport, taking into consideration that which was converted into constitutional requirement, to justify intrusion into athletes' fundamental rights. Athletes, on the other hand, will point out to the rights outlined under the Charter, and the conflict of different values will take place within the objective justification framework of the two sets of TFEU economic provisions.

After the insertion of sport in Article 165 TFEU, the Council of the EU has become a pro-active player in relation to doping-related discussions at EU level. An

---

[99] The appeal against the suspension was first launched before the CAS, which confirmed the decision of the doping panel, but later when scientific experiments showed that nandrolone's metabolites can be produced endogenously by the human body at a level that may exceed the accepted limit when certain foods have been consumed, they reduced the sanctions to 2 years. In 2001, however, the applicants launched the complaint with the Commission, whose decision they appealed to the General Court, and finally the decision of the General Court was brought before the Court.

[100] C-519/04 *Meca-Medina*, paras. 16–17.

EU Expert Group on Anti-Doping was set up under European Union Work Plan for Sport for 2011–2014. It prepared the first EU contribution to the revision of the WADC, which was submitted by the Danish EU Presidency to WADA in March 2012. The following observations were made:

> Although the prevention of doping constitutes a legitimate goal, the goal-driven provisions on RTPs and whereabouts regrettably do not set any limits to their application as no notion of proportionality can be found in these prescriptions. This sets them into conflict with applicable EU laws such as Article 52(1) of the EU Charter of Fundamental Rights and Article 6(1)(c) of the Directive 95/46/EC that render the processing of personal data under the requirement of necessity and proportionality to the legitimate goals pursued.[101]

The Council has extended the mandate of the Expert Group on Anti-Doping, tasking it with the revision of the World Anti-Doping Code until its end in late 2013.

The contributions made by the Expert Group represent a non-binding opinion, but it will take a legal challenge before the EU Courts to confirm the legality under EU law of any of the controversial aspects related to the WADA's anti-doping programme.

10 Concluding Remarks

In EU law, individual athlete's interests are safeguarded by the free movement and free competition principles spelled out in the TFEU economic provisions, whereas the protection of sport federations' interests rest on the objective justification framework under those provisions. Within the scope of those opposing ends lies the heart of the conflict between athletes' fundamental rights enshrined under the Charter and sporting autonomy as represented by the concept of "specificity of sport" in Article 165(1) TFEU.

Any sporting rule can be challenged under the EU law as long as it has effect on the economic activity. Sporting activity that constitutes such economic activity thus falls within the scope of the TFEU, and the conditions for engaging in it as laid down by the governing bodies are subject to all the obligations that result from the various TFEU provisions.

Governing bodies often impose the terms of contracts of adhesion, which cannot be negotiated, and are the first such condition for engaging in the economic sporting activity. More often than not, these one-page standard contracts lead to the application of the number of detailed rulebooks and regulations that include clauses constituting a waiver of basic fundamental rights, such as the right to fair trial.

Principles of fair trial as *a condition sine qua non* for the protection of fundamental rights of athletes should be possible to depart from only partly and only in

---

[101] Council of the European Union, EU contribution to the revision of the World Anti-Doping Code, 13516/12 SPORT 47 DOPAGE 13 SAN 193 JAI 606 DATAPROTECT 104, Brussels 26 September 2012, para. 2.1.3.

circumstances that involve a waiver in the full knowledge and on the basis of good faith negotiations and representation of both sides of the industry. Sport-governing bodies have a positive duty to ensure that such social dialogue takes place, as their autonomy depends on the respect for the principles of good governance.

Whereas doping and match fixing strike at the core of sport and fighting against these forms of corruption remains one of the centrally important issues in preserving the integrity of sport, it should not be overlooked that protecting the economic rights of athletes from adoption and enforcement of disproportionate anti-corruption and anti-doping rules by the sport-governing bodies is equally important. The breaches of athletes' rights cannot be adequately addressed at the national court level as any national court is likely to refuse a jurisdiction over the cases that involve interfering with the regulations of the international sporting bodies or be very reluctant to rule against the sporting regulations having global impact. Thus, the increased Commission diligence in its role as a guardian of the TFEU in pursuing the rules and practices that go beyond what is necessary for the attainment of the legitimate sporting goals appears indispensable.

References

Backe Madsen L, Johansson JM (2008) Den Forsvunne Diamanten (The Lost Diamond). Tiden Norsk Forlag, Norway

Blackshaw I (2009) Sport, mediation and arbitration. T.M.C. Asser Press, The Hague

Brems E, Lavrysen L (ed) (2012) Human rights & international legal discourse. Hum Rights Sport Special Issue 226–228

Černič JL (2012) Fair trial guarantees before the court of arbitration for sport. Human rights & international legal discourse. Hum Rights Sport Special Issue 259–283

De Mol M (2012) Dominguez: a deafening silence. Eur Constitut Law Rev 8:280–303

De Montmollin J, Pentsov D (2011) Do athletes really have the right to a fair trial in "Non-Analytical Positive" Doping Cases? Am Rev Int Arbitrat 22(2):239

Gardiner S et al (2005) Sports Law, 3rd edn. Cavendish Publishing, London

Greenfield S, Osborn G (eds) (2004) Readings in law and popular culture. Routledge, London

Halgreen L (2004) European Sports Law – a comparative analyses of the European and American Models of Sport. Forlaget Thomson, Copenhagen

Landrove JC (2006) European Convention on human rights impact on consensual arbitration. In: Besson S, Hottelier M, Werro F (eds) Human rights at the center. Zürich: Schulthess, Basel, pp 73–101

Morel M (2012) Displaced in the name of sports: Human Rights Law comes to the rescue. Human Rights & International Legal Discourse. Human Rights Sport Special Issue 229–258

Palmer W (2011) Balancing athletes' fundamental rights against specific nature of sport. Sport and citizenship. Special issue. European Social Dialogue in Sport 15

Papadopoulous T (2011) Criticizing the horisontal direct effect of the EU general principle of equality. Eur Hum Rights Law Rev 4:437–447

Pijetlovic K (2010) Another classic of EU sports Jurisprudence: legal implications of *Olympique Lyonnais SASP v. Olivier Bernard and Newcastle UFC* (C-325/08). Eur Law Rev 35:858–869

Safjan M, Miklaszewicz P (2008) Horisontal effect of the general principles of EU Law in the sphere of private law. Eur Rev Private Law 18:475–486

Soek J (2008) Is the professional athlete's right to privacy being tacitly ignored? Int Sports Law J 1–2:100

Idolatry of Rights and Freedoms

Reflections on the Autopoietic Role of Fundamental Rights Within Constitutionalization of the European Union

Ondrej Hamuläk

1 Introduction

European integration—through its elementary method, i.e., transfer/conferral of powers from the building units (Member States) to the centre (Union)—is basically programmed and predisposed to cut the powers out of the Member States and thus materially narrow their capability to regulate society (or—if you want—their sovereignty in the classical sense). Integration is based on the establishment and existence of an entity distinct from the states, which is authorized to manage autonomously the sum of powers transferred on it.

Autonomy (legal, decision making, and financial) of this body not only creates the preconditions for the gradual competition among the Member States and Union and between EU law and national law[1] but also opens the space for the encroachment of the supranational public authority into the private spheres of individuals. And option of regulating individuals' rights gives rise to the necessity of building the barriers to this regulative force. Those barriers are traditionally made of fundamental rights and freedoms.[2]

This paper deals with the role of the fundamental rights notion within the process of democratization and legitimation of the Union's political and legal systems. The first part covers the general meaning of the material constitutionality of the European Union. The second part presents the structure of the mechanisms designed to

---

[1] Maduro (1998), p. 31.

[2] This feature is described as republican standard or republican idea of constitutionalism. See Mac Amhlaigh (2011), pp. 27–28.

O. Hamuläk (✉)
Faculty of Law, Palacký University in Olomouc, tr. 17. listopadu 8, Olomouc 77111, Czech Republic
e-mail: ondrej.hamulak@upol.cz

T. Kerikmäe (ed.), *Protecting Human Rights in the EU*, 187
DOI 10.1007/978-3-642-38902-3_11, © Springer-Verlag Berlin Heidelberg 2014

secure the respect of fundamental rights on the supranational level—the Charter, the Convention, and General Principles.

2 Constitutionalism Beyond the State[3]

The supranational impetus associated with the creation of European Communities and the evolution of the integration leads us to some theoretical assumptions according to which international law in European region has entered into post-Westphalian period.[4] This means the necessity of rejecting the classical conception of the state sovereignty (indivisible, exclusive, highest power) and acceptance of some supranational political and legal will. European integration is something like planned and controlled deconstruction of the content of the sovereignty of Member States. This phenomenon then logically opens the debate about the nature of the European Union itself. The central point of this debate is the question whether the European Union is on the track to be a state-like organization. I am not going to claim that the European Union is a "superstate" that replaced or is replacing the Member States. But on the other side, one has to accept that the European Union is an autonomous entity, the original political structure that has its own efficient construction of the internal organization and distinctive goals and instruments leading to them.

The unique characteristic of the Union gives rise to the notion of constitutional movement that accompanies the European integration. "Constitutionality", "Constitutional Law", "Constitutional System"—all these terms currently exceeds beyond the borders of national states and thus cannot be regarded as sole objectives of the national law and jurisprudence.[5] Certainly, there is no classical pouvoir constituant behind the creation of the European Union. But this claim does not contest the fact that the integration entities display characteristics of a distinct constitutional system. The evidence of existence of such system may be found in the specific structural elements that the European Union differ from the traditional international organizations.

We may find the social/institutional, normative, and material/meta-legal arguments in favor of assertion that European Union has its own substantive Constitution. It has its own internal organization of relations between main participating players (the European Union and its Member States) between institutions of the Union and between the Union and the individuals/citizens of

---

[3] In this section, I am dealing with the wide understanding of constitutionality as a new approach to this term. See further Klabbers et al. (2011).

[4] From the plethora of literature on this phenomena, see Maccormick (1999), pp. 123–136; Walker (2003), pp. 9–10; or Jakab (2006), pp. 375–397.

[5] For deep analysis of the several approaches to the supranational constitutionalism, see De Búrca et al. (2012).

the Union. Here, the assertion of material constitutionality should sound like this: where society exists, i.e., political and societal structure, there is a Constitution. Another point is connected with the ability of the Union to manifest its own will by the adoption of law and making of administrative decisions. The Union has its own independent legal framework that lays down rules of adoption of binding provisions. These provisions express the Union powers in the outer world, and they are internally applicable within the Member States practice. The autonomous legal system gives rise to an argument of this sort: where a law is present, i.e., autonomous legal system is working, there is a Constitution. The last argument is connected with the allegation according to which where a rule of law is respected (i.e., democratic system based on the rule of law and protection of the fundamental rights), there is a Constitution. Here, the role of mechanisms of promotion and respecting the fundamental rights is crucial without any doubts. The focus on the developments in this field will be given later on.

The constitutional system and the constitutional law of the European Union predict the existence of fundamental rules of organization of social structures. It indicates that the Union may be foreseen as a legal community, an equivalent of the rule-of-law-based state. It is a constitutional structure of a kind that acts and behaves in accordance with and is regulated by a set of rules that have its own democratic ethos. The key role in determining the contours of the constitutionality of the European Union was and still is played by the Court of Justice of the European Union.[6] The Court of Justice promoted independence and some practical domination of European Union law as a prerequisite for the functionality of the entire project of European integration. It served as the agent of emancipation of supranational law and supranational entities.[7] And it was the Court itself who played the pioneer role within the notion of respecting the fundamental rights as general principles within the supranational legal and political structure.

Having in mind the complex sum of arguments mentioned above, the existence of the Constitutional system of the European Union is a hardly contestable phenomenon. Of course, it goes about the constitutionality in the substantive sense of the word, the constitutionality based on principles, separation of powers, and the human rights protection system, i.e., a respected constitutionality and not one that was formally enacted or literally stated.

---

[6] The Court supported its quest for understanding European Law as an autonomous constitutional system also by some semantic turnovers. In Judgment 294/83 Les Verts or Opinion 1/91 on the Treaty on a European Economic Area, it expressly referred to the Treaty as constitutional charter of the integration entities. See commentary in Lenaerts (2010), pp. 295–315.

[7] This is playing the role of "Constitutional Court of the European Union". See Lenaerts and Van Nuffel (2011), p. 22.

3 "Cerberus" Guarding the Fundamental Rights and Advocating the Supranational Constitutionalization

Nowadays, the key provisions that define the Union as a constitutional community based on respect for human rights are included in the Treaty on European Union. The most important are article 2 TEU (which defines the values of European Union and presents human rights as the fundamental core of the integration), article 6 TEU (which defines or summarizes the sources and several instruments of human rights protection within the European Union), and article 7 (which introduces the mechanism of control and sanctioning of the Member States in the cases of grave violation of the fundamental rights by them).

The central provision is the second aforementioned article (art. 6 TEU), which defines the three cornerstones of the protection of fundamental rights at the supranational level. These three totems seem to provide Union within the most complex system of the promotion of fundamental rights that shall work as the one body of tools with three different heads—like the Cerberus guarding the mythic underworld.

Moreover, this strong impetus on the role of fundamental rights within the supranational legal order serves as an indirect tool of defence of supranational (Court's) view on the nature of the legal system of the Community/Union.[8] The recognition of fundamental rights as immanent part of supranational law and establishment of the complex system of their protection rendered to the supranational legal system the nature of the constitutional order. Therefore, it was suitable to be accepted by the national courts in their practice as the law applicable in their judicial decision making. The big lesson here was learned in connection with the famous Solange saga of German Federal Constitutional Court.[9] The German court primarily rejected the possibility of unlimited application of Community law within the national legal practice by the argument that supranational law showed serious deficiencies in the field of protection of individuals. It stated that as long as Community system will show the deficiencies (in comparison with German level), it will not accept its general internal effects (case Solange I, 1974[10]). Once the Community system improved and the doctrine of fundamental rights was introduced, the Federal Constitutional Court changed its opinion and accepted the application of Community rules (case Solange II, 1986[11]), but once more with the objection that it will serve as the ultima ratio guardian of the structural quality of this reached level. In case serious structural discrepancies will appear within the

---

[8] See also Craig (2010), pp. 194–197.

[9] See further Frowein (1988), pp. 201–206.

[10] Solange I - Internationale Handelsgesellschaft von Einfuhr- und Vorratsstelle für Getreide und Futtermittel, decision of 29 May 1974, BVerfGE 37, 271.

[11] Solange II - Wünsche Handelsgesellschaft decision of 22 October 1986, BVerfGE 73, 339.

supranational system, the German court reserves itself the right not to accept the internal applicability of certain rules of EU law within the German system.[12] This raised finger is still valid (see its repetitions in the cases Maastricht, 1993,[13] and Lisbon, 2009[14]) and transmitted also to the approach of other Member States courts (the Czech Constitutional Court may serve as one of the most influenced examples; see cases Sugar Quotas, 2006[15]; European Arrest Warrant, 2006[16]; Lisbon I, 2008[17]; and Lisbon II, 2009[18]).[19] And within this atmosphere of permanent control from the national level, the supranational approach to the protection of fundamental rights has to develop perpetually nowadays and in the future. Therefore, the Union is bound by the sources and mechanisms, and therefore it is still willing to go further—mainly by the accession to the European Convention.

3.1 Charter of Fundamental Rights of the European Union: Internal Pillar

According to the first paragraph of article 6 TEU, the effect of the Lisbon Treaty (1st December 2009), the Union catalogue of human rights—the Charter of Fundamental Rights of the European Union has become a legally binding document and a regular part of European Union law. Thanks to this legal cornerstone, the Union obtained an internal instrument of identification and protection of human rights, which is the first pillar of the whole system. The role of the Charter is crucial. On one side, it confirmed the attitude of the Court of Justice towards the fundamental rights from the previous decades. From another point of view, it fulfilled the requirement of legal certainty of the holder of fundamental rights by making them visible and manifested. The great deal made by the Court of Justice by the introduction of the fundamental rights as General Principles (see further) was always connected with the risk of uncertainty and unpredictability. As AG Mazák rightly stressed (AG Opinion in C-411/05 Palacios): "in the nature of general principles of law, which are to be sought rather in the Platonic heaven of law than in the law books, that both their existence and their substantive content are marked by uncertainty".[20] The Charter is the tool for minimalizing that uncertainty, and this seems to be its crucial added value.

---

[12] See closer Lebeck (2006), pp. 908–912.

[13] Maastricht-Urteil decision of 12 October 1993, BVerfGE 89, 155.

[14] Lissabon-Urteil decision of 30 June 2009, 2 BvE 2/08.

[15] Sugar Quotas Regulation III decision of 8 March 2006, Pl. ÚS 50/04.

[16] European Arrest Warrant decision of 3 May 2006, Pl. ÚS 66/04.

[17] Lisbon Treaty I decision of 26 November 2008, Pl. ÚS 19/08.

[18] Lisbon Treaty II decision of 3 November 2009, Pl. ÚS 29/09.

[19] See closer Hamulak (2011), pp. 279–303.

[20] Opinion in Case C-411/05 Félix Palacios de la Villa, [2007] ECR I-08531, point 86.

3.1.1 The Creation of the Charter

The Charter was adopted in the December 2000 as a mere political declaration without a legally binding nature. First attempt to make it legally binding came in connection with the Treaty establishing Constitution for Europe. Here, the Charter was included directly to the text of European Constitution. But because this reform document was rejected by the French and Dutch people in referendums in 2005, the question of the binding force of the Charter was not resolved yet. Second (successful) attempt was made in connection with the Treaty of Lisbon. This document changed the wording of article 6 TEU and introduced the "legalization" clause according to which the Charter got the same legal value as the Treaties. By 1st December 2009 (when the Treaty of Lisbon entered into force), the Charter of fundamental rights of the European Union became legally binding.

3.1.2 The Scope of the Charter

The Charter is a very complex and quite an ambitious document. It includes tens of human rights from all generations (from classical division of human rights to the three generations of rights: civil and political; economic, social and cultural; modern/solidarity rights). It has its own special structure that does not follow the classical division of human rights to types or generations. The "body of Charter" includes 50 material and 4 horizontal provisions (plus explanations that are attached to the catalogue). It is internally structured into the seven titles.

- The first title called "dignity" (articles 1–5) is inspired by "Kantian" ideal concepts, i.e., human dignity at the first place. It includes the hard-core rights as rights to life, protection of personal integrity, prohibition of torture, etc.
- The second title entitled "freedoms" (articles 6–19) deals with the various examples of personal liberties like personal freedom, protection of private spheres, freedom of thought and expression, freedom of association and assembly, etc.
- The third title called "equality" (articles 20–26) stresses the fact that antidiscrimination policy is one of the most important fields of activity of the Union. There is big variety of equality clauses that ensure, for example, equality before law, general antidiscrimination clause, equality between men and women, special protection of vulnerable groups—children, elderly, and people with disabilities etc.
- The fourth title marked "solidarity" (articles 27–38) includes mainly economic and social rights, e.g., collective bargaining and action, fair and just working conditions, access to health care, etc.
- The fifth title called "citizen's rights" (articles 39–46) is inspired by the Treaty provisions on Union's citizenship. It repeats the classical group of rights of Union's citizens (electorate rights, free movement, political rights, and diplomatic protection) and adds quite detail provision on the right to good administration.

- The sixth title is identified as "justice" (articles 47–50) and includes the procedural safeguards as right to fair trial, presumption of innocence, legality and proportionality of criminal justice, *ne bis in idem* principle.
- The seventh title includes the so-called horizontal provision, which determines the general rules of application and interpretation of the Charter and presents the sources of inspiration for the adoption of this document (articles 51–54).

A Very important provision that has to be mentioned is art. 51, paragraph 1. It defines the addresees of obligation to respect the rights included in the Charter. There are two categories of addresees that have obligation to respect the Charter:

- Institutions, bodies, offices, and agencies of the Union—here the Charter serves as a tool of fortification of rule of law and democratic legitimacy of the supranational governance. It is the goal of long path on which Communities and the Union were finding the ideal tool for the protection of fundamental rights.
- Member States—here we need to point out limited scope on the application of the Charter because member States are obliged to respect this document only "when they are implementing Union law". It means that Member States have to follow the Charter in circumstances where they are acting as "Union agents" (either they hold a direct obligation under EU law norms—see 222/84 Johnston,[21] 43/75 Defrenne,[22] or they hold implicit obligation in connection with the implementation of EU law norms—see 5/88 Wachauf,[23] C-84/95 Bosphorus[24]). Additionally, according to the case law of the Court of Justice, Member States have to respect fundamental rights that form part of general principles of EU law also in cases where they are derogating the rights flowing from EU law (C-260/89 ERT,[25] C-368/95 Familiapress[26]).

3.2 European Convention for the Protection of Human Rights and Fundamental Freedoms: External Pillar

In the second paragraph, we may find the commitment of the Union to accede to the European Convention for the Protection of Human Rights and Fundamental

---

[21] Judgement 222/84 Johnston/Chief Constable of the Royal Ulster Constabulary of 15 May 1986, [1986] ECR, p. 1651).

[22] Judgment 43/75 Defrenne/SABENA of 8 April 1976, [1976] ECR, p. 455.

[23] Judgment 5/88 Wachauf/Bundesamt für Ernährung und Forstwirtschaft of 13 July 1989, [1989] ECR, p. 2609.

[24] Judgment C-84/95 Bosphorus/Minister for Transport, Energy and Communications and others of 30 July 1996, [1996] ECR, p. I-3953.

[25] Judgment C-260/89 ERT/DEP of 18 June 1991, [1991] ECR, p. I-2925.

[26] Judgment C-368/95 Vereinigte Familiapress Zeitungsverlags-und vertriebs GmbH/Bauer Verlag of 26 June 1997, [1997] ECR, p. I-3689.

Freedoms. This provision is a reflection of established practice, when the Court in its case law commonly refers to the Convention as the source of its inspiration.[27] Intensive accession negotiations have been ongoing since the beginning of 2010, and on 19 June 2011 the first complete version of the draft Agreement on the Accession of the European Union to the Convention was published on the website of the Council of Europe.[28] Currently, there are ongoing negotiations between the representatives of the Member States of the Council of Europe and European Union institutions primarily on procedural details of the adoption of this document. But it seems that deliberations are being finalized and the final agreement is close.[29] The importance of the accession is, to some extent a symbolic act, when the Union shows the will and readiness to be subject to the same control mechanism as its Member (and other European) countries. But it will have also practical consequences because new mechanism of protection will appear then. It is clear even from the statement of the Committee preparing the accession that says that "As a result of the accession, the acts, measures and omissions of the EU, like every other High Contracting Party, will be subject to the external control exercised by the Court in the light of the rights guaranteed under the Convention. This is all the more important since the EU member States have transferred substantial powers to the EU".[30]

3.3 Unwritten General Principles: Eternal Pillar

3.3.1 The Role of Principles

The third paragraph then identifies the last (but historically oldest) pillar of human rights protection on supranational level—the unwritten rules contained in the general principles of law. Even if the Union has its written catalogue (the Charter) now, the importance of general principles is still high. First of all, even when the Fathers of the treaty decided to state down explicitly the list of protected rights, there is always a risk of deficiencies and incompleteness. There is also the phenomenon that may be determined by the phrase "society overtake the law", which means that legal regulation is always somehow behind the evolutional features in technology and society that bring the new unknown problems. And the open category—as the principles are—is the best instrument for the flexible reaction and protection of individuals' rights in these circumstances. The development of the

---

[27] See further Douglas-Scott (2006), pp. 629–665.

[28] See commentary on this document Králová (2011), pp. 127–142.

[29] See press release of the CoE: "Milestone reached in negotiations on accession of EU to the European Convention on Human Rights" from the 5 April 2013. Available here: http://hub.coe.int/what-we-do/human-rights/eu-accession-to-the-convention.

[30] Paragraph 5 of the DRAFT Explanatory report to the Agreement on the Accession of the European Union to the Convention for the Protection of Human Rights and Fundamental Freedoms.

doctrine of fundamental rights as part of the general principles of law played a crucial role in building the constitutionality of supranational entities.

Contours of material constitutionality of the European Union (remember that our third claim is "where a rule of law is secured there is a constitution") are defined primarily by the system of protection of fundamental rights. The question of the role and place of fundamental rights within the European Communities and the European Union has undergone major developments during the history of integration.

3.3.2   The Success Story of the General Principles Doctrine

The original text of founding documents did not pay any attention to this issue. Also, the Court of Justice was originally very strict and, by using precise formal approach, rejected the possibility of protection of fundamental rights within the Community legal system. The Court believed that then sources of Community law contained no (neither explicit nor implicit) basis for the protection of fundamental rights (1/58 Stork,[31] 36/59 Geitling[32]). The most quoted reasons for this initial resistance were:

- The dominant focus on economic integration,
- The existence of the Council of Europe (another European organization that was established primarily for the protection and promotion of democracy, rule of law, and fundamental freedoms),
- Fundamental rights as a traditional domain of national constitutional law,
- Absence of legal competence of the Community in the field of fundamental rights.

The silence of the Treaties and reluctance of the Court of Justice to the possibility of fundamental rights protection had a negative impact in several aspects. It led to the reduction in quality of protection of individuals, tension between Community law and national law, and decrease of legitimacy and democratic nature of European Communities. Therefore, this undesirable situation (with its negative consequences) was not sustainable for a long time. And it was the Court of Justice who brought the revolution and caused the end of the "dark era" in the approach to the fundamental rights.

In the seminal Decision 29/69 Stauder,[33] the Court of Justice turned its approach from strictly formal and positive to material and stated that fundamental rights form part of general principles of law on which the Community is based and prescribed itself the assignment to be their guardian. Court's doctrine of fundamental rights as part of the general principles of law laid the foundations of inner (supranational) prism to human rights protection.

---

[31] Judgment 1/58 Stork & Cie ECSC High Authority of 4 February 1959, [1959] ECR, p. 17.

[32] Judgment 36–58, 37–58, 38–59 and 40–59 Präsident Ruhrkohlen-Verkaufsgesellschaft and others/ECSC High Authority of 15 July 1960, [1960] ECR, p. 423.

[33] Judgment 29/69 Stauder/Stadt Ulm of 12 November 1969, [1969] ECR, p. 419.

The importance of the Stauder ruling is that the Court of Justice found a way to safeguard the rule of law in cases of alleged violation of fundamental rights by actions of Community authorities. The court denied its own initial assertion that Community law does not contain any (neither explicit nor implicit) rules providing for protection of fundamental rights.

In the next period of the evolution of this doctrine, the Court of Justice primarily pointed out particular sources of inspiration[34] that filled the unspecified category of general principles of law. These sources of inspirations were:

- Constitutional traditions common to the Member States (11/70 Internationale Handelsgesellshaft,[35] 4/73 Nold[36]) and
- International treaties on human rights on which the Member States participate or are their signatories. The particular importance was given to the European Convention for the Protection of Human Rights and Fundamental Freedoms (36/75 Rutili,[37] 44/79 Hauer[38]).

Fundamental rights encoded in the unwritten general principles of law become the only source of protection for long decades of existence of supranational entities. Recognition of human rights was important not only in terms of individuals and their protection. As I mentioned above, the doctrine of fundamental rights as a general principle served also as certain self-reference, the autonomous claim for the constitutionality of European integration entities that supported their accountability and legitimacy of their actions.

4   Conclusion

Establishment of the complex structure of tools serving to protect and promote fundamental rights at the supranational level had (still has) several reasons. From the political point of view, the most important reason for the open approach is the

---

[34] It is important to stress the notion of "inspiration" here. Even though the Court of Justice was and still is open to draw inspiration from the national constitutional traditions and international sources, it does not mean that all acknowledged rights are transposed to the supranational level automatically. The Court of Justice understands the fundamental rights autonomously as the original part of supranational legal order and also offers an autonomous interpretation of the content of the fundamental rights. We may call it a "Community/Union view" with regard to the objectives of the Community/Union, which in some way limits the scope of protection afforded to fundamental rights (see 4/73 Nold or 44/79 Hauer, where fundamental right to property was to some extent suppressed by the Community economic and market interests).

[35] Judgment 11/70 Internationale Handelsgesellschaft mbH Einfuhr- und Vorratsstelle für Getreide und Futtermittel of 17 December 1970, [1970] ECR, p. 1125.

[36] Judgment 4/73 Nold KG/Commission of 14 May 1974, [1974] ECR 1974 p. 491.

[37] Judgment 36/75 Rutili/Ministre de l'intérieur of 28 October 1975, [1975] ECR, p. 1219.

[38] Judgment 44/79 Hauer/Land Rheinland-Pfalz of 13 December 1979, [1979] ECR, p. 3727.

need to legitimize supranational governance. The Union uses its powers and interferes with the increasing range of fields of human activities and therefore touches directly the individuals in the Member States. The new public power appears that has to be fettered by bonds of fundamental rights. From the legal point of view, without a system of protection of fundamental rights there is a serious risk of the *denegatio iustitiae* problem because fundamental rights encoded in national constitutional norms are not applicable in connection with the supranational legislative and administrative rules. The lacuna that appeared because of non-applicability of national standards towards the EU rules needed the necessary reaction within the supranational legal order itself. The petrification of the character of Community/Union law as an independent and self-sufficient legal system was another important motivation. At the end of 1960s, the autonomy of Community legal system was developing in a rapid way. The principles of direct applicability, direct effect, and primacy were already introduced by the Court of Justice. The lack of fundamental rights protection at the Community level could impair the growing independence of whole Community legal system because it could lead to the reluctance of national courts (which were the main addresses of the principles of application of Community law). Therefore, fundamental rights protection played also the crucial role as the autopoietic argument and feature accompanying the evolution of independent supranational legal order and its constitutionality.

References

Craig P (2010) The Lisbon treaty, law, politics, and treaty reform. Oxford University Press, New York

De Búrca G et al (2012) The Worlds of European Constitutionalism. Cambridge University Press, New York

Douglas-Scott S (2006) A tale of two courts: Luxembourg, Strasbourg and the Growing European Human Rights Acquis. Common Market Law Rev 3:629–665

DRAFT Explanatory report to the agreement on the accession of the European Union to the convention for the protection of human rights and fundamental freedoms, document CDDH-UE (2011) 16fin. http://www.coe.int/t/dghl/standardsetting/hrpolicy/Accession/Working_documents/CDDH-UE_2011_16_final_en.pdf. Accessed 29 Mar 2013

Frowein J (1988) Solange II, (BVerfGE 73, 339) Constitutional complaint Firma W. Common Market Law Rev 1:201–206

Hamulak O (2011) New fighter in the ring: the relationship between European Union Law and Constitutional Law of Member States from the perspective of the Czech Constitutional Court. J Eur Law 2:279–303

Jakab A (2006) Neutralizing the sovereignty question; compromise strategies in constitutional argumentations before European integration and since. Eur Constitut Law Rev 2:375–397

Klabbers J et al (2011) The constitutionalisation of international law. Oxford University Press, New York

Králová J (2011) Comments on the draft agreement on the accession of the European Union to the convention for the protection of human rights and fundamental freedoms. CYIL 2:127–142

Lebeck C (2006) National constitutionalism, openness to international law and pragmatic limits of European Integration – European Law in the German Constitutional Court from the EEC to PJCC. German Law J 11:908–912

Lenaerts K (2010) The basic constitutional charter of a community based on the rule of law. In: Maduro MP, Azoulai L (eds) The past and future of EU law, the classics of EU law revisited on the 50th Anniversary of the Rome Treaty. Hart Publishing, Portland, pp 295–315

Lenaerts K, Van Nuffel P (2011) European Union Law, 3rd edn. Sweet and Maxwell, London

Mac Amhlaigh C (2011) The European Union's Constitutional Mosaic: Big 'C' or Small 'c', Is that a Question? In: Walker N (ed) Europe's Constitutional Mosaic. Hart Publishing, Oxford, pp 21–47

Maccormick N (1999) Questioning Sovereignty. Law, state, and nation in the European Commonwealth. Oxford University Press, New York

Maduro MP (1998) We the court. The European Court of Justice and the European Economic Constitution. A critical reading of Article 30 of the EC Treaty. Hart Publishing, Portland

Walker N (2003) Late Sovereignty in the European Union. In: Walker N (ed) Sovereignty in transition. Hart Publishing, Portland, pp 3–32

Printed by Printforce, the Netherlands